The League to Enforce Peace

THE LEAGUE TO ENFORCE PEACE

Ruhl J. Bartlett

PROFESSOR OF HISTORY
TUFTS COLLEGE

CHAPEL HILL

The University of North Carolina Press

1944

Copyright, 1944, by
The University of North Carolina Press

THE WILLIAM BYRD PRESS, INC.
RICHMOND, VIRGINIA

Preface

IN THE CRITICAL YEARS between 1914 and 1920 when the world was in turmoil and the United States was obliged to decide what place it should take in world affairs, the League to Enforce Peace was the principal organized support for a league of nations. It advocated American leadership in the establishment of a league with sufficient strength to protect each nation against aggression and to enforce peace. It reached into every state, absorbed the majority of American political and intellectual leaders, and secured nearly a million dollars in gifts. It urged American political parties to pledge their support to the league idea, strongly upheld the government in its league pledge to Germany, backed the President in his struggle to sustain this pledge at Paris, and for a time steadfastly supported the League once it had been established. In May, 1919, it was on the verge of complete success. The reasons why it did not fully succeed offer perhaps the principal explanation of the default of the United States in the League of Nations movement, which in turn largely explains the failure of the League as a world organization.

The League to Enforce Peace influenced some people profoundly and aroused in them deep and sustained convictions that the failure of the United States to add its strength to the structure of a world organization would be fatal to peace. It stirred many other people into momentary acceptance of this view, but their interest in world peace was transitory, and their thoughts, directed by their trusted leaders, quickly and easily turned back into familiar channels of traditional thinking. "We produced," wrote A. Lawrence Lowell, "no substantial effect on the great mass of voters who were, indeed, thankful when the whole thing [The League of Nations] was killed and buried by the Republicans and by President Harding."

The League to Enforce Peace failed, and the League of Nations, less sturdy than it ought to have been because of that failure, showed signs of deterioration almost immediately upon its establishment. It is obvious, therefore, that the work of the League to Enforce Peace must be taken up again, this time more firmly, with larger promise, and it must succeed. This task must be borne by men and women who have the right and the necessity to know why their predecessors failed, what they themselves must avoid, and what they must achieve.

In the mechanics of this presentation, one particular difficulty arose regarding terminology. The League to Enforce Peace was organized for the purpose of promoting the establishment of an international association which might bear the same name. When this purpose was actually realized, the English title given to it was the "League of Nations." It was obvious to me that confusion would arise over the meaning of the word *league*, since it refers sometimes to the American and sometimes to the international organization. In order to avoid this confusion, without reverting to the cumbersome expedient of repeating the full title for each reference, the term "the *l*eague" is used throughout to mean the League to Enforce Peace, and "the League" for the League of Nations. While this does not quite solve the problem of terminology, for it is necessary to refer to "*a* league of nations" and to "the league *idea*," it is hoped that the context in which the word "league" appears will make the meaning clear.

The most important collection of materials for the study of the League to Enforce Peace is its central office files, referred to here as the *League Collection*, now located in the Widener Library of Harvard University. The Edward A. Filene collection is in the Woodrow Wilson Foundation Library, and a virtually complete file of the league's *Bulletin* is in the Edwin

PREFACE

Ginn Library at the Fletcher School of Law and Diplomacy, Tufts College.

Dr. A. Lawrence Lowell, who was chairman of the executive committee of the League to Enforce Peace and intimately connected with its entire history, gave me the unrestricted use of his papers dealing with the league, illuminated its history during many pleasant conversations in his Marlborough Street home, and treated me with every courtesy and consideration. He read the first draft of the manuscript, offered many helpful suggestions, and was generous in his conclusion that the work had been done with "extreme diligence and impartiality." It is a disappointment to me that he did not live to see its publication, for he followed the progress of the study with great interest and urged me repeatedly to make haste.

To other people who were intimately connected with the league and who supplied me with documents, memoranda, or personal recollections about its history I am very grateful. These were the following: George Grafton Wilson, Vance C. McCormick, Denys P. Myers, George A. Bellamy, Theodore Marburg, Hamilton Holt, and Professor Irving Fisher. The Chief of the Division of Manuscripts of the Library of Congress, Dr. St. George L. Sioussat, kindly assisted me in securing permission to use the Elihu Root, William Howard Taft, and William J. Bryan papers, and Miss Katherine Brand, Custodian of the Woodrow Wilson papers, Herbert S. Houston, Albert Shaw, Henry W. Taft, and President W. C. Dennis of Earlham College patiently answered inquiries that I addressed to them.

In addition to Dr. Lowell, several people generously consented to read all or parts of the manuscript. I am especially obliged to Dr. Hamilton Holt, now President of Rollins College, who went over the entire manuscript with me page by page. No one connected with the league contributed more than Dr. Holt to its origin or more steadfastly supported its cause. No one else now living has his intimate knowledge of the events connected with its history. Unlike Dr. Lowell, who favored the "Lodge reservations" and supported the candidacy of Senator Harding, Dr. Holt opposed the reservations and, along with Irving Fisher, Theodore Marburg, and others, led the pro-

League Republican opposition to Harding. I am greatly indebted to Professor Irving Fisher, who read the last two chapters of the manuscript and shared with me his unrivaled knowledge of the struggle for the League, particularly during the political campaign of 1920. I am equally indebted to Mr. Denys P. Myers for his suggestions during the early stages of the study and for his critical comments on the last two chapters of the manuscript. Mr. Myers was a member of the Washington Bureau of the league and had therefore a close-up view of the contest in the Senate over the League issue. Professor Paul Birdsall and Dr. Edward A. Jamison of Williams College read the first four chapters, and Professors Albert H. Imlah and Albert E. Irving of Tufts College read the entire manuscript. I gratefully acknowledge the helpful criticisms of all those who read the manuscript but place no burden upon them for any of the errors or shortcomings of the work.

I particularly appreciate the aid which I have received from Mr. Raymond L. Walkley and the staff of the Eaton Library at Tufts College, and from Mrs. Ralph M. Manning, who typed the manuscript, checked some of its content, and saved me from many errors.

R. J. B.

Tufts College
October, 1943

Contents

CHAPTER		PAGE
	Preface	v
I	The American Peace Movement	3
II	The Founding of the League to Enforce Peace	25
III	Response to the League Idea	48
IV	The League as a War Aim	83
V	The Crucial Test	113
VI	Confusion and Failure	167
VII	Perspective	205
	Appendices	215
	Index	231

THE LEAGUE TO ENFORCE PEACE

CHAPTER ONE

The American Peace Movement

IN A NARROW VIEW, the League to Enforce Peace was a product of the First World War. In a broad view it was a part, many people hoped the culmination, of an old and honorable peace enterprise. For centuries ecclesiastics, statesmen, and scholars had searched in vain for the way to world peace. They had tried to establish it through a universal political or ecclesiastical state; they had preached it, written about it, and formulated plans for it, all with but transient success. While Americans of the nineteenth century were not interested in a modern *Pax Romana* or a *Pax Christiana*, many of them were seriously concerned about the recurrence of war and, with world peace as their goal, labored actively and systematically during the hundred years prior to 1915. This great peace movement, quickened by the war, reached its farthest extent in the United States in the League to Enforce Peace and its crucial test in the struggle for the League of Nations.

The devastating Napoleonic Wars in Europe and the War of 1812 in the United States stirred many people in different places, often working independently without knowledge of the efforts of others, to consider the problem of war. They found no lack of arguments and plans for peace but a great dearth of unified effort on the part of peace advocates. Organization was the first need of the hour, and this they intended to provide. The New York Peace Society and the Massachusetts Peace Society were founded in 1815, and a year later the Society for the Promotion of Permanent and Universal Peace was established in London. The movement grew rapidly. In the United States the advocates of peace followed the examples of the pioneer movements in New York and Massachusetts, and in 1828 organized the American Peace Society. By 1850 no less than fifty distinct peace societies existed in the United States.[1]

The difficulty was that at no time during the century did the advocates of peace unite on means or ends. They dissipated much of their total strength in disagreements not only regarding the instruments through which their policies should be applied but also with respect to the policies themselves. Some were out-and-out pacifists,[2] some were avowed internationalists, and some believed in the application of economic force but only through national unilateral action. The pacifists formulated able arguments against war and advocated campaigns of education designed gradually to convince all men that war is evil. Certain pacifists proposed to accelerate the arrival of peace by the establishment of machinery for the peaceful settlement of disputes, but they contemplated no use of force or compulsion. Still others, who observed the growth of war preparations and the increase of trade barriers and who understood the enormous influence of these two factors in the promotion of wars, put their faith in the reduction of armaments and in the establishment of free trade. A few bold individuals advocated obligatory arbitration and the use of boycotts against belligerents through international action.

Notwithstanding these dissensions, the leaders of the peace

---

[1] A large part of the materials for this chapter has been drawn from the following excellent works dealing with the peace movements of the eighteenth century: Merle Eugene Curti, *The American Peace Crusade, 1815-1860* (Durham, Duke University Press, 1929), and *Peace or War, the American Struggle* (New York, W. W. Norton Company, 1936); A. C. F. Beales, *The History of Peace* (New York, The Dial Press, 1931); Christina Phelps, *Anglo-American Peace Movement in the Mid-Nineteenth Century* (New York, Columbia University Press, 1930).

[2] There is a lack of consistency among writers on peace and on international relations regarding the use of the word *pacifist*. It is often used to mean a person opposed to war as an instrument of national policy who is willing, however, for force to be employed against aggression. It is also used to indicate a person opposed to the use of military or any other kind of force in international affairs. Since the word must be used frequently in this study, it is important to note that it has been used consistently to connote the second of the two meanings referred to above.

movement had cause to be proud of their accomplishments during the first half of the nineteenth century. They had given their ideas a substantial place in the humanitarian thought of the time and had extended the interest in peace to a large number of common people who had everything to lose and nothing to gain from war.

Strong as it was, however, the peace movement at the mid-century mark was still relatively weak in comparison with other forces in society. In the United States, abolitionism and the economic and political factors that produced sectionalism loomed larger in the minds of even the most notable leaders of the movement than did peace itself. Peace societies neither threw their weight behind the proposals for a peaceful settlement of the sectional dispute nor offered practical suggestions of their own. The Civil War in the United States and the Crimean War in Europe closed the first phase of the movement for peace in the nineteenth century.

Although the American Peace Society survived the Civil War, and the peace movement had strength enough to establish the Universal Peace Union in 1866, public education for peace was feeble. Schools and churches could have acted as media for the spread of ideas on the subject of world peace, but they offered very little assistance. In the public schools no one thought of instructing students in the causes and cures of war. American history was taught largely for purposes of formal discipline or to stimulate patriotism. The writers of history textbooks frequently knew little history, and the teachers generally knew less. School leadership was woefully lacking in an understanding of the responsibilities of education in a democracy.

The peace movement fared no better among the churches. Such popular churchmen as Phillips Brooks and Dwight L. Moody were concerned with applying the principles of Christianity to individual morality but not to international morality. Not until after 1880 did any of the great ecclesiastical institutions pay serious attention to organizations for peace. Newspapers, magazines, and popular literature gave little consideration to the movement until after 1890.

The most powerful stimulus to the renewal of popular interest in peace came not so much from the activity of the peace organizations as from the widely heralded success of the *Alabama* arbitration. The settlement, in 1872, of the *Alabama* claims controversy brought to an end a decade of dispute between the United States and Great Britain and provided a much-needed and magnificent example of the fact that even the most serious international controversies can be settled by pacific means. Particularly it immensely stimulated the idea that arbitration was the most promising method of peaceful settlement. The Institute for International Law was founded at Ghent in 1873, and the rules for arbitral procedure that were shortly drawn up by that organization provided a pattern for arbitration treaties which began to appear by 1900. By 1914 more than 200 treaties of arbitration had been ratified.

The closing years of the nineteenth century were marked, as were the earlier years, by both victory and defeat for the peace movement. Each victory meant progress, and no temporary setback, however striking, retarded the determination of the peace leaders. The Universal Peace Congress and the Interparliamentary Union conferences were working for the development of arbitration, and both of these organizations held meetings in London in 1896 and in Rome in 1897. The International Peace Bureau was opened at Bern in 1892, and resolutions were adopted advocating the establishment of a "Confederation of European States" on the model proposed by the Geneva League of Peace and Liberty in 1867. In nearly every nation of western Europe at least one peace society existed. In most places the leaders of these organizations were men and women of sufficient prominence to give prestige to the movement for peace and to attract attention generally.

During the last years of the century, arbitration as a method for settling international disputes won the support of both private and public organizations in the United States and in England. In 1887 William Randall Cremer secured the signatures of 232 members of the House of Commons to a memorial which was presented to both houses of the American Congress. The memorial pledged the active support of its signers to proposals that had been introduced into Congress favoring a treaty of arbitration between the United States and Great Britain. During the next three years resolutions favoring arbitration were introduced into the Senate by Senators James F. Wilson, William B. Allison, and John Sherman. As a result of such proposals, which also received support in the House of Representatives, the following concurrent resolution was adopted by both Houses in 1890:

> Resolved by the Senate (the House of Representatives concurring), that the President be, and is hereby, requested to invite, from time to time as fit occasions may arise, negotiations with any government with which the United States has or may have diplomatic relations, to the end that any differences or disputes arising between the two governments which cannot be adjusted by diplomatic agency may be referred to arbitration, and be peaceably adjusted by such means.

In England, the House of Commons, responding to a flood of petitions from the people, adopted a resolution, in 1893, supporting the congressional proposal and calling upon the British government to coöperate in a movement for arbitration. Two years later, the French Chamber of Deputies requested the government of France to negotiate a permanent treaty of arbitration with the United States.

Private organizations continued to advocate arbitration. Albert K. Smiley organized the first Lake Mohonk Conference on International Arbitration in June, 1895, and the American Peace Society sponsored the first National Conference on Arbitration, which met in Washington in 1896. These organizations provided the opportunity for distinguished citizens, students of international law, and other interested people to gain a hearing before the nation on the subject of peace, and they aided in the crystallization of public opinion.

In the midst of these developments the long-standing controversy between the United States and Great Britain over the Venezuelan boundary suddenly flared into a serious dispute which threatened the friendly relations of the two powers. The difficulty was settled peacefully, largely because Great Britain for various reasons gave way to the resolute determination of the United States. Nevertheless, it brought home the fact that governments had given more attention to preparation for military than for peaceful solutions of such controversies. As a result of this episode and of the discussion that preceded it, Secretary of State Richard Olney and the British Ambassador, Sir Julian Pauncefote, negotiated the Olney-Pauncefote Arbitration Treaty. The treaty was presented to the Senate under what appeared to be exceptionally favorable circumstances, for the concurrent resolutions which had initiated it had passed the Senate by unanimous vote.

The treaty was more American than British in that it conformed more closely to the wishes of Secretary Olney than to those of the British government. Under its terms all disputes were *prima facie* arbitrable, and those which were not settled by diplomacy were to be submitted to arbitration unless either nation decided that the dispute involved "questions of principle of grave general importance affecting the national rights of such party," or pecuniary claims of more than £100,000, or territorial claims.[3]

From the very beginning of the debate on the treaty it was evident that the Senate was determined either to defeat the treaty or to emasculate it beyond recognition. It has been said that the Senate's consideration of the treaty "was less a debate than a parliamentary exercise."[4] Senators talked to no purpose, proposed amendments, engaged in tricks designed to delay action, and finally managed to stop all consideration of the treaty during the final days of Cleveland's administration.

This policy of delay, however, did not put an end to the fight. Although the treaty had been negotiated under a Democratic administration, President McKinley warmly praised

[3] This is a general analysis of the broad meaning of the treaty. It provided for three types of tribunals. The text of the treaty and relevant documents are given in Henry James, *Richard Olney and His Public Service* (Boston, Houghton Mifflin Company, 1923), Appendix V.
[4] *Arbitration and the United States* (Boston, World Peace Foundation, 1926), IX, pamphlets nos. 6-7, 455.

it in his inaugural address, mentioned the concurrent resolution of 1890, and declared that arbitration followed a principle of peaceful settlement of disputes which had been the leading feature of American foreign policy throughout the entire history of the nation. He urged the ratification of the treaty "not merely as a matter of policy, but as a duty to mankind." The Republican Committee on Foreign Relations, however, reported the treaty with fifteen amendments, and individual members of the committee advocated additional changes. The Senate debated intermittently for two months, amended the treaty with shameless irresponsibility, and then rejected it entirely.

Secretary Olney was sadly disappointed, not only because the treaty had been defeated but also because, as he said, it had "been done to its death not by open enemies but by professed friends." Clever senators who wanted to defeat the treaty realized that they must do so without incurring public disapproval. No one recognized this situation with clearer insight than Secretary Olney, and no one stated it with greater precision. "The method of assault," he said, "has been as insidious as it has been deadly. A single sound objection to the Treaty as signed has yet to be stated. Yet, awed by the universal public sentiment for the Treaty and feeling compelled to seem to defer to it while in reality plotting to defeat it, Senators have exhausted their ingenuity in devising amendments to the Treaty. Hence before the Treaty came to a final vote, the Senate brand had been put upon every part of it, and the original instrument had been mutilated and destroyed beyond all possibility of recognition."[5]

No simple reason accounts for the conduct of the Senate. The explanation lies in the intricate complex of domestic politics, in personal animosities, in partisan influences, in selfish sectional demands, and in the determination of the Senate to assert its powers.[6] The defeat of the treaty was more than a

[5] This was stated in a letter to Henry White, May 14, 1897. It is quoted in W. S. Holt, *Treaties Defeated by the Senate* (Baltimore, Johns Hopkins Press, 1933), pp. 154-162.
[6] For a more complete analysis of the reasons for the Senate's action

victory of the Senate over the executive branch of the government; it was a victory of the extreme nationalists in both major parties over the internationalists. But most of all, it was a full dress rehearsal for Senator Henry Cabot Lodge for the rôle he was to play supremely well in the defeat of the League of Nations.

The Spanish-American War followed close upon the failure of the Olney-Pauncefote Treaty. While the war was precipitated over controveries relative to Cuba, it resulted in the annexation of Puerto Rico, Hawaii, and the Philippine Islands. Many of the people who vigorously opposed the Olney Treaty were the most insistent advocates of intervention in Cuba and the most vocal supporters of the acquisition of new possessions. These people, adherents to the so-called "large policy of 1898," may properly be called imperialists whose fundamental principles were the antithesis of the Olney Treaty.

The discussions and debates attendant upon the Olney Treaty and the Spanish-American War served to accelerate the division of American opinion on foreign policy into three principal categories: imperialism, internationalism, and pacifism. The imperialists thought in terms of force and advocated unrestrained nationalism, with the United States dispensing justice to the world from the quarter-deck. The internationalists thought in terms of law and advocated the establishment of political organizations for the preservation of peace. The pacifists thought in terms of Christian ethics and advocated the moral regeneration of the world through individual action.

The failure of most Americans to think through the implications of these three main categories of opinion resulted in an uncertainty of purpose as the nation entered upon the great stage of world affairs at the close of the nineteenth century. Many people selected ideas from each category, used similar arguments for different ends, and either misjudged or misrepresented the ends which would follow particular means. Thus the pacifists rejected the argument of humanitarianism as

---

see Denna Frank Fleming, *The Treaty Veto of the American Senate* (New York, G. P. Putnams Sons, 1930), pp. 77-84; and W. S. Holt, *op. cit.*, pp. 154-162.

applied to the acquisition of the Philippines but accepted it as applied to Cuba. The imperialists justified their expansionist policies on the ground that America could no longer be isolated from world affairs in a world of growing economic interdependence, and at the same time advocated higher tariff barriers. Thus the confusion of thought and the lack of centrality of program among those who were sincerely non-imperialists made it possible for the imperialists to dominate American policy.

This fact is well illustrated by comparing the fate of the Olney Treaty with the success of the imperialists in ratifying the Spanish Treaty. Although President McKinley favored the Olney Treaty he did not seriously attempt to control his political followers who led the opposition to it. The anti-treaty forces controlled the important Senate committees and had the votes to enact nullifying amendments, but the anti-imperialists, in 1898, neither controlled committees nor had the unity of purpose to force through their desired changes. The advocates of the "large policy" in 1898 not only controlled the Senate but also boldly denounced the anti-imperialists for trying to defeat the treaty of peace with Spain by using the same methods they themselves had used to defeat the arbitration treaty. Senator Lodge even complained that by defeating the Spanish treaty the Senate would repudiate the President, and would demonstrate the unfitness of the United States for a place among the great powers.[7] He had been quite willing to repudiate the same president in the defeat of the Olney Treaty and was more than willing, later, to repudiate President Wilson.

While the people of the United States were accommodating themselves both to the imperialism and to the world position implicit in the treaty with Spain, the government was preparing to join with the governments of twenty-five other nations at the first Hague Conference. Although the idea of an international conference on the limitation of armaments had been discussed in Russia as far back as 1894, the first public an-

[7] Fleming, *op. cit.*, p. 120.

nouncement of such a proposal was made in August, 1898, when Russia sent invitations to the nations who had diplomats in Russia. The reasons for Russia's initiation of the conference were varied. Relations with Germany and Austria were strained, and Russo-British relations in the Far East were less cordial than formerly. European armaments were rapidly increasing, particularly land equipment in Austria and naval preparation in Germany, and the internal situation in Russia was such that an enormous expenditure of money for rearmament might prove to be disastrous. Perhaps the general European uneasiness which might lead to war and the Tsar's interest in peace, which had been aroused by the monumental treatise on war written by Jean de Bloch,[8] were also important considerations. The Tsar's first, rather vague, rescript did not receive very enthusiastic reception, and a more specific statement was issued in January, 1899. In this invitation it was proposed that the nations participating in the conference consider the desirability of declaring an armament holiday, the outlawry of certain new weapons, the adoption of rules of war, and the use of good offices, mediation, and voluntary arbitration in the settlement of disputes between nations.

The conference met and after deliberating for two months adopted the "Final Act," which included three conventions, three declarations, one resolution, and three expressions of hope regarding future action. How much the conference accomplished is a matter of point of view. On the credit side of the ledger it could be pointed out with unquestioned accuracy that the assembling in peace time of an international conference in the interest of peace was unprecedented and that it was of some value even to have recognition of the fact that

[8] The Tsar had either read this work or knew the main points of M. Bloch's thesis. See Ford, "The Genesis of the First Hague Conference," *Political Science Quarterly* (Sept., 1936), LI, 355, and A. F. Beales, *The History of Peace* (New York, The Dial Press, 1931), pp. 230-231. The Tsar may have been influenced also by Suttner's great anti-war novel, *Die Waffen Nieder*, which had tremendous vogue all over the world.

international problems existed which might be settled by peaceful means. Moreover the actual accomplishments were substantial. The conference drew up a convention for the settlement of international disputes which placed a stamp of approval upon the use of good offices, mediation, and commissions of inquiry, provided for a permanent court of arbitration, and established rules of arbitral procedure. It recommended the adoption of certain rules of war and made declarations concerning what should receive further consideration. The conference gave important direction to subsequent development of international law, and in fact most of its work bore fruit in actual application.[9]

Viewed from the debit side of the ledger the conference was pedestrian in its advance toward the goal of international peace. Some of the individual members of the conference, for example Andrew D. White from the United States and Léon Bourgeois and Baron d'Estournelles de Constant from France, would probably have done more had the situation not been dominated by stronger personalities and specific instructions. The fact is very clear, and it becomes even clearer with the addition of each new piece of evidence from hitherto unpublished documents, that the conference was completely dominated by the military mind.[10] This does not mean that the military were in control of the civil governments of the various states. It means that the responsible statesmen of the great powers did not have sufficient confidence in existing peaceful international procedures or the will to strike out for the development of new processes in which they would have confidence, to induce them to risk the loss of whatever military

---

[9] The most important study of the Hague conferences in relation to their influence on the development of international law is Walther Schücking, *The International Union of the Hague Conferences*, translated by C. G. Fenwick (Oxford, The Clarendon Press, 1918).

[10] Captain W. D. Puleston, *Mahan, the Life and Work of Captain Alfred Thayer Mahan* (New Haven, Yale University Press, 1939), pp. 204-217. See also Lionel M. Gelber, *The Rise of Anglo-American Friendship* (London, Oxford University Press, 1938), p. 62; and J. A. Spender, *Great Britain: Empire and Commonwealth, 1886-1935* (London, Cassel, 1935), pp. 136 ff.

advantage their nations possessed. There was no distinction among the powers in this respect.

On the main question of armaments, Captain Mahan made it quite clear to the conference that the United States intended not only to maintain its existing military and naval strength but to increase it.[11] The United States was not interested in agreements limiting or abolishing the use of certain new destructive weapons of warfare, and an American delegate cast the only dissenting vote in a sub-committee which considered the proposal to outlaw the use of gas projectiles. Secretary of State John Hay had instructed the American delegates to press for an agreement exempting non-contraband private property from destruction or capture either on the seas or on land in time of war. Although Mr. White presented this proposition to the conference it was not seriously considered and was postponed for later consideration, for Captain Mahan did not approve of the idea, and other delegates regarded it as being of peculiar interest to the United States.

If nothing could be done toward the limitation of armaments, perhaps something could be accomplished toward the development of arbitration. Secretary Hay favored this part of the Russian proposal, and even the military technicians were anxious that the conference should not *appear* to be a complete failure. They were very willing that the governments of the world, applauded by their countrymen, walk blithely along the road marked as leading toward peaceful solution of disputes as long as that road was only a camouflaged treadmill. The proposal for the use of mediation, good offices, commissions of inquiry, and arbitration was carefully drawn so as to omit any compulsion whatsoever. Good offices were to be used "as far as circumstances allow," and commissions of inquiry might be employed with reference to problems "involving neither honor nor vital interests." The convention on arbitration did not constitute a promise to resort to arbitration; it only established a usable court of arbitration.

[11] On this point Mahan was following the formal instructions from Secretary Hay, and he took pains to amplify the instructions in private conversations.

The French delegation hoped to make at least a gesture toward the idea of the collective responsibility of nations, and to that end proposed what became Article 27 of the Convention for the Pacific Settlement of International Disputes. The article stated that if a serious dispute threatened to break out between two or more of the signatory powers, the other signatory powers should consider it their duty to remind the disputants that the Permanent Court was open to them. Such a reminder, the article added, should not be regarded as unfriendly.

Captain Mahan easily convinced his colleagues that this was too extreme a measure, and he was instrumental in securing the consent of the conference to an American reservation. The reservation was worded so as to free the United States from any responsibility abroad and to protect it from any interference from outside influences in the solution of American problems. The United States government thus adhered stubbornly to a policy of non-coöperation, non-recognition of any international responsibility, and complete indifference to the danger of competitive armaments.

The accomplishments and failures of any international conference must necessarily be measured against the announced objectives. If the objectives are far-reaching and beyond the practical possibilities of the moment, even substantial accomplishments may be overlooked, with the result that the whole effort is regarded with disillusionment and cynicism. To a considerable extent this was the situation at the first Hague Conference. But the substantial achievements of the conference were encouraging even to those who were disappointed that it had not utilized all its opportunities.

In the United States the leaders of the "large policy," although somewhat attracted by the accomplishments of the Hague Conference, had not fully learned that a great rôle in world affairs could be played through enlightened leadership in international coöperation. They were not isolationists. They looked abroad and saw the opportunities for American influence and perhaps realized American responsibilities, but the only rôle within their vision was that of imperialism. A brief catalogue of events will illustrate the actual course of developments. In Far Eastern affairs there were the "open door" negotiations, intervention in China to suppress the Boxer uprising, Roosevelt's mediation in the Portsmouth Peace Conference, the Taft-Katsura and the Root-Takahira agreements, and "dollar diplomacy." Theodore Roosevelt "took Panama," intervened in Santo Domingo, participated in the Algeciras Conference, reorganized the army, strengthened the navy and boldly displayed its power to the whole world by means of the famous around-the-world cruise. Thus the United States moved rapidly into a position of world influence, but slowly toward world coöperation.

During the years between the first Hague Conference and the First World War, the peace movement in the United States did not appear to be in decline. It advanced along three fronts: (1) private and semi-public internationalism of the so-called non-political variety, (2) the continued activity of peace societies in the realm of education and public enlightenment, and (3) the work of the national government in promoting the second Hague Conference, in further attempts to establish arbitration treaties, and in negotiating the Bryan treaties of conciliation. In the field of private and semi-public internationalism the activity was notable. More than 1,500 international conferences were held between 1899 and 1914. Almost all the varied interests and activities of civilized people were considered in these conferences. The subjects embraced history, religion, peace, law, science, education, agriculture, public administration, labor, and many other items.[12] While the value of these conferences in the peace movement cannot be accurately measured, it can scarcely be doubted that they were a force for better international understanding.

The organized peace movement expanded its activity. Local and national peace conferences were held, and some of them attracted nation-wide attention. Several new organizations were

[12] See Herbert Newhard Shenton, *Cosmopolitan Conversation* (New York, Columbia University Press, 1933), for an exhaustive study of these conferences together with the language problems connected with them.

established, most notably the Carnegie Endowment for the Advancement of Peace, the World Peace Foundation, and the American Society for Judicial Settlement of International Disputes. In December, 1910, Mr. Andrew Carnegie transferred to the Carnegie Peace Fund $10,000,000 to be used "to hasten the abolition of international war, the foulest blot upon our civilization." The distinguished American Society for Judicial Settlement of International Disputes held a series of conferences, the purpose of which was to strengthen existing sentiment and to create sentiment in favor of judicial settlement of disputes rather than arbitral adjustments or the compromises of diplomacy. Some peace societies, by dint of large endowments and professional staffs, were able to maintain, even in years of public apathy, their programs of systematic study and publicity of problems of international affairs.

The peace societies, however important, were not ends in themselves. The leaders realized that the ends they sought could be brought about only through the action of national governments. With this in mind Mr. T. E. Burton induced the Interparliamentary Conference, meeting at St. Louis, to pass a resolution asking President Theodore Roosevelt to call a second Hague Conference. After some delay, the conference was called, although not directly by President Roosevelt. Three hundred delegates, representing forty-four nations, assembled in the Hall of Knights at The Hague on June 15, 1907. They remained in session for four months. The United States government had hoped that something might be done at the conference concerning disarmament and arbitration, but this hope was not realized. Disarmament was not really considered at all, and whatever hope there had been of even a gesture toward compulsory arbitration was blasted by the German delegate, Marshall von Bieberstein. But for those who were content to take the long view of the peace movement the conference was not a failure. Progress was made in the field of international law, and a convention was drawn for the establishment of a judicial court of arbitration to parallel the Permanent Court established earlier.

In the meantime, prior to the second Hague Conference,

another attempt had been made in the United States to advance the cause of arbitration. Momentum, favorable to arbitration and stimulated during the struggle for the treaty of 1897, had not disappeared. The Anglo-French treaty of 1903 and the Second American Conference on International Arbitration, held in Washington in 1904, tended to keep interest alive. Backed by President Roosevelt, Secretary Hay negotiated a series of arbitration treaties designed to be first steps toward the significant use of arbitration. Questions regarding vital interest, independence, or national honor were removed from the scope of the treaties. They were utterly harmless, but the Senate amended them so as to necessitate the negotiation of a new treaty requiring the Senate's approval whenever any question was to be submitted to arbitration. Roosevelt, in high dudgeon, removed the treaties from the Senate.

These treaties were not fundamentally very important, but two things regarding the episode are significant. The obvious thing was that the Senate rejected them, that is, amended them so as to change their character, notwithstanding their milk-and-water nature. The reasons were believed to be similar to those that had influenced the Senate to reject the Olney Treaty of 1897. More important was the reason given by Roosevelt for withdrawing them from the Senate. He stated that to amend the treaties as the Senate had done was in reality to oppose the principle of general arbitration and that it would be hypocrisy and deception to pretend otherwise.[13] In a letter to Senator Shelby M. Cullom, Chairman of the Committee on Foreign Relations, the President explained his position fully. He declared that if in the opinion of the President an amendment nullified a treaty, it was clearly the President's duty "to refrain from endeavoring to secure ratification, by the other contracting power or powers, of the amended treaty.[14] Three years later, however, Mr. Root persuaded Roosevelt to consent to the negotiation of other treaties, including the Senate's amendments.

[13] Philip C. Jessup, *Elihu Root* (New York, Dodd, Mead, and Company, 1938), II, 80.
[14] "Arbitration and the United States," p. 520.

The movement for international arbitration reached its highest point in the Taft treaties of 1911. At a dinner in New York on March 22, 1910, President Taft had remarked that he did not see why questions of national honor should not be submitted to international tribunals. Later on, in December of the same year, he had referred to the matter again and had stated that he saw no reason why "every issue" that could not be settled by negotiation could not be referred to arbitration courts established by treaty agreement.[15] Both England and France expressed interest in such agreements, and Taft was hopeful that he might be able to conclude treaties with all the great powers and that other nations might take up the movement until a network of treaties was made. Thus the objectives of universal arbitration treaties might be reached by piecemeal methods.

During the summer of 1911, Secretary of State Knox carried on negotiations with France and England and, for a while, with Germany. Efforts to draw Germany into the treaty network were not fruitful, but on August 3, 1911, identical treaties were signed with England and France. In general the treaties provided that all differences between the contracting parties, justiciable in nature and not settled by diplomacy, should be submitted to arbitration, and that a commission should be established with authority to determine, either unanimously or with only one dissenting vote, whether a question was justiciable.[16] President Taft thought that one of the most significant causes for past failures of arbitration treaties, the opposition of the Senate to any curtailment of its power, had been avoided by a stipulation that every case referred to arbitration had to be submitted under an agreement approved by the Senate. It was also hoped that German-American and Irish-American dislike of Anglo-American friendship would be nullified by the fact that a treaty was also signed with France and by the clearly

[15] Henry F. Pringle, *The Life and Times of William Howard Taft* (New York, Farrar and Rinehart, 1939), II, 738.
[16] The text of these treaties may be found in many places, for example, *International Conciliation* (New York, Carnegie Endowment for International Peace, 1911), No. 48.

expressed desire to sign similar treaties with Germany and other nations.[17]

It is as certain as anything can be in the realm of public opinion that the vast majority of the American people favored the Taft treaties.[18] This was admitted by senators, stated by newspapers, and affirmed by organizations that reflected public opinion. Nevertheless the Senate thwarted the will of the people with impunity as it had done before, and it accomplished its purpose in the same way. It attached to the acts of ratification resolutions which nullified the essential character of the treaties so that the President could not in good faith ask either England or France to accept the mutilated agreements.

Senator Henry Cabot Lodge, Theodore Roosevelt, and Captain Mahan formed the spearhead of the anti-treaty forces. Senator Lodge marshaled the opposition in the Senate and spun out tenuous legalistic arguments against the treaties. As in earlier contests he worked for the defeat of the treaties while he pretended to support the principles of arbitration. Although Senator Root, with compelling logic, pointed out the fallacies of Lodge's arguments, he rendered little real assistance to the pro-treaty forces. He refused to participate in public discussions, and while he disliked Lodge's reservations he had reservations of his own which were only less objectionable than those of the more outspoken opponents of the treaties.[19] Roosevelt, with remarkable disregard for either truth or reason, thundered against the treaties with prodigious verbosity well-studded with such words as righteousness, national honor, patriotism, and hypocrisy. Captain Mahan's position, however, was clear and understandable. He did not favor the treaties for the simple reason that he did not believe in the development of law as an instrument of natural international adjustment. He favored armaments, the "free play of forces," and the rule of might.[20] He believed that arbitration

[17] *British Documents on the Origins of the World War*, VIII, Chap. LXX, Doc. Nos. 499, 503, 510.
[18] The evidence is cited in Fleming, *op. cit.*, pp. 10-109; Holt, *op. cit.*, pp. 230-235; Pringle, *op. cit.*, II, 738-755.
[19] Jessup, *op. cit.*, II, 273.
[20] Puleston, *op. cit.*, p. 318.

and disarmament would lead to "a socialistic community of states" in which civilization would decay for want of national initiative engendered by competition.[21] He declared that it would be better "to depend upon great armaments, as institutions maintaining peace, which they have done effectually for forty years in Europe itself, and not to demoralize the European peoples by the flood of socialistic measures which will follow upon the release to a beneficiary system of the sums now spent on armament."[22]

Mahan's argument against arbitration is notable, not for its merit but because it was made by a person who was a member of the American delegation to the first Hague Conference and who was the mentor of both Roosevelt and Lodge.[23] His argument consisted of three assumptions, all of them manifestly vulnerable. It is highly doubtful that competitive armament significantly contributed to the peace of Europe prior to 1911. On the contrary, the re-armament race was the reason why many people believed that peace was precarious and that the need existed for the Hague Conference. The second assumption was that if money was not spent for armament it must necessarily be spent for something else. This was virtually a thesis that it was necessary for the people to be taxed. The third assumption was that what Mahan called a "beneficiary system" was an evil. The beneficiary systems that existed included such things as old age pensions, social insurance laws, labor laws, and greater educational opportunities for the less wealthy classes. What Mahan was apparently trying to do by his "beneficiary" argument was to associate peace with socialism and to mobilize against the treaties the fear that a private-property-owning public might feel for the danger of anything that could be labelled socialistic. This was an effective argument, for only nine years later Taft used the bogey of socialism to explain his desertion of Wilson and the League of Nations.

[21] Captain A. T. Mahan, *Armaments and Arbitration* (New York, Harper and Brothers, 1912), p. 10.
[22] *Ibid.*, p. 13.
[23] Puleston, *op. cit.*, pp. 318-330.

Escorted by such arguments as Mahan's, the treaties went down to defeat. Taft, thinking that he could bring pressure upon the Senate by appealing to public opinion, made a tour of the country. But it was the Senate and not public opinion that failed to support the treaties, even though very vocal anti-British groups made whatever public denunciation they could.

The peace movement in this era experienced one meagre victory, the Bryan treaties. No secretary of state had been a more sincere advocate of peace than William Jennings Bryan.[24] His contribution to the peace movement was the development into definite form of the idea of delaying the use of force until a commission of inquiry could investigate the causes of a dispute and suggest possible lines of peaceful solution. He proposed the establishment of permanent commissions with jurisdiction over all questions not otherwise provided for. His proposal amounted to compulsory investigation, but the recommendations of the investigating commissions would carry no sanction other than that of public opinion. Having secured approval for his idea from at least some European statesmen, from President Wilson, and from the Committee on Foreign Relations of the Senate, he submitted his proposal to the nations which had diplomatic representatives in Washington. Between August 7 and October 13, 1914, thirty treaties embodying his principles were signed, and twenty of them were ratified by the Senate and proclaimed by the President.

While Mr. Bryan's accomplishment was an undoubted victory for the peace movement, its importance can easily be exaggerated. The outbreak of the First World War just after the first group of treaties had been submitted to the Senate tended to center senatorial interest elsewhere. No treaty was signed with the Central Powers or with Japan, and one reason for the lack of strong opposition to the treaties was the belief that they were too unimportant to bother about. Senator Lodge

---

[24] An excellent short treatise on the Bryan treaties may be found in James Brown Scott, *Treaties for the Advancement of Peace* (New York, Oxford University Press, 1920). A more complete analysis of the work of Bryan is Merle E. Curti, *Bryan and World Peace* (Northampton, Department of History of Smith College, 1931).

thought they were "fatuous" and did not go to Washington to oppose them. It is notable, however, that Senators Borah, Bristow, Fall, Jones, and Poindexter voted in the negative in the test vote on the first treaty of the group. These treaties were not tested during the war era and they have had no significant application, but they formed a part of the experience out of which peace machinery could be built.

Thus during the hundred years prior to 1914, conditions, factors, and ideas making for war competed with those that promised peace. Unbridled nationalism, strident imperialism, competitive armament, and increasing impediments to the free flow of world commerce, contained the seeds of war. These flourished in an atmosphere of indifference among people too busy with the affairs of a new industrial society to consider seriously the consequences of such policies. Their growth was favored also by the enormous power of traditional thinking which caused many thoughtful men to cling to established institutions until new ones were proved both safe and superior. Had not poverty and war always existed? And were not plans for peace the utopia of the idealist and the mirage of the impractical?

But the seeds of peace had been planted too, and in greater quantity than during any other previous hundred years in history. If, as Shakespeare had said, war was "a game which were their subjects wise, kings would not play at" then war was losing the race with peace, for democracy was on the offensive in many countries in 1914, and education, both a cause and an effect of democracy, was spreading rapidly. True and therefore liberal education in all of its far-reaching aspects contained within itself the power to sterilize and thus to render impotent all the forces making for war. Moreover, in an atmosphere of liberal education, science flourished, and in its wake the advance of technology tended to increase the interdependence of nations. Well organized and increasingly well led peace societies were becoming more and more capable of exerting a wide influence among the people as they came to realize the fact that perils of war were real and not imaginary.

One of the great tragedies of 1914 was the arrival of war just as the forces for peace were beginning to make greater headway than at any time during the preceding century. In the United States such fundamental causes of war as tariffs, imperialism, militarism, and extreme nationalism were under serious assault, and the spirit that produced this assault had its counterpart in far-flung areas of the world, the British Empire, Latin America, China, and, to some extent, even in Russia and in Central Europe. Ideas still paid some revenue at the frontiers of nations, but the prospect was never better that they would soon pass duty free. And the ideas that were on the wing in 1914 were those making for peace. Unfortunately, however, it takes but one nation to start a war, and once the war had started it had to be fought through to the end. Could it be used to further the peace-making gains of the century, or would the forces of reaction retain or regain their power in the end and submerge the rising tide of peace? This was the problem that the League to Enforce Peace undertook to solve.

CHAPTER TWO

The Founding of the League to Enforce Peace

AT NO TIME in the course of the preceding century were peace discussions more widespread or peace proposals more urgent than in the decade which closed in 1914. Recurrent crises aroused people to a realization of the imminence of war and to calculations of the consequences. Undoubtedly the peace movement of the past century contributed to this activity. But what galvanized thoughtful people of high and low degree with earnest effort was the nightmare vision of Armageddon itself. Thus on the eve of war the intense concentration of activity concerning peace was in fact a barometer revealing the sense of danger. When the League to Enforce Peace was established, the majority of its founders were men who had been connected with prior peace efforts. The new organization inherited, therefore, impetus that antedated its own creation.

While proposals were being made in Europe for the establishment of an European federation,[1] or European unity league,[2] plans were being considered in the United States for calling a third Hague conference. The movement for the latter was sponsored by Andrew D. White and Joseph H. Choate, chairmen respectively of the American delegations to the first and second conferences at The Hague. At a meeting held in the Hotel Astor on January 21, 1914, it was decided to organize a citizens' committee of 100 to urge the President to issue the call. This committee was later informed that the government had already done as much as was prudent and possible to pro-

[1] "The League to Enforce Peace," *The Independent*, LXXXVI (June 5, 1916), 358.
[2] The London *Times*, Jan. 31, 1914.

mote such a conference. The outbreak of war undoubtedly prevented the calling of a third conference.

One of the most ingenious attempts to stimulate a worldwide movement for peace was connected with a dramatic and notable speech made by Theodore Roosevelt at Christiania, Norway, on May 5, 1910, in connection with his reception of the Nobel Prize. The attention evoked by this address was so great that a considerable number of people have been misled into thinking that it was the origin of the League to Enforce Peace.[3] Roosevelt declared, among other things, that it would be a "master stroke" if those great powers honestly bent on peace "would form a League of Peace, not only to keep the peace among themselves, but to prevent, by force if necessary, its being broken by others." He went on to advocate some form of international police force and the formation of a "combination of nations" to command peace.[4] Roosevelt's speech was well received by the press. *The Independent* was especially delighted with the address and pointed out that in an editorial of February 17, 1910, it had urged many of the ideas mentioned by Mr. Roosevelt. It thought that Roosevelt's plea was for nothing less than the "Federation of the World" and that since the "Great Design" of Henry IV of France early in the seventeenth century, no one comparable to Roosevelt had proposed such a comprehensive plan for world peace.[5] It thought also that Roosevelt was the ideal person to lead the movement for the creation of the federation that he proposed.

The Independent had good reason to be pleased with Roosevelt's Christiania address, for the similarity of the address to

---

[3] This statement has frequently been made. See, for example, Felix Morley, *The Society of Nations* (Washington, Brookings Institute, 1932), p. 5; also John M. Mathews, *American Foreign Relations* (New York, The Century Company, 1928), p. 121; Denna F. Fleming, *The United States and the League of Nations* (New York, G. P. Putnam's Sons, 1932), p. 4. Mr. Roosevelt was awarded the Nobel Peace Prize in 1906 in consideration of his efforts for the conclusion of the Russo-Japanese War. The usual requirement of personal attendance at the time of the award was waived in Mr. Roosevelt's case.

[4] *The Independent*, LXVIII (May 12, 1910), 1027-1029.

[5] *Ibid.*, p. 1043.

the editorial of February 17 was not merely a coincidence. Andrew Carnegie had learned that Roosevelt, when he emerged from Africa, planned to make speeches in Rome, Paris, and Berlin, and that the Nobel Peace Committee was outraged because he had given no indication of going to Norway. Mr. Carnegie discussed the problem with Hamilton Holt, editor of *The Independent* and a fellow member of the New York Peace Society. They agreed that Mr. Holt would write an editorial addressed to the world in general but intended for Mr. Roosevelt in particular, and that Mr. Carnegie would see to it that Mr. Roosevelt received a copy. As soon as the editorial could be prepared, a copy of the galley proof was hurried off to Roosevelt. The Christiania address was virtually the Holt editorial with some shift of emphasis.[6]

There is no reason to suppose, however, that the Christiania address had anything to do directly with the origin of the League to Enforce Peace. At most it illustrates that Roosevelt was impressed with the current of ideas about peace, particularly with the idea that world peace required constructive international activity rather than mere anti-war sentiment. But he was not sufficiently impressed to devote his time or attention to the development of world peace. The movement went on without him under the leadership of men who for a long time had been devoting themselves to it. They were directly responsible for the idea of the Taft arbitration treaties, and they loyally supported President Taft in his struggle to secure the Senate's approval of those treaties. When the treaties failed, the peace advocates simply took up their task anew.

In this work probably no one was more tireless than Hamilton Holt, and no one was more responsible for the organization of the League to Enforce Peace. He was one of the principal leaders of the New York Peace Society, an influential member of the First and Second National Peace Congresses, and was the president of the Third National Peace Congress held in

---

[6] This was related to the author by Mr. Holt. See also William Short to Raymond V. Ingersoll, Apr. 15, 1919, *League to Enforce Peace Collection*, Harvard University Library, hereafter referred to as the *League Collection*.

Baltimore in 1911. In his presidential address before the Baltimore meeting, Holt made a carefully prepared statement, in the original draft of which he had proposed that force should be used in carrying out the decisions of a properly organized international body. He was advised by Theodore Marburg, however, not to say anything about force. Marburg argued that in the opinion of international law authorities, nations joining an agreement for general arbitration would perform their obligations without being forced to do so. Holt conceded this point of view for the time being, and the idea of the use of force was omitted from the address. After the outbreak of the European War, however, he rewrote the Baltimore address and published it in *The Independent* under the title "The Way to Disarm: A Practical Proposal."[7] He started with the assumption that universal peace could not become a reality until the world was politically organized on the basis of law. In this work the United States was destined to play a great part, for it was already a "world in miniature." Perhaps federalism would not be possible, but a league of peace could be formed more or less on the pattern of the Articles of Confederation, and such a league should be prepared to use force against nations that would not submit to peaceful procedures for the settlement of disputes. Force, Holt continued, is not an evil in itself. It is bad when used for aggression, but it is necessary for defense and wholly good when used for the sanction of law. Holt suggested that the constitution of such a league might be based upon the following five principles:

> First: The nations of the League shall mutually agree to respect the territory and sovereignty of each other.
> Second: All questions that cannot be settled by diplomacy shall be arbitrated.
> Third: The nations of the League shall provide a periodical assembly to make all rules to become law unless vetoed by a nation within a stated period.
> Fourth: The nations shall disarm to the point where the

[7] Hamilton Holt to the author; also *The Independent*, LXXIX (Sept. 28, 1914), 427-429.

combined forces of the League shall be a certain per cent higher than those of the most heavily armed nations or alliance outside the League. Detailed rules for this pro rata disarmament shall be formulated by the Assembly.

Fifth: Any member of the League shall have the right to withdraw on due notice, or may be expelled by the unanimous vote of the others.

In many respects Mr. Holt's plan for a league was not unique or significantly different from other plans that were current. Three months earlier, on the eve of the war, *The Independent* had published an editorial under the title "A Basis for a League of Peace" in which it was pointed out that the idea of such a league was not new, for federal and confederate governments were essentially leagues of peace and that from ancient times various attempts had been made to form such leagues. Specifically, however, four recent proposals for the formation of a world organization were reviewed, and it was noted that all of them involved the use of force to provide sanction for the decisions of the league.[8]

Hamilton Holt's proposals for a league of nations, coming as they did just before and shortly after the outbreak of war in Europe, were interspaced by an independent suggestion of Professor Irving Fisher of Yale University. As a graduate student at Yale, Mr. Fisher had read a paper before the Political Science Club on May 17, 1890, advocating a league of nations and predicting that sooner or later without one a world war would break out. When the prediction was fulfilled, he revised the article in a few minor ways and sent it to *The New York Times*.[9] Professor Fisher argued that the war had resulted from rather fundamental causes inherent in the world economic order and that the peace settlement at the end of the war should be made the occasion for the creation of some kind of league of peace that would form an international government with an arbitral court and international police power. He suggested that Alsace-Lorraine might be neutralized to form a

[8] *The Independent*, LXXIX (July 20, 1914), 83-84.
[9] Irving Fisher to the author, Aug. 4, 1939.

"District of Columbia" for a union of nations. Members of the world league would agree to submit all disputes to a court of arbitration. Decrees of the court would be enforced by the international police force and by the military power of all member nations.[10]

Since these proposals of Hamilton Holt and Irving Fisher for a league of nations were the first public pronouncements on the subject to be made in the United States after the outbreak of the war in Europe, the origin of the League to Enforce Peace might be traced to either one or to both. Both articles attracted attention and caused public comment. Both authors were encouraged by their friends to initiate some organized support for their ideas. It is possibly true, however, that neither proposal was the cause of the league movement. They represented opinions that were current among many men on the eve of the war, reflected the impact of the war upon constructive minds, and stimulated action.

Since Mr. Holt was an active member of the New York Peace Society, it is rather natural that his suggestions concerning a league of nations led to a discussion among the directors of that society on the whole subject of what the peace societies could do with advantage toward the promotion of his proposals. A meeting called for such a discussion took place on October 7, 1914. Mr. Holt, John Bates Clark, Frederick Lynch, Henry N. McCracken, and Robert Underwood Johnson were among those present at the meeting. Discussion centered particularly around the idea of having the society declare its support of the establishment of an international police force in connection with a league of peace at the end of the war. At Mr. Holt's suggestion, a Plan of Action Committee was appointed to consider what the society could do and to report to the executive committee. This was the initial action out of which the League to Enforce Peace evolved.[11]

---

[10] *The New York Times*, Aug. 16, 1914.
[11] Copy of the *Minutes* of the meeting of the Directors of the New York Peace Society, *Edward A. Filene Collection*, Woodrow Wilson Foundation Library. Hereafter referred to as *Filene MSS*.

FOUNDING OF THE LEAGUE TO ENFORCE PEACE 31

The first meeting of the Plan of Action Committee was held on October 28, 1914. Of the twenty-eight people who had been invited to the meeting ten were not heard from, eighteen accepted the invitation, and seven actually attended.[12] Professor George W. Kirchwey was chairman of the meeting, and for some reason Mr. Holt was not present. The committee decided that a movement should be inaugurated among the neutral nations to induce the belligerents to send delegates to a peace conference at which attempts would be made to find solutions for the controversies that had caused the war. It was decided that a manifesto to that effect should be drawn. This proposal was reconsidered at length at a second meeting of the committee held on November 4, and objection was raised to it by Mr. Holt and other members. It was decided to make a full report of the discussion to the executive committee at its meeting on December 22, 1914.

At this meeting Mr. Holt reported for the Plan of Action Committee. The majority of that committee believed that one of two things would have to happen before a peace conference could be held: a victory for one side or an impasse. They therefore did not favor the idea of attempting to secure a conference at that time. They believed that there was a rapidly growing desire among the people for the reduction of armaments and for "the establishment of permanent security through international law and sanctions." This aspiration could be realized only through the creation of "a union of sufficient number of powers to guarantee the preservation of peace by the maintenance of military force which can be used at need as a police, against any power which threatens hostilities." Certain necessary features of the arrangement to bring about such a union could, in their opinion, be foreseen with some certainty, and should include the following:

> 1. A treaty which shall not only arrange the boundaries of the states but shall guarantee the territories so established against attack, either from within or from without the League. Under such a treaty a country whose territory

[12] *Minutes*, meeting of Oct. 28, 1914, *Filene MSS*.

should be attacked by one or more Powers would have a right to call remaining powers in the League to assist in defending it.

2. The avoidance of lasting enmities due either to the present war or to the terms of settlement, by—

   a. making peace in a generous spirit and before the forces on either side shall have been completely crushed.

   b. respecting racial affiliations in the adjustment of territory made in the treaty of peace.

3. The reduction of armaments so that each state would have only its part of a police force.

4. A treaty under which member nations would agree to refer all differences between them to arbitration or to a permanent court.

Professor Kirchwey presented a minority report, signed only by himself, in which he argued again for calling a conference of the belligerents at once. He urged that in such a conference national boundaries and colonial claims could be settled, and that a concert of powers could be established which would be the germ of a federation of Europe and possibly the federation of the world. Both reports were considered at length, with the result that the entire problem of a plan of action was referred to a Committee of Four, which was to draft a new report and present it to the Plan of Action Committee. William H. Short, secretary of the New York Peace Society, Professor Kirchwey, John Bates Clark, and Hamilton Holt were appointed as the new committee.

This new committee presented its report on January 6, 1915, at a meeting held at the Hotel Astor. Essentially it was an elaboration of the majority report given to the executive committee on December 22. Some additional emphasis was given to the holding of annual conferences and to the establishment of a standing committee of the powers for the consideration of incipient disputes. The report urged strongly that nations should not disarm until some other form of security was developed and that international political organization was absolutely essential for the establishment of such security. The committee proposed that a copy of its report be sent to all members of the society and that a larger committee be formed for the purpose of waging an active campaign in behalf of the program outlined. This proposal was adopted.[13]

Up to this time, January 6, 1915, the events that led to the formation of the League to Enforce Peace had taken place within the New York Peace Society. Although the Society authorized the continuance of its activity for a league of nations, events took a somewhat different turn and resulted in the formation of an independent movement that emanated from a series of dinner conferences which were held at the New York Century Club. Writing to William Howard Taft about these dinners a few years later, Hamilton Holt described the events as follows:

> I was very much interested in the interview that Donald Wilhelm had with you in The New York Times of Sunday. The matter is not of very great importance, but I presume in the interest of strict accuracy you might be interested to know that there were four dinners given at the Century Club instead of three which you mentioned. The first was given by Mr. Howland and myself. It came about in this way. Mr. Howland and I were lunching at the Century and Marburg happened to come along and sit down beside us. He had been reading my *Independent* article in which I proposed a concrete plan for a league of nations, the first article, I think, that appeared in the country on the subject since the war broke out. He suggested that my article was sound but he thought we ought to get it criticized. Then if the critics agreed that there was anything in it, we could take it to another group of men who could tell us whether it was practical. Marburg suggested that I give the first dinner. When I got home Mr. Howland came and said that he would like to share the expense with me, so we gave the first dinner together. I presided as I remember. We got nowhere at that dinner and Mr. Marburg invited the same group to the second dinner. At the third dinner Marburg suggested that we invite in Mr. Howland, and Mr. John Hays Hammond, so we four gave the third dinner. You and the gentleman you mentioned were at the fourth dinner and the same four

[13] *Minutes*, meeting of Jan. 6, 1915, *Filene MSS;* also in the *League Collection.*

who served as hosts at the third dinner served at the fourth. The rest of the progress of events you know as well as I do.

The first two dinners only paved the way for the third dinner, but the third got a fairly good program, tho it needed the fourth to complete it. The idea really did not get anywhere until the dinner at which you were present.

The first conference at the Century Club was held on January 25, 1915. Among those present in addition to the hosts, were Theodore Marburg, Franklin H. Giddings, W. W. Willoughby, Theodore S. Woolsey, James L. Tryon, H. J. Howland, Frederick Lynch, John Bates Clark, William I. Hull, Irving Fisher, George A. Plimpton, Frank Crane, James A. Stewart, and William H. Short. Mr. Holt acted as chairman and opened the meeting with a plea for the establishment of a league of peace. Mr. Crane supported Holt's ideas, advocated the leadership of the United States in a league movement, and expressed the belief that President Wilson would favor such a program since he already advocated the creation of a Pan-American league to replace the Monroe Doctrine.

The discussion that followed ranged over the many problems of world peace. Arguments were presented for and against including all nations in a league, the establishment of world government as against the idea of territorial guarantee, and the propriety of American action to initiate a movement for a league of peace. The general sentiment was that the time was ripe for such a movement and that the United States should take the lead. Resolutions were passed to the effect that the league should be so constituted as to bring about the amicable settlement of all disputes between nations, and a guarantee of each member of the league against invasion or impairment of its independence.

In his letter, quoted above, Mr. Holt stated that the same guests who were present at the first conference were invited to attend the second. Although the same people may have been invited, several did not attend, while others were present who had not attended the first dinner. The latter included Jeremiah W. Jenks, John Hays Hammond, George C. Holt, and Everett P. Wheeler. At the second dinner, held on January 31, Hamilton Holt again acted as chairman and the discussion continued to be of a general nature. The third dinner was not held until two months later, March 30, 1915. In the meantime Theodore Marburg had sent summaries of the first two Century Club conferences to a number of people including Lord Bryce, William H. Taft, and President Wilson. He had received a copy of Bryce's "Proposals for the Prevention of Future Wars," and was able, therefore, to place that document before the third dinner conference. The final result of the third meeting was the adoption of the following program:

1. The function of the League of Peace shall be to guarantee that no dispute to which a member of the League is a party shall be settled by other than amicable means, the guarantee to be maintained when necessary by the use against the offending nation of the united forces of the nations of the League.

2. Disputes not settled by diplomacy to which a member of the League may be a party shall be referred for settlement to existing institutions, such as the International Committee of Inquiry, the Permanent Court of Arbitration, good offices, mediation, or to other institutions to be established for that purpose. The early creation of an International Court of Justice is held to be especially important.

3. The League ought to be formed as soon as practicable but not until the nations adhering to its constitution shall represent a sufficient preponderance of power to enable it to maintain the guarantees of the League.

4. Initiative for the formation of a League of Peace ought to be taken by the United States immediately without waiting for the ending of the present war.

5. The nations of the League shall provide an assembly to meet periodically to discuss affairs of common concern.[14]

It was agreed that the next step would be to submit the program to a group of "practical" men who would be invited to attend a fourth conference. This, the last of the Century Club conferences, was held on April 9, with such men in attendance as William Howard Taft, James M. Beck, J. Reuben Clark, Jr., A. Lawrence Lowell, Albert Shaw, John Bates Clark,

[14] *Minutes*, meeting of Mar. 30, 1915, *League Collection*.

William C. Dennis, and Leo S. Rowe, in addition to a few of the members of previous conferences, including Hamilton Holt and Theodore Marburg. Mr. Marburg explained to the conference the proposals for a league of peace that had been approved at the previous meeting. He argued that a voluntary international court would not insure peace, that machinery was needed to force the submission of disputes to the court, and that an international police force, a standing army of the league, was necessary.[15]

Mr. Taft was startled at the ambitious nature of the proposals. They involved, he said, the entrance of the United States into an offensive alliance. Perhaps it would be better to establish an international court and trust that sometime in the future they could establish a league to stand behind it. In the general discussion that followed, Mr. Shaw advocated compulsory arbitration and Mr. Beck denounced American isolation, the false tradition of Washington, and expressed the hope that one great good would result from the war—a league of peace.[16] The main discussion took place, however, between Dr. Lowell and Mr. Taft, Dr. Lowell stating firmly that he believed in the use of force to compel the reference of a dispute among nations to judicial decision under international law and in the need for a world league to settle non-justiciable questions.[17] Dr. Lowell later expressed the belief that his main contribution to the meeting was the idea that "the use of force should be automatic instead of subject to the decision of a meeting of powers," for in his opinion such a meeting of powers was likely to hesitate and do nothing at all. Other people, present at the Century Club conference, have emphasized Dr. Lowell's skillful work in leading Mr. Taft to support his general program.[18] Agreement was finally reached on the following resolutions.

[15] *Minutes*, meeting of Apr. 9, 1914, *League Collection*.
[16] *Ibid.*
[17] A. Lawrence Lowell to Theodore Marburg, Mar. 21, 1921 (copy), Lowell MSS.
[18] William C. Dennis to the author, July 18, 1939; Hamilton Holt's account of the meeting in conversation with the author.

1. That it is the opinion of those present that it is desirable for the United States to form a League of all the great nations in which all justiciable questions between them would be submitted to a judicial tribunal.
2. That members of the League shall jointly use their military force to prevent any one of their number from going to war or committing acts of hostility against any member before the question at issue has been submitted to the tribunal.
3. That nations shall be compelled to submit non-justiciable questions to a Council of Conciliation before going to war, under the same penalty as provided above.
4. That conferences between the parties to this agreement shall be held from time to time to formulate and to codify rules of international law which, unless some nation shall signify its dissent within a stated period, shall thereafter govern in the decision of the aforementioned tribunal.

Henry Pritchett and J. Reuben Clark, Jr. objected to the second resolution on the basis that it would involve the United States in entangling alliances.[19] Otherwise the resolutions were adopted without dissent, although some of the people present may not have been enthusiastic about them.[20]

Careful consideration was given to plans for future action. It was agreed finally that Mr. Taft should edit the resolutions and send them to the members of the conference for their signatures. They should then be presented to a large group of influential citizens, a hundred or more, who would be asked to sponsor a larger meeting to which men of position and prominence would be invited. At this meeting attempts would be made to bring the proposals to the attention of the nation at large and to launch the movement for a league of peace into a national campaign. Since it would take some time to secure the support of the sponsoring group and to arrange for and organize the proposed meeting, the date selected was Bunker Hill Day, June 17, and the place chosen was Independence Hall, Philadelphia. The date and the place were thought to symbolize

---

[19] J. Reuben Clark, Jr. to the author, July 5, 1939; *Minutes* of the meeting, *League Collection.*
[20] Albert Shaw to the author, July 14, 1939.

events in American experience which were logical steps toward the goal of world peace.

The movement to initiate the Philadelphia conference did not take place in a vacuum. Newspapers and magazines were filled with accounts of the war in Europe, of destruction, of battles, and of the fate of civilians who were in the path of invading armies. The *Lusitania* episode, early in May, brought war close to the United States and fortified the momentous decision of the government to defend American maritime rights. Five peace conferences were held between February and June, 1915, and all of them adopted resolutions showing that the trend of thought was in the direction proposed by the league of peace movement. These conferences were the National Peace Conference at Chicago, February 26-28, the Central Organization for Durable Peace at The Hague, April 28-30, the World Court Congress, at Cleveland, May 13-14, and the Lake Mohonk Arbitration Conference where Theodore Marburg, Professor John B. Clark of Columbia University, Dr. Samuel A. Eliot, and Hamilton Holt presented the league of peace project.[21]

The league group carried on its work as rapidly as possible. The resolutions adopted at the meeting of April 9 were edited by Mr. Taft, and submitted to a group of prominent men who were asked to endorse them and also to sponsor the Philadelphia meeting. The resolutions, as edited by Mr. Taft, were as follows:

> It is desirable for the United States to join a League of all the great nations, binding the signatories to the following:
> First: All justiciable questions arising between the signatory powers, not settled by negotiation, shall be submitted to a judicial tribunal for hearing and judgment both upon the merits and upon any issue as to its jurisdiction of the question.
> Second: All non-justiciable questions arising between the signatories, and not settled by negotiation, shall be submitted to a judicial Council of Conciliation for hearing, consideration, and recommendation.
> Third: The signatory powers shall jointly use their mili-

[21] *The Independent*, LXXXII (May 31, 1915), 340.

tary forces to prevent any one of their number from going to war, or committing acts of hostility, against another of the signatories before any question arising shall be submitted as provided in the foregoing.

Fourth: Conferences between the signatory powers shall be held from time to time to formulate and codify rules of international law, which, unless some signatory shall signify its dissent within a stated period, shall thereafter govern in the decisions of the Judicial Tribunal mentioned in Article One.

Over a hundred sponsors were easily secured,[22] and other arrangements for the meeting were made.

Approximately 300 people assembled in Independence Hall on June 17 under the temporary chairmanship of Thomas Raeburn White. Mr. Taft was elected president of the conference, and a resolutions committee of fifteen members was appointed with A. Lawrence Lowell as chairman. Other members of this committee included Hamilton Holt, Newton D. Baker, James M. Beck, George Grafton Wilson, J. M. Dickinson, and John Bates Clark. Mr. Taft was a member *ex officio*.

For the most part the committee accepted the resolutions used in the call for the convention. Only three changes were made. It was agreed that the league, now officially called the League to *Enforce* Peace rather than the League *of* Peace, should not be limited to the *great* nations but should be open to membership by all nations. Under Article II the words "subject to the limitation of treaties" were added, because it was believed that otherwise the world court might hold a question justiciable in spite of a specific treaty provision to the contrary. And it was agreed that economic as well as military pressure should be used against any member that violated its obligations under the agreement. In answer to the contention that economic pressure might be an alternative to other forms of force, Dr. Lowell expressed what became the prevailing view, that if the members of the league had to meet and consider whether, in a given instance, economic or military pressure should be employed, delay and intrigue might very well permit the guilty nation to escape punishment. The

[22] See Appendix I.

convention adopted the following statement as the official platform of the League to Enforce Peace.

Warrant from History

Throughout five thousand years of recorded history peace, here and there established, has been kept, and its area has been widened, in one way only. Individuals have combined their efforts to suppress violence in the local community. Communities have co-operated to maintain the authoritative state and to preserve peace within its borders. States have formed leagues or confederations, or have otherwise co-operated, to establish peace among themselves. Always peace has been made and kept, when made and kept at all, by the superior power of superior numbers acting in unity for the common good.

Mindful of this teaching of experience, we believe and solemnly urge that the time has come to devise and to create a working union of sovereign nations to establish peace among themselves and to guarantee it by all known and available sanctions at their command, to the end that civilization may be conserved, and the progress of mankind in comfort, enlightenment and happiness may continue.

It is desirable for the United States to join a league of nations binding the signatories to the following:

First: All justiciable questions arising between the signatory powers, not settled by negotiation, shall, subject to the limitations of treaties, be submitted to a judicial tribunal for hearing and judgment, both upon the merits and upon any issue as to its jurisdiction of the question.

Second: All other questions arising between the signatories and not settled by negotiation, shall be submitted to a Council of Conciliation for hearing, consideration and recommendation.

Third: The signatory powers shall jointly use forthwith both their economic and military forces against any one of their number that goes to war, or commits acts of hostility against another of the signatories before any question arising shall be submitted as provided in the foregoing.*

---

* The executive committee later authorized the following interpretation of Article 3.

"The signatory Powers shall jointly employ diplomatic and economic pressure against any one of their number that threatens war against a

Fourth: Conferences between the signatory powers shall be held from time to time to formulate and codify rules of international law, which, unless some signatory shall signify its dissent within a stated period, shall thereafter govern in the decisions of the Judicial Tribunal mentioned in Article One.

Among the speeches made at Philadelphia, probably those by Messrs. Taft, Lowell, Marburg, and Holt were the most important. Mr. Taft made it very clear that so-called neutral nations were inescapably influenced by wars among their neighbors. The interests and needs of neutrals, he said, could easily be developed to the point where international law would recognize their rights to be consulted about the wars of their neighbors. The fundamental idea of the League to Enforce Peace was that "no war can take place between its members until they have resorted to the machinery that the League proposes to furnish to settle the controversy likely to lead to war."[23]

Theodore Marburg dwelt particularly upon the reasons why other world leagues of the past had failed and traced the evolution of world organization. First, he said, came the creation of international institutions; second, the agreement to use them; third, the use of force to bring about their use; and fourth, the use of force as a sanction for international law and legislations. The Hague conferences had taken the world through the first two stages of development, the program of the League to Enforce Peace provided the third stage, and people had a right to expect that the fourth stage would be reached soon. He felt that the success of the league system depended upon the loyal support of the most democratically progressive states, Great Britain, France, and the United States.

---

fellow signatory without having first submitted its dispute for international inquiry, conciliation, arbitration, or judicial hearing, and awaited a conclusion, or without having in good faith offered to submit it. They shall follow this forthwith by the joint use of their military forces against that nation if it actually goes to war or commits acts of hostility, against another of the signatories before any question arising shall be dealt with as provided in the foregoing."

[23] *The Philadelphia Conference* (pamphlet), *League Collection.*

Dr. Lowell emphasized again the difference between agreeing to go to war against a nation that violated its obligations under the league and agreeing to consult about what should be done when a case arose. He compared the latter with the ludicrous situation that would exist if a policeman who observed a street fight should suggest that the problem of what to do with the participants be referred to the city council. To those who feared that the American policies of isolation would be violated by the league system, he declared that the Atlantic Ocean was no longer a barrier; it was a lake, and soon would be a river.

Hamilton Holt referred to Immanuel Kant's essay of 1795, *Perpetual Peace*, and agreed with Kant that peace would be established only when nations are hospitably disposed toward one another, have representative governments, and are politically organized. He considered the various uses of force and made a clear distinction between force used by an aggressor state and force used by the nations of the world as international police power. He compared the need for world organization to the need for union in the United States at the time of the formation of the Constitution and drew a picture of what would have happened if each American state had decided to provide for its own safety through its own armament.

The Philadelphia meeting did not create a news sensation, but it received considerable attention in the press, probably more attention, all things considered, than might have been expected. "Never before," declared one journal, "has the idea of permanent peace been set forth with the united support of so many advocates or in so complete a form, or at so opportune a moment as in the recent formation of the League to Enforce Peace." The consideration given to the movement was surprising when compared with the rather cold reception given to Secretary Bryan's peace treaties and to older peace movements. More papers commented favorably than otherwise. Among the former were the *Philadelphia Inquirer*, the *New York World*, the *Brooklyn Eagle*, the *Buffalo Courier*, the *Pittsburgh Dispatch*, the *Baltimore American*, the *Washington Post*, and the *Indianapolis Star*. Journals that commented unfavorably generally stated that the program of the league was vague, that American participation would bring about "entangling alliances," end the Monroe Doctrine, and necessitate amendments to the Constitution.

The first task of the League to Enforce Peace, following its official establishment, was the creation of a permanent organization. For this purpose the first meeting of the executive committee was held in New York on June 29, 1915. Mr. Taft had already accepted the presidency of the organization, and it was understood that Dr. Lowell would accept the chairmanship of the executive committee. The committee elected Hamilton Holt and Theodore Marburg vice-chairmen, Herbert S. Houston, treasurer, and William H. Short, secretary. The following committees were established: (1) Committee on Information, Mr. Houston, Chairman; (2) Committee on Finance, Darwin P. Kingsley, Chairman; (3) Committee on Home Organization, Alton B. Parker, Chairman; (4) Committee on Foreign Organization, Theodore Marburg, Chairman. It was agreed that the president of the league, Mr. Taft, the five other national officers mentioned above, and the chairmen of the four committees should constitute a Committee on Management with *ad interim* full power between meetings of the executive committee.

It is notable that in addition to the work of organization, the only other important action taken at the first official meeting of the executive committee was the decision to invite Nicholas Murray Butler and Elihu Root to become members of the league and of its executive committee.[24] Neither invitation was accepted. Mr. Root expressed doubts as to the wisdom of the league's program. He disliked giving to a world court power over its own jurisdiction, and he felt that Article III would involve the United States in entangling alliances. He believed that a court of justice should be established for the determination of judicial questions, that there should be a "tribunal of conciliation for hearing and recommendation upon all other questions," and that "some kind of sanction for the enforcement of the judgment of the court should be estab-

[24] *Minutes*, Executive Committee, June 29, 1915, *League Collection*.

lished by general international agreement."[25] Mr. Root, therefore, appeared to believe in the principles of the league, while he refused to join in its efforts to establish them in fact and practise. The question of the jurisdiction of the court was not vital, as Dr. Lowell pointed out to him,[26] since the agreement called only for submission of questions to the court. And if he believed in the enforcement of judicial decisions by sanctions established through international agreement, as he clearly said he did, then he could not have been seriously opposed to American participation in "entangling alliances."

For one reason or another, in the United States and perhaps elsewhere, Mr. Root was regarded with exceptionally high esteem as a statesman, lawyer, and student of international affairs. He was one of the comparatively few people in the United States who could not remain really neutral regarding a movement like the League to Enforce Peace. If he said nothing whatsoever publicly, people like Lord Bryce in England and thousands of people in America wondered why he said nothing.[27] When proponents of the league quoted, from his letters or speeches, statements favoring the principles of the league, the inquiry obviously arose regarding what objection he had to its program. In fact the question may reasonably be raised whether his open opposition would not have been less damaging to the league than his silence. Open opposition would have required him to state his objections publicly, and the league forces would have had an opportunity to analyse and counter them. The significance of Elihu Root in the whole history of the League to Enforce Peace is second to that of no other individual, although he was never a member of the organization.

Having launched the movement and established the nucleus for a national organization, the next task before the league was to present its program to the people of the nation. Enough funds had been raised at the Philadelphia meeting to start a pamphlet series, and efforts were immediately directed toward

[25] Elihu Root to A. Lawrence Lowell, Aug. 9, 1915, *Lowell MSS.*
[26] A. Lawrence Lowell to Elihu Root, Aug. 18, 1915 (copy), *Lowell MSS.*
[27] Taft to Root, Jan. 4, 1915 (copy), *Taft MSS.*

securing the support of other organizations with established machinery for the dissemination of information. The first pamphlets were prepared by Taft, Lowell, and the treasurer, Herbert S. Houston. They outlined the league's program and produced strong arguments in support of it. The most complete analysis of the movement in this early stage, however, was Dr. Lowell's article, "A League to Enforce Peace" in the *Atlantic Monthly* for September, 1915. This article was reprinted in pamphlet form and widely distributed at the expense of the World Peace Foundation. In addition it was referred to and summarized elsewhere.[28] By reason of its author's position in the league and because of its extensive reporting in the press, the article acquired the force of an official statement.

In his moderate and reasoned argument Dr. Lowell stated that the program of the league was not designed to stop the existing war but to prevent future wars. It was admittedly imperfect and incomplete, but it was the most "promising plan for maintaining peace" that had been brought forward. He explained the uses of arbitration and conciliation, and pointed out the unique feature of the league's plan—the agreement to use force against a nation that violated the agreement. He illustrated the problem of international collective security by the analogy of the rôle of the vigilance committee on the American frontier—and the responsibility of one nation in a collective scheme—by comparing it with the position of a citizen who is called upon to serve on a *posse comitatus*.

It was hoped that the movement for the League to Enforce Peace would secure the active and enthusiastic support of the older peace societies. This hope was only partially realized. The World Peace Foundation gave its whole-hearted and complete coöperation, but the American Peace Society had divided counsels on the question. The latter organization and many other similar bodies contained among their membership ardent pacifists who did not agree with the fundamental idea of the league, the use of force. Other members realized fully that peace had to be a constructive effort, and they were quite willing to join the movement. This conflict of opinion was

[28] *Literary Digest*, LI (Sept. 18, 1915), 594-595.

observed in the meeting of the Fifth American Peace Conference held in San Francisco, October 10-13, 1915. The American Peace Society, the Church Peace Union, and other organizations had joined in the conference. But the program of the league was ably presented and in the end was substantially introduced into the resolutions of the conference.[29]

Through the efforts of Edward A. Filene and others, the United States Chamber of Commerce gave timely support to a large part of the league's program. The activity of the Chamber of Commerce on the subject of peace began with a resolution offered to the chamber at its Washington meeting, January, 1915, "urging that the power of international commerce and finance, applied as economic pressure, be employed to compel nations to bring their differences before an international tribunal before going to war." A committee was appointed to "examine into the relations between the present war and business and to submit suggestions as to the future." The committee studied the problem and drew up a series of resolutions which were submitted to the members of the United States Chamber of Commerce for their approval. The first three resolutions were adopted by nearly all of the 282 chambers of commerce that answered the referendum. These resolutions approved of calling a conference of neutral nations to define the rules for the protection of life and property upon the sea, declared that the United States should join in the establishment of an international court for the settlement of justiciable questions, and called upon the United States to take the initiative in establishing a council of conciliation for the consideration of non-justiciable questions.

The fourth resolution provided that the United States should take the initiative in bringing about an agreement among the nations to "bring concerted economic pressure to bear upon any nation or nations which resort to military measures without submitting their differences to an international court or council of conciliation, and awaiting the decision of the court or recommendation of the council, as circumstances make the more appropriate." This resolution was approved by about

[29] *Proceedings*, Fifth American Peace Conference, New York, 1915.

a three-to-one vote. The fifth resolution urged the United States to take the intiative in bringing about an agreement "to use concerted military force in the event that concerted economic pressure exercised by the signatory nations is not sufficient to compel nations which have proceeded to war to desist from military operations and submit the questions at issue to an International Court or to a Council of Conciliation, as circumstances make the more appropriate." This was approved by about a two-to-one vote. Although the Chamber of Commerce resolutions did not specifically endorse the program of the league, they served to advertise and to support its principles. Mr. Filene did not object to the use of military force but believed that economic force should be tried first.

CHAPTER THREE

Response to the League Idea

From the time of its founding until the declaration of war in April, 1917, the League to Enforce Peace waged a campaign of education. Its task was to show the American people that their safety and welfare depended upon the existence of a peaceful world, that such a world could not be established without American coöperation, and that the league's program offered a practical solution for the problem of world peace. This task was not easy, for many people, some of them in organized groups, contended with zeal and often with effectiveness that the affairs of the rest of the world were of no immediate concern to the United States. The sincerity of these people may be conceded; their motives were certainly diverse. Among them were the simon-pure isolationists who relied for their ideas upon certain phrases of Washington and Jefferson without regard to the context in which the phrases were used. Pacifists saw in the isolationist doctrine the hope for escape from involvement in war. The Anglophobes feared that concern for world peace might lead to coöperation with Great Britain, and the Germanophiles feared that it might lead to opposition to the Central Powers. Some people thought that the league advocated too much and others that it attempted too little. And still others like James Brown Scott and Elihu Root held themselves coldly aloof from the enterprise. Thus the struggles of the league in its early days were against covert as well as overt hostility.

The high point of the league's activity during this period was the First National Assembly, which was held in Washington on May 26 and 27, 1916. No possible effort was spared to make the meeting a success. Formal invitations were sent to the chambers of commerce of the United States, to college presidents, to the governors of the states, to the mayors of cities, to learned societies, to clergymen, to fraternal, patriotic, labor, and religious leaders, to bar associations and other societies, to leading publicists, to educators, and to many other individuals. Public officials were asked to send representatives if they could not attend in person, and organizations were asked to send delegates. The total resources of the league were used in securing as large an attendance as possible. Literally thousands of letters were sent. These efforts were fruitful. More than 2,000 people assembled in the Belasco Theatre for the first meeting of the assembly.

The speeches were of two kinds, those dealing with the organization and activity of the league and those dealing with its objectives or with criticism which had been leveled against its plans. Prominent among those who dealt with organization and activity were Philip H. Gadsden, a Charleston, South Carolina, business executive, Herbert S. Houston, vice-president of Doubleday, Page and Company, and Theodore Marburg. It was realized, however, that organizational activity was the day-by-day task of league workers. Interest centered, therefore, in the discussion of ideas.[1]

These speeches in defense of the league's program present a catalog of the objections that had been advanced against it. They explained simply and clearly that the submission of a dispute to judicial decision was not a violation of the Monroe Doctrine; that American participation in an international organization for the preservation of peace was not entering into an "entangling alliance" as Jefferson used the term; that the league's program did not deprive Congress of its power to declare war or to control domestic affairs. Mr. Taft stated very clearly, however, the principle that unless Congress, through treaties, was willing to promise to act in certain ways under certain specified circumstances, no hope for international agreement concerning enforced peace could be contemplated. This

[1] Speeches of George Grafton Wilson, William H. Taft, Thomas Raeburn White.

idea was the basis for Article 10 in the League of Nations Covenant, an article that Mr. Taft later denounced.

Edward A. Filene, in a speech distinguished for its clarity and for its prophetic vision, drew a picture of the post-war world as it would be if a regime of peace under law and a far-seeing international economic policy were not followed. There would ensue, he said, the greatest depression in history, the erection of tariffs in the United States and abroad, a new era of competitive armament, burdensome taxation, and eventually war. He recounted the story of the Good Samaritan and declared that it was the duty of the United States not only to play the rôle of the Good Samaritan but also "to rid the Jericho Road of thieves." The United States, he said, must lead the way to a new world order or be dragged into an undesirable order by those who would lead the way.

The dinner session of the assembly was presided over by William Howard Taft, and the first speaker was Senator Henry Cabot Lodge. Both on account of the importance attached to it at the moment and because of later events, the address of Senator Lodge is notable. He had expressed himself on the use of force in national affairs in an address delivered at Union College just prior to the Philadelphia meeting of the League to Enforce Peace in 1915.[2] At that time he paid tribute to men who look facts in the face and give heed to stern realities. He denounced treaties for the settlement of international disputes which provided no force to support the obligations behind them. The way to have peace was through the establishment of international force behind treaties. The Senator referred to this earlier speech and reaffirmed what he had said. He declared that voluntary arbitration agreements had gone as far as they could go and that the next step was the one proposed by the league, the use of force behind international peace. "We may not solve it that way," he continued, "but if we cannot solve it that way it can be solved in no other." He admitted that there would be objections to the league program. "I know," he said, "the difficulties which arise when we

[2] Henry Cabot Lodge, *War Addresses, 1914-1917* (Boston, Houghton Mifflin Company, 1917), pp. 23-48.

speak of anything which seems to involve an alliance. But I do not believe that when Washington warned us against entangling alliances he meant for one moment that we should not join with the other civilized nations of the world if a method could be found to diminish war and encourage peace." Thus Senator Lodge took a strong stand in favor of the principles as well as the proposals of the league.[3]

Sitting on the platform with Mr. Taft and Senator Lodge was President Wilson. Although it had not been foreseen and was not fully appreciated at the time, one of the great dramatic moments in American and world history had arrived when the President arose to speak. The scene itself was not remarkable. Other distinguished banquet audiences had gathered at the Willard Hotel. Other men, notable for their intellectual attainments, had discussed the subject of world peace not only during the First National Assembly of the League to Enforce Peace but also at other times and places over a period of several thousand years. In the realm of ideas the President's address contained nothing that was new. All that he said had already been said by Lowell or Taft or Holt or other members of the league movement. Nevertheless the President's address, in his own opinion the most important that he had ever been called upon to make,[4] was the most significant pronouncement on the subject of American foreign policy since President Monroe's famous message to Congress.[5] It was not only the first formal commitment of President Wilson to the league of nations idea but also the first time in history that the responsible head of a great world power had proposed to lead that power into a commonwealth of nations. In this sense his address marked an epoch in the moral evolution of civilization.

President Wilson's pronouncement was not the result of sudden conversion to the idea of collective security. Rather it

[3] This and the other addresses given at the First National Assembly of the League to Enforce Peace were printed in a pamphlet entitled *Enforced Peace* (New York, 1916).
[4] Ray Stannard Baker, *Woodrow Wilson, Life and Letters* (New York, Doubleday, Doran Company, 1927-39), VI, 216.
[5] Harley Notter, *Origins of the Foreign Policy of Woodrow Wilson* (Baltimore, Johns Hopkins Press, 1937), p. 521.

represented the slow evolution of his thought dating back at least to 1887, when he had spoken of "governments joined with governments for the pursuit of common purposes, in honorary equality and honorable subordination."[6] He had joined the American Peace Society in 1908, had sponsored the Bryan treaties, and had taken an active part in the negotiation of the Pan-American Pact. Sometime during the fall of 1914 he had stated his ideas regarding a league of nations in a conversation with his brother-in-law, Dr. Stockton Axson. As Dr. Axson later recalled the scene, he and the President were alone in the President's office in the White House. The President arose from his desk and walked over to the fireplace. He said he was troubled about the war, for he believed that nothing would be permanently settled by it, and that the real settlement would have to be made later. Four things, he said, would have to be done:

> First, that small nations shall have equal rights with great nations; second, that never again must it be permitted for a foot of ground to be obtained by conquest; third, that the manufacture of munitions of war must be by government and not by private enterprise; and fourth, that all nations must be absorbed into some great association of nations whereby all shall guarantee the integrity of each so that any one nation violating the agreement between all of them shall bring punishment on itself automatically.

Dr. Axson could not be certain whether the President had used the word "league" or "association," although he had tried to recall the exact words of the President's statement.[7]

By November, 1915, the President was convinced that provision for some form of a league of nations was absolutely necessary in any European peace program, and by February, 1916, he was ready to express publicly the hope that some form of joint guarantee of peace would result from the war.[8] On May 8, 1916, in response to a delegation from the American

[6] Notter, *op. cit.*, p. 43.
[7] *The New York Times*, Feb. 4, 1924.
[8] See Notter, *op. cit.*, for a more complete history of the evolution of Wilson's thought.

Union Against Militarism, he came out openly and emphatically for the use of force for the preservation of peace. "In the last analysis," he said, "the peace of society is obtained by force, and when action comes,—it comes by opinion but back of opinion is the ultimate application of force."[9]

President Wilson prepared his address of May 27 with unusual care. Clippings and shorthand notes relative to the subject of his address had been kept in his study in a folder which no one was allowed to touch.[10] But it is impossible to connect particular ideas expressed in the address with precise sources of inspiration. As an historian, he was familiar with the constitutional history of the United States and could not have escaped thinking about the analogy between the American system of federal government and a possible confederation of world states. Also as an historian he was reasonably familiar with the various movements for world peace that had taken place in the past. Through correspondence, conversations, and study, he was in touch with the pronouncements of the various peace groups and was well acquainted with the program of the League to Enforce Peace.[11]

When first approached by the league, he had declined the invitation to speak at the Washington meeting. But as the time for the meeting approached, he changed his mind. The reasons seem to have been his own crystallizing conviction, the trend of world events, and the deepening public interest in the subject of peace. Secretary Lansing had disapproved of his speaking at the league meeting, and Colonel House had advised against giving public approval to the league program in detail.

[9] *The Independent*, LXXXVI (May 22, 1916), 264.
[10] Baker, *op. cit.*, VI, 217.
[11] Colonel House made suggestions for the address and many of them were approved by Wilson. See Charles Seymour, *The Intimate Papers of Colonel House* (Boston, Houghton Mifflin Company, 1926), II, 337-338. To show, however, that the President's address followed on various points the ideas contained in the House memorandum does not demonstrate that the President took the ideas from the memorandum. Since most of the points in the address had been either implicit or explicit in former addresses and statements of the President, it would be easy to exaggerate the rôle played by Colonel House.

This advice was probably not needed, for it would have been inexpedient for a person in the President's position to have committed himself to precise phrases. But having made up his mind to speak, to endorse the principles and ideals of the league's program, he went forward, and during the remainder of his life he did not turn away from the road that he had taken.

After a few opening remarks, the President came directly to the crucial conclusion which he had decided to assert: that American isolation from world affairs was a figment of the imagination. He said that we were not merely onlookers in the existing war. Our rights, privileges, liberties, and property had been affected. We could not be onlookers at the peace, for both peace and war thereafter would be the common interest of mankind. "We are," he continued, "participants, whether we would or not, in the life of the world. The interests of all nations are our own also. We are partners with the rest. What affects mankind is inevitably our affair as well as the affair of the nations of Europe and of Asia." A little later on he phrased his whole thesis into one sentence: "The nations of the world have become each other's neighbors."

The President was not content with an academic analysis. He was concerned with deeds, with action, and announced a "new and more wholesome diplomacy" based upon the ideas he had expressed. Under this new diplomacy the nations of the world would seek agreements covering their fundamental common interests and formulate methods of dealing with any nation or group of nations that sought to disturb those interests. They should insist upon three fundamental rights of nations:

> 1. the right of every people to choose the sovereignty under which they live.
> 2. the right of small nations to enjoy the same respect for their sovereignty and territorial integrity that great nations insist upon.
> 3. the right of all the nations of the world to be free from war resulting from aggression and the disregard of the rights of peoples and nations.

The President believed that the American people were prepared to support the new diplomacy, to accept the fundamental principles by which it would be directed, and would be willing, therefore, that the United States should become a "partner in any feasible association of nations formed to realize these objectives and make them secure against violation." This association would maintain the freedom of the seas for the use of all peoples and would prevent aggressive war in such a way as virtually to guarantee to all nations their territorial integrity and political independence.[12]

The President began his address by saying that it would not be expected of him to discuss in detail the program of the League to Enforce Peace. During the course of his remarks, he nevertheless managed to endorse virtually all the league's proposals. He favored the use of force, moral, economic, and in certain circumstances, physical. He advocated the formulation of international rights and the creation of an association of nations to make them secure. He did not mention specifically the idea of a judicial tribunal, but privately, in a letter to Colonel House, he defended that part of the league's program also. The idea of the guarantee of independence and territorial integrity was not in the league's platform, but it had been included in the early drafts of the platform. *The Independent* called the President's address a "Declaration of Interdependence" which should be added to the Declaration of Independence.[13]

It could not have escaped the attention of observant people that the majority of the founders of the League to Enforce Peace were Republicans. Among its most active spirits were Taft, Lowell, Holt, and Marburg. Moreover on January 4, 1915, Theodore Roosevelt had expanded his Christiania statement to include the advocacy of a league of nations, an international court, the use of international force, and the guarantee

---

[12] Ray Stannard Baker and William E. Dodd, editors, *The Public Papers of Woodrow Wilson* (New York, Harper and Brothers, 1925-1927), IV, 184-188.
[13] *The Independent*, LXXXVI (June 5, 1916), 357.

of territorial integrity and independence.[14] Now Senator Lodge had joined in advocating the league's principles. Thus a reasonable basis existed for the statement frequently made later by Taft and Lowell that the movement in the United States for the League of Nations was more Republican than Democratic in origin. If President Wilson had desired to make the league issue a partisan one and to secure political capital out of the nationalistic tendencies of the people, he had the opportunity. But the fact that he spoke for the league from the same platform with Senator Lodge at a meeting presided over by ex-President Taft, demonstrated his hope that a great issue of foreign policy could be advanced in a non-partisan spirit.

The President was very anxious that the subject of world peace should not become a matter of political debate. Congressman David J. Lewis of Maryland offered to introduce a resolution in Congress stating that Congress favored the President's idea of some sort of guarantee of peace following the war and that the United States should take the initiative in securing such a guarantee. The executive committee of the league authorized Messrs. Taft, Lowell, and Marburg to consider Mr. Lewis' proposal after having discussed the matter with the President. The President urged that the resolution should not be introduced for the reason that it would offer an opportunity for the opponents of the league to stir up opposition to it. Mr. Taft agreed with the President, and the proposal was dropped. The President discussed the subject again with both Mr. Taft and Mr. Marburg at the Washington meeting.[15]

The league, too, hoped to avoid partisan political difficulties over the league issue by securing the unqualified endorsement of the major parties. In two cases their efforts were wholly successful; in the third their efforts failed.

The Progressive Party was still in existence, and plans were

---

[14] *The Independent*, LXXXVI (May 22, 1916), 264.

[15] *Minutes*, Executive Committee, May 12, 1916; Marburg to Judge Parker, June 20, 1916 (copy); Taft to Marburg, June 6, 1916 (copy), *Filene MSS*. Also John H. Latané, *Development of the League of Nations Idea; Documents and Correspondence of Theodore Marburg* (New York, The Macmillan Company, 1932), I, 161.

made to secure the support of that group through the efforts of Oscar Straus.[16] Statements in the Progressive Party platform concerning the league issue were interwoven with bristling demands for thorough military preparedness and vigorous defense of American rights. The league issue, nevertheless, was clearly met. The platform declared that the "tradition of isolation has been ended," that the "United States is now a part of a world-system of civilization," that "it is the supreme duty of civilization to create conditions that will make peace permanent," and that the country "must be able and ready to take its part in that work."[17]

The support of the Republican Party for the league's program was sought through several avenues of approach. Mr. Taft sent letters to prominent leaders of the party.[18] Charles Stewart Davison, New York lawyer and author, communicated with Senator Lodge. Henry Lane Wilson, former Ambassador in Mexico, was designated as the official league representative at the convention.[19] Judge William H. Wadhams of the Court of General Sessions of New York talked with Nicholas Murray Butler and gave him a draft of a plank which would meet the desires of the league.[20] Through these and perhaps other influences a tentative draft of the platform which was to be presented to the Republican convention contained an endorsement of the league's program.[21] That endorsement was removed from the platform, however, at the insistence of Senator Lodge, who became the chairman of the committee on resolutions.[22] What reasons led Lodge, who supported the league up to the moment President Wilson endorsed it, to make the

[16] *Memorandum* on the National Conventions, dated June 2, 1916, *Filene MSS.*

[17] Edward Stanwood, *A History of the Presidency* (Boston, Houghton Mifflin Company, 1916), pp. 346-350.

[18] *Memorandum* on the National Conventions, dated June 2, 1916, *Filene MSS.*

[19] C. C. Michener to Edward Filene, June 2, 1916, *Filene MSS.*

[20] Judge Wadhams to Edward Filene, June 3, 1916, *Filene MSS.*

[21] William Short to Dr. Lowell (copy), July 18, 1916, *League Collection.* Also Judge Wadhams to Edward Filene, June 3, 1916, *Filene MSS.*

[22] William Short to Dr. Lowell, July 18, 1916 (copy), *League Collection.*

deletion can only be surmised. As adopted, the platform contained only one sentence on the subject of world organization that could in any way be construed as a reference to the program of the league. "We believe," ran the sentence, "in the pacific settlement of international disputes and favor the establishment of a world court for that purpose." This statement was so general and so limited in scope that under the circumstances it was nothing but the expression of a pious wish. Mr. Taft, however, congratulated the League to Enforce Peace on the action of the Republican Party in adopting the principles of the league.[23] His willingness to place such a fanciful construction on the platform may be explained partly by his intense and almost boundless personal dislike of the President and partly by his hope that the Republican Party would ultimately espouse the principles of the league.[24]

The failure of the Republican Party to take a stand in its platform on the league issue probably did not appear to the public at that time to be important. Other factors tended to obscure the omissions of the platform. Charles E. Hughes, in accepting the Republican nomination for the presidency, spoke at considerable length on what he termed the "organization of peace." War, he said, could not be prevented by pious wishes, but only through international organization designed to provide justice and "to safeguard so far as practicable the peace of the world." He declared that it was "worse than folly" to ignore the limitations of arbitration treaties as adequate means of preventing war. There was need, he continued, for the establishment of international judicial tribunals for the settlement of justiciable disputes and for "conferences of the nations to formulate international rules, to establish principles, to modify and extend international law so as to adapt it to new conditions, to remove causes of international disputes." Back of this organization there had to be the "cooperation of nations . . . the preventive power of a common purpose . . . some practical

---

[23] *Ibid.*

[24] William H. Taft to Calvin Cobb, July 19, 1916 (copy); Taft to Colonel Gordon McCabe, June 19, 1916 (copy); Taft to Gus J. Karger, Jan. 11, 1916 (copy), *Taft MSS.*

guarantee of international order." There is, he said, "no national isolation in the world of the twentieth century ... the peace of the world is our interest as well as the interest of others, and in developing the necessary agencies for the prevention of war, we shall be glad to have an appropriate share."[25]

Another factor in the Republican situation was the activity of Mr. Taft. He was delighted with the nomination of Mr. Hughes, consented to a public reconciliation with Theodore Roosevelt,[26] and entered wholeheartedly into the support of the Republican candidate. At the same time he continued to give tireless support to the league and spoke constantly in its behalf. His support of both the league and Mr. Hughes, together with the latter's New York speech of acceptance and later occasional references to the desirability of world organization for peace, tended to minimize the failure of the party platform to support the ideas of the league.

The Democratic Party's platform on the league issue was lifted almost verbatim from the President's league speech of May 27. It referred to the "new day of international relationships," to the duty of the United States to use its power "in the interests of humanity to assist the world in securing settled peace and justice," to the fundamental rights of nations that the President had mentioned, and to the duty of the United States to join with other nations "in any feasible association" of nations that would serve the principles stated and maintain the freedom of the seas.

During the remainder of the campaign, the President referred again and again to the problem of peace.[27] As the summer advanced and his difficulties in maintaining American rights became greater, his concern for the problem of world peace increased. His address of October 12 at Indianapolis was, directly and indirectly, entirely devoted to the future rôle of the United States in world affairs. He spoke about the "rebirth of America ... the task ahead for us for which we must be

[25] For complete text of the address see *The Commercial and Financial Chronicle*, CIII (Aug. 5, 1916), 457-460.
[26] Henry F. Pringle, *op. cit.*, II, 898.
[27] References to address listed in Notter, *op. cit.*, pp. 541-542.

soberly prepared . . . the duty of America to join with other nations of the world in some kind of a league for the maintenance of peace," and the part that the nation needed to play in the world by supplying it with conceptions of justice and liberty.[28] In Cincinnati, on October 26 he declared that from "this time on, in or out of office," he was going to preach that the United States must lend her "moral influence" and her "physical force, if other nations will join her, to see to it that no nation or group of nations tries to take advantage of another nation or group of nations. . . ." This "is the last war of the kind or of any kind that involves the world that the United States can keep out of."[29] Speaking at Shadow Lawn on November 4, just before the close of the campaign, he declared that the United States could never again enjoy "splendid isolation" and could never again be "unconnected with the great forces of the world. . . ."[30]

It would be a mistake to emphasize the differences between the two major parties on the question of the precise program of the league. Neither party endorsed its program in detail. Both, either through platforms or statements of party spokesmen, endorsed its guiding principles. The people at large probably made no distinction between the two parties on this issue. It is significant that no prominent political figure dissented publicly from the internationalism of his party spokesmen. It must be assumed, therefore, that practical politicians sensed that the people were willing to launch upon the broad policy of the league's objectives.[31] How much the League to Enforce Peace was responsible for this public attitude, how much it was due to Wilson's influence, and how much it was an effect of the world situation, no one can say. Only one thing is certain—all these factors were conducive to the same end.

In the meantime, the league's membership and influence were growing rapidly. The policy, however, concerning membership was very loose. Since it was believed that funds should

---

[28] Baker and Dodd, *op. cit.*, IV, 356-363.
[29] *Ibid.*, pp. 380-381.
[30] *Ibid.*, p. 391.
[31] Notter, *op. cit.*, p. 532.

be raised by voluntary subscription, drives to increase its personnel, so necessary in many organizations for financial reasons, were not employed.[32] The league wanted to influence people to support its cause and was rather indifferent about their enrollment as members. In order to influence people, however, it needed a widespread working organization, in many cases with salaried secretaries, and that required funds.

From the very beginning the New York Peace Society was of immense assistance. It gave office space, contributed to the cost of additional space, and virtually exhausted its funds through gifts or advances prior to the Washington meeting of May, 1916.[33] The World Peace Foundation was generous in its assistance,[34] and when Edward A. Filene became interested in the league movement he gave $25,000, the largest individual contribution during the entire history of the organization. Following the Washington meeting, contributions increased rapidly. Total receipts for the year 1916 amounted to $111,783.39,[35] and at the end of the year the league had about $240,000.00 in pledges.[36] The anticipated expenditure for the year beginning May, 1916, was $291,750.00.[37]

The organizational management of the league was under the direction of William H. Short, who served as general secretary throughout the existence of the movement. He did not escape criticism, at times from his subordinates and at other times from his superiors, but he was intelligent, energetic, and faithful to the ideals of the organization.[38] By the end of 1916, he had associated with him in the national office in New York an assistant secretary-treasurer, a director of field work, a secretary for the committee on information, and the vice-chairman

---

[32] William Short to Dr. Lowell, Dec. 15, 1916, *Lowell MSS.*
[33] William Short to C. C. Jackson, May 5, 1916, *Filene MSS.*
[34] It contributed $10,000. *Minutes*, Executive Committee, Jan. 20, 1916, *League Collection.*
[35] Treasurer's Report, May, 1917, *Filene MSS.*
[36] *Minutes*, Executive Committee, Sept. 13, 1916, *League Collection.*
[37] *Ibid.*, May 24, 1916, *League Collection.*
[38] Hamilton Holt to Dr. Lowell, Apr. 19, 1916; Herbert S. Houston to Dr. Lowell, Mar. 14, 1917; C. C. Michener to Dr. Lowell, Apr. 3, 1917, *Lowell MSS.*

of the finance committee. The stenographic office force numbered fourteen.[39] In addition there were four district field secretaries [40] whose main function was to organize state branches of the league.

By the end of 1916, branches had been organized on paper in all but three states, Minnesota, Nebraska, and Nevada.[41] But it was recognized by the national office that a great difference existed between a group actively functioning with headquarters, a permanent staff, and reasonably adequate funds and one that existed largely on paper. Probably twenty states had groups of the former kind. The strong branches, at this time, were in New England, the Middle West, New York, Maryland, West Virginia, California, Oregon, and South Dakota.[42] It was intended that each state branch should raise its own funds and have, in general, control over its own area.

The Massachusetts branch was particularly well managed and was used, in many cases at least, as a model for the establishment of other branches. It will serve as an illustration of what was being done or attempted throughout the nation. The Massachusetts branch was directed by James Mott Hallowell, an enthusiastic and able leader. He had the assistance of the World Peace Foundation and the Massachusetts Peace Society, whose president was Bliss Perry and whose vice-president was George H. Blakeslee. Both of these organizations contributed money, office space, staff assistance, and other valuable aid to Mr. Hallowell. At the outset a central committee was established with a chairman, secretary, and treasurer, and chairmen

[39] William Short to Dr. Lowell, June 12, 1917, *Lowell MSS; Bulletin,* League to Enforce Peace, Dec. 7, 1916; Short to Glenn Frank, July 17, 1915, *Filene MSS.*
[40] Report of Field Director C. C. Michener, Jan. 20, 1917, *Filene MSS.* The district secretaries of this time were John C. Leach, former Commissioner of Education for the Philippines, John C. Burg, former Assistant to the President of Northwestern University, Walter E. Dorland, formerly a secretary of the Chamber of Commerce of the United States, and W. R. Boyd, Jr.
[41] *Bulletin,* League to Enforce Peace, Nov. 22, 1916.
[42] Report to Executive Committee of Committee on Field Work, Oct. 11, 1916 and Jan. 20, 1917, *Filene MSS.*

of various sub-committees. This committee secured the support of about seventy-five prominent men who agreed to serve as vice-presidents,[43] and who contributed generously themselves and secured funds from others.[44] Plans were made for a large public meeting at which the state branch would be inaugurated.

The meeting, held in Boston on March 8, was a great success.[45] In spite of a snow storm, Symphony Hall was filled, and an overflow meeting was held in a near-by building.[46]

With the state branch thus established, plans were made for the prompt organization of local branches in the cities and towns of the state. The procedure used in starting the state branch was followed in developing local units. Both Taft and Lowell spoke at many of the local meetings, especially in the larger cities.

After the organization meeting in a given locality had been held, other devices were used to provide a hearing for the league's program. Whenever it was possible, mayors of cities were persuaded to proclaim a League to Enforce Peace Day, and clergymen were encouraged to establish League to Enforce Peace Sundays. On the former occasion it was the custom to hold not one meeting but a whole series of meetings throughout the area involved. Thus at Worcester, Massachusetts, on November 28, 1916, fifty speakers held meetings at various places in the city, and Mr. Taft spoke many times. A large evening meeting at Mechanics Hall concluded the day's activity. Thus it was hardly possible that anyone in the city was unaware of the league when the day was over. League to Enforce Peace Days were proclaimed in New Bedford, Fall River, Pittsfield, Salem, Lynn, Springfield, Amherst, Lowell, and in other cities and towns. During 1916, the Massachusetts branch organized 132 local meetings. By the end of the year, political leaders

[43] *Minutes*, Executive Committee, Feb. 25, 1916, *League Collection*.
[44] Ten people subscribed $5,000. *Ibid.*, Mar. 22, 1916.
[45] J. M. Hallowell to Edward A. Filene, Mar. 17, 1916, *Filene MSS*. Hallowell was asked to supply this information concerning his methods. A pamphlet containing the data was prepared and sent to other state chairmen with the suggestion that the methods used in Massachusetts could be followed elsewhere.
[46] Dr. Lowell to Short (copy), Mar. 9, 1916, *Lowell MSS*.

were making it a point to attend.[47] League Day meetings were for the purpose of general advertising. Later, similar group and educational work could be carried on.

With varying degrees of success, depending on the ability and energy of local chairmen, the activity in Massachusetts was duplicated in other states. During the fall of 1916 and the early months of 1917, Mr. Taft made speaking tours through New England, the Middle West, and the South. Dr. Lowell addressed meetings in Chicago, Milwaukee, Minneapolis, and St. Paul in January, 1917. The president of the Chicago Corn Exchange Bank, Charles L. Hutchinson, said that the league's Chicago dinner of January 6, 1917, was the most notable gathering that had been held in Chicago in five years,[48] and similar remarks were made about meetings in Detroit, Baltimore, New York, Wheeling, Hartford, Topeka, and a number of other places. In some states governors proclaimed League Sundays and League to Enforce Peace Days.[49]

The increasing activity of the league and the discussion of world peace by political candidates during the election, elicited considerable comment in the press. There was a tendency for editors to be noncommittal or obscure in their statements on the league issue. Those who were explicit in their approval outnumbered those who opposed, however, about four to one. A careful analysis was made of editorial comment concerning the Washington meeting of May, 1916. Of the ninety-nine editorials read by the league's committee on information, ninety-one favored the league and eight opposed it. In general there was no concerted press objection to the league, and there was some well-informed, intelligent support.[50] Articles analyzing the league's program continued to appear in leading journals,[51] and the general subject of world peace provided a

[47] *Bulletin*, League to Enforce Peace, Nov. 9, 23, 29, 1916; Mar. 1, 8, 1917.
[48] *Ibid.*, Jan. 11, 1917.
[49] For example, Kansas, Jan. 28, 29, 1916.
[50] *Report*, Committee on Information, Jan., 1917, *Filene MSS; Bulletin*, League to Enforce Peace, Nov. 23, 29, 1916.
[51] Herbert Croley, Hamilton Holt, and A. Lawrence Lowell, for example, wrote articles for the *New Republic, The Independent*, and *The North American Review*, respectively.

topic for discussion by learned societies and other groups. Under the general topic of "Preparedness and America's International Program," the American Academy of Political and Social Science devoted a meeting largely to the world peace program.[52] The league distributed a great quantity of literature.[53]

The league's influence was increased by the fact that practically all other programs for peace that were being seriously considered in the United States embraced most of the league's program and agreed with its principles. A few serious students of international affairs earnestly advocated an Anglo-American alliance as the most essential development of American foreign policy. This alliance, it was thought, would check the power of predatory nations, lead to the development of equal economic opportunities for all nations in the undeveloped areas of the world, and thus remove the world's danger zones.[54] Some people, particularly those who had actively supported the American Society for the Judicial Settlement of International Disputes, tended to favor the program of the Central Organization for a Durable Peace.[55] This organization was formed at The Hague in 1915. Its so-called "minimum program" called for the open door policy for colonies and spheres of influence, the protection of the rights of minority national groups in the various states, the submission of all disputes to judicial settlement, concerted action "diplomatic, economic, or military," against a state that refused to submit its disputes to judicial settlement or to mediation, the control of foreign policies by parliaments, the freedom of the seas, the reduction of armaments, and the abolition of secret treaties.[56] None of these

[52] *The Annals of the American Academy of Political and Social Science*, LXVI, July, 1916.

[53] During 1916 more than one and a half million league booklets were printed. *Report*, Finance Committee, Nov. 8, 1916, *Filene MSS*.

[54] Variations of this theory were advocated by Roland G. Usher, *The Challenge of the Future* (Boston, Houghton Mifflin Company, 1916) and by Walter Lippmann, *The Stakes of Diplomacy* (New York, Henry Holt Company, 1915).

[55] William I. Hull, "Three Plans for a Durable Peace," *Annals of the American Academy of Political and Social Science*, LXVI, 12-15.

[56] *The Independent*, LXXXVI (June 12, 1916), 446-447.

groups opposed the league nor were they opposed by it. They were complementary societies working toward the same ends.

In the meantime, the ideas of the league were making some headway in Europe. Hamilton Holt was probably over-enthusiastic when he declared that the credit for bringing the League of Nations idea before the world was "unquestionably due" to the League to Enforce Peace.[57] The idea was as indigenous to Britain as it was to America, and probably no group could say that it had led the way. But it is true that the United States became the leader and the champion of the idea. Three particular groups in England were studying the problem of peace: the Bryce Group, largely a study group that circulated its reports privately, the Fabian Society, and the League of Nations Society. Theodore Marburg, who spent a part of the summer of 1916 in England in the interest of the League to Enforce Peace, held conferences with many of the leaders of these groups, and spoke before the British League of Nations Society.[58] Public support for the league idea in England was hampered by the prevailing belief that the league movement was a stop-the-war movement and that such action would be to the advantage of Britain's enemies.[59] In Germany, a League to Enforce Peace representative was told that the league was generally regarded there as pro-ally.[60]

Undoubtedly the first and best friend of the League to Enforce Peace among the European statesmen was Sir Edward Grey,[61] the British Foreign Secretary. In March, 1916, Theodore Marburg reported to Taft, after an hour's conference with Grey, that "he goes the whole way with us" and that he

[57] *Ibid.*, LXXXIX (Feb. 5, 1917), 213.

[58] Theodore Marburg to William Short, Sept. 11, 1916, *League Collection*. Mr. Marburg recounted the history of his activity in England in his book *The League of Nations*, and much of his correspondence is given in Latané, *op. cit.*

[59] Lord Bryce to Theodore Marburg, Dec. 7, 1916 (copy), *League Collection;* Marburg to William Short, Sept. 11, 1916, *League Collection*.

[60] Unsigned memorandum of a report by Dr. Charles S. Macfarland, dated Nov. 11, 1916, *League MSS;* see also *Literary Digest*, LIII (Nov. 11, 1916).

[61] He had proposed a league of nations as early as Nov., 1914. See Latané, *op. cit.*, II, 767.

would go even further.[62] In an interview with the *Chicago Daily News* on May 13, in an open letter to Herman Bernstein, June 5, 1916, and in a speech before the Foreign Press Association in London on October 23, 1916, Grey referred to the policy of the League to Enforce Peace and in general advocated it.[63] Grey's one hesitancy about a future league of nations was the question of American support. He felt that unless the United States would be a member and could be counted upon to uphold treaties and agreements by force, the world would not be more secure under a league than it had been before 1914.[64]

Apparently in answer to Grey's speech of October 23 and President Wilson's Cincinnati speech of October 26, the German Chancellor, von Bethmann-Hollweg, announced in the Reichstag that "Germany is at all times ready to join a league of nations. . . ."[65] The British, French, and German governments all sent messages to be read at the League to Enforce Peace dinner in New York on November 24.[66] This European support of the league idea together with the increasing indication of American support[67] encouraged President Wilson to send his note of December 18 to the belligerent nations asking them to state their peace aims.[68] He mentioned that statesmen of the belligerents on both sides had expressed willingness "to

[62] Theodore Marburg to William Howard Taft, Mar. 23, 1916 (copy), *League Collection*.
[63] Sir Edward Grey to Theodore Marburg, Sept. 16, 1916 (copy), *Filene MSS;* The *Outlook*, CXIV (Nov. 8, 1916), 524-526; *The New Republic*, VIII (Oct. 28, 1916), 309. Grey was talking of a league as early as Jan. 2, 1916, and after his retirement from office became the first president of the League of Nations Union. See George M. Trevelyan, *Grey of Falloden* (Boston, Houghton Mifflin Company, 1937), pp. 354, 359-361.
[64] Grey to Theodore Marburg, Sept. 16, 1916 (copy), *Filene MSS*.
[65] *Literary Digest*, LIII (Nov. 25, 1916), 1398. See also "History of the German Peace Moves," *Literary Digest*, LIII (Dec. 30, 1916), 1696-1697.
[66] Latané, *op. cit.*, I, 234.
[67] *The Independent*, LXXXVIII (Dec. 11, 1916); Notter, *op. cit.*, p. 579.
[68] There were, of course, other reasons for the President's actions. Every day the position of the United States as a neutral became more difficult.

consider the formation of a league of nations, to insure peace and justice throughout the world," that the United States was interested in measures "to secure the future peace of the world" and to relieve weaker peoples of the peril of wrong and violence, and that the United States was "ready, and even eager, to coöperate in the accomplishment of these ends."[69]

The President's peace effort came to nothing. The German government refused to state its peace aims. It declared, however, that after the war, and apparently after the belligerents had themselves arranged peace, Germany would be willing to coöperate with the United States in the work of preventing future wars.[70] The Allied Governments replied to the President's note through the French Foreign Office. They did not think it was possible to have an immediate peace that would assure them reparation, restitution, and guarantees against future aggression. They declared, however, that they "associate themselves with all their hopes with the project for the creation of a league of nations to insure peace and justice throughout the world."[71] The President realized how dim the chance was for a negotiated peace, but he refused to regard the situation as hopeless. He continued to offer opportunities to Germany to state her peace objectives, not knowing that the German government, without waiting for the allied reply to his peace note, had decided upon unrestricted submarine warfare. The President also decided to make a last desperate effort for peace —an appeal to the world.[72]

In December, 1916, the League to Enforce Peace, taking stock of its accomplishments, might have viewed the results with a great deal of encouragement and satisfaction. It had developed a nation-wide organization, and its fundamental tenet, the enforcement of world peace through concerted international action, had been accepted by a remarkably large American following as well as by belligerents and many neutral

[69] Baker and Dodd, *op. cit.*, IV, 404.
[70] *Foreign Relations*, 1916, Supplement, p. 118.
[71] *Ibid.*, 1917, Supplement, p. 6.
[72] See Baker, *op. cit.*, VI, 365-434, for detailed discussion of events during Dec., 1916. Also Notter, *op. cit.*, pp. 560-561.

nations. Its principles had become, in the words of A. Lawrence Lowell, "a matter on which the President has virtually staked his reputation before posterity."[73] This astounding growth of the league idea was not due solely to the work of the League to Enforce Peace. History is a vast complex, and no event is a "link in a chain of necessity." It would be quite impossible to weigh with precision the relative force of Wilson's pro-league influence on public opinion and the influence of that opinion, once aroused, on the President's course of action. The relation was clearly reciprocal. This would be equally true of other public men. But no one could question that the League to Enforce Peace was the chief organization in the world devoted to the idea of the enforcement of peace.

Undoubtedly one of the most significant facts about the history of the league up to December, 1916, was the absence in the United States of any concerted or organized opposition to it or to its ideas. Many people, it is true, were opposed to the abandonment of isolation. A few of them had written articles or otherwise voiced their disapproval of the league, but their arguments had been answered by the pro-league forces, and they had not created a known following. With the exception of William Jennings Bryan, who was a pacifist, no prominent political figure of either major party had taken up the anti-league cause. A few people, notably Charles W. Eliot, refused to support the league because it did not go far enough, but they did not oppose the league idea.[74]

Most of what scattered opposition there was to the league came from the pacifists, who objected to the use of force of any kind.[75] The league forces had recognized this faction from

[73] *Minutes*, Executive Committee of the League to Enforce Peace, Mar. 16, 1917, *League Collection*.

[74] Many people who discussed the league publicly found fault with some part of its program or favored some other approach to the enforcement of peace. Dr. Felix Adler, for example, thought that emphasis should be on a parliament of parliaments. *The Nation*, CIV (Jan. 4, 1917), 5-6. It was common, also, for writers to discuss the league without saying anything worth reading on either side of the subject.

[75] See, for example, H. Begbie, "Can Man Abolish War?" *North American Review*, CCV (June, 1917), 886-894.

the outset, and they had made no attempt to appease or to compromise with it. The league, said Dr. Lowell at the inaugural meeting in Philadelphia, "exists for the purpose of enforcing peace or it exists for nothing at all." The American Peace Society [76] and some of the church organizations were parts of the pacifist opposition. But the most influential spokesman for the group was Bryan, who believed that peace could not be enforced and that the effort to do so had been responsible for most modern wars.[77]

Bryan was extremely active against both the League to Enforce Peace and the preservation of American rights upon the seas. One of the best examples of the character of his thought and mind is his written debate with Mr. Taft. In December, 1916, Soloman Fieldman, President of Press Forum Incorporated, asked Taft and Bryan to debate the league problem in writing. They agreed to three debates, one each on the following topics:

1. Is the platform of the League to Enforce Peace feasible?
2. Does it offer the most practicable plan for securing permanent peace?
3. Should the United States join a League to Enforce Peace? [78]

Mr. Bryan's first paper was not really a discussion of the platform of the league, but rather an affirmation of his belief that the use of force by an international body was not different from its use by a nation or an alliance. The league's plan was therefore not a new principle but only an enlargement of what the world had outgrown. "For this nation," he said, "to exchange its moral prestige for the expensive privilege of putting its army and navy at the command of European monarchs, to

---

[76] Theodore Marburg resigned as a director of the society. See Latané, *op. cit.*, I, 273.

[77] Curti, *op. cit.*, p. 248.

[78] The debates were printed in various papers and later in pamphlet form, *World Peace* (New York, George H. Doran Company, 1917). Practically all the arguments used by Bryan in the debates had been used by him elsewhere, for example at the Lake Mohonk Conference, May, 1916.

be used in settling European quarrels, would be retrogression, not progress—a stepping down, not ascent to a higher plane." In his second paper he continued his affirmations against the use of force, and for proof of its uselessness, he cited the "fact" that when men ceased to carry weapons to defend themselves "but cultivated friendship instead of trying to excite fear," strife among individuals declined.

Mr. Taft had no difficulty in answering the argument concerning the use of force. After all, no one had proposed to place American armed forces at the command of European monarchs. The idea that the use of force by a world league acting under international law was analogous in any way to the use of force in the past was obviously absurd. The whole argument for a league of nations had to be based upon the assumption that it would exist in fact. To assume, as Bryan did, that some great powers would not join, was to assume the non-existence of a league and was no argument against the idea. Bryan's "redemption" of the gun-toting individual was especially unfortunate for his side of the case; no argument was historically more suitable for Mr. Taft. People ceased carrying weapons only when collective security replaced self-help.

Bryan made no attempt to refute Taft's arguments. He discussed matters that had no perceptible relevance to the subject, reaffirmed his views, and in the end moved to other ground. His final argument was a shift from pacifist to isolationist dogma. To join a league would be to abandon the teachings of Washington and Jefferson and also to abandon the Monroe Doctrine. The abandonment of the latter would leave the Latin-American nations unprotected, and they would then become either the colonies of European aggressor states or militarize themselves for protection. This was an admission of the efficacy of force, a refutation of the crux of his whole former argument, and incidentally a *non sequitur* as far as principles and proposals of the league were concerned. Finally Bryan proposed to establish peace by adjudication, arbitration, and conciliation, by referenda on war, and by the reduction of armaments.

Possibly at no time in his career was Bryan less the master of his subject than in these debates with Taft. His thought was a curious mixture. Primarily he was a pacifist, opposed to the use of force in international affairs, opposed to the defense of American rights on the seas, and opposed to the preparedness measures advocated by President Wilson. Yet he did not favor pacifism in the realm of domestic affairs. He believed in police power, for example, in the enforcement of prohibition laws, and he did not oppose the use of force in the protection of Latin America. But he opposed the preparedness which would provide the force which he advocated. He appealed to history but omitted data most pertinent to the league issue. He opposed the league idea but advocated referenda on war and the reduction of armaments without considering the means through which these remedies for war would be achieved. Like many other people Bryan disliked war, but his thought was distorted by emotional enthusiasm and intellectual confusion.

Bryan's influence, however, should not be measured by the lack of intrinsic merit in his argument. His *ex parte* historical analysis, his statements regarding "European quarrels" and American soldiers being ordered about by "European monarchs," his references to the alleged isolationist advice of Washington and Jefferson, and his theoretical substitutes for a league of nations, all became a part of the ammunition of the anti-league forces. Bryan plowed and seeded fertile soil in 1916 and 1917, but the harvest of the isolationist and pacifist doctrines was reaped in 1919 and 1920.

Another type of argument which began to appear in 1916 was neither pacifist nor isolationist but defeatist in theory. The pacifists held that no attempt should be made to bring about world peace through the use of force, because force had been tried and had failed. The defeatists held that force could be effectively used only through the instrumentality of a unitary world state. The modern world, however, was too large and too complicated for the establishment of a new Roman empire. The idea of a confederate or federal world state for the purpose of enforcing peace was, in their opinion, stuff and nonsense, because in the minds of men everywhere in the world the forces of nationalism were stronger than the forces of internationalism. Since it was impossible to establish a unitary state and futile to try to establish a confederate state, nothing could be done about war save through the gradual change of the hearts of men.[79]

Thus the defeatists arrived at the same conclusion as did the pacifists, but they were not of them. They posed as disinterested observers, hard-headed realists who looked facts in the face, practical men who had plumbed the depths of human nature. Their significance rests with the use that could be made of their arguments by pacifists, by imperialists such as Albert J. Beveridge,[80] and by militarists of the Captain Mahan school, as well as by the self-styled intelligentsia, who delighted in casting a cold eye upon all enthusiasts for causes and reforms. Their chief weapon was ridicule. The advocates of the League to Enforce Peace were simple-minded idealists, impractical and visionary. The program of the league was an "untutored expedient" which betrayed "a grotesque misapprehension of the real problem to be faced." The defeatists added powerfully to the nationalism which they professed to deplore. They too planted seeds for others to harvest.

In an article entitled "The Opposition Gathers," *The New Republic* analyzed the forces that were beginning to oppose the League to Enforce Peace. It declared that the "very success" of the league movement had created the "inevitable opposition" and that soon as many people would be engaged in attempting to discredit it as had hitherto advocated its policies. *The New Republic's* analysis of the opposition is worth quoting in full: [81]

> As we have indicated, the opposition springs from many diverse sources. It derives from pacifists who repudiate use

---

[79] See, for example, Sidney Brooks, "The Dream of Universal Peace," *Harpers Magazine*, CXXXIII (Nov., 1916), 862-869.

[80] Claude G. Bowers, *Beveridge and the Progressive Era* (Boston, Houghton Miffllin Company, 1932), pp. 494, 496.

[81] *The New Republic*, IX (Jan. 6, 1917), 255-257. With regard to the so-called legalistic group, *The New Republic's* charges are perhaps too sweeping, but they were not without some basis. See *Current Opinion*, LXII (Feb., 1917), 82-85.

of force even in the interests of international order, from militarists who refuse to seek peace even by means of possible coercion, and lawyers who resent any attempt to find a basis for international law except abstract right, recognized precedent and the voluntary consent of free and absolute sovereigns. Of these three classes of opponents the second will prove in all probability to be the least formidable. Certain men always have and always will oppose any form of international organization for the discouragement of war, because peace seems to them inseparable from moral and political stagnation. But in the future their opposition will not count for much, because the tragic costs of the present war have convinced American public opinion that the future of civilization depends absolutely on the organization of peace. Far more dangerous will be the opposition of the other two groups. Together they will deprive the program of the League of the support of thousands of people who are sincerely desirous of contributing to the abolition of war. Both of these groups expect to institute peace without calling force to the aid of the institution, the first because it regards the use of force, even for the achievement of excellent purposes, as a compromise with the devil, and the second because it regards certain general principles of international rights as so intrinsically reasonable and of such general and victorious application that their exposition by a court will impose itself upon the consciences of the sovereign nations. They are the same two classes of opponents which have hampered American experimental liberalism in its laborious work of domestic reconstruction—on the one hand the sentimental idealists like Mr. Bryan, whose aspirations are admirable, but who spends them in agitation and declamation rather than in the organization of results; on the other hand, the legalists who expect peace like other ultimate social goods to be deduced by judges from abstract principles rather than gradually wrought by purposive national action out of the living forces prevailing in international politics.

Among other evidences of the gathering of opposition to the league, two items were significant, a debate in the Senate and an article by Theodore Roosevelt. The Senate debate began over a resolution offered by Senator Hitchcock approving the

President's note of December 18.[82] After Senator Borah had blocked the immediate consideration of it, the resolution was referred to the Committee on Foreign Relations. Senator Hitchcock brought up the subject again on January 2, pointing out that his resolution simply expressed approval of the President's request for peace terms.[83] Senator Lodge objected to the consideration of the resolution, and Senator J. H. Gallinger of New Hampshire read into the record an editorial from the *New York Sun*, in which the President's offer of December 18 to coöperate with the world in securing peace was denounced as a violation of the Monroe Doctrine.[84]

Senator Lodge took up the opposition on July 3. He pointed out that the resolution projected Congress into the "field of foreign negotiations" reserved by the Constitution to the Executive, involved the nation in European affairs, and committed the Senate to an endorsement of the President's note. The policy inherent in the note meant an abandonment of "the policy we have hitherto pursued of confining ourselves to our own hemisphere and makes us a part of the political system of another hemisphere, with the inevitable corollary that the nations of that other hemisphere will become a part of our system." The Senator hinted, by using quotations, that the President wanted to commit the nation to this policy without the consent of the Senate. He admitted that he had supported the settlement of international disputes by international tribunals backed by force. But great obstacles presented themselves in regard to this problem, and he now doubted that anything could be done about it.[85] Continuing his speech on July 4, he secured consent to place into the record the *New*

---

[82] *Congressional Record*, 64 Congress, 2nd Session, Vol. 54, part I, p. 635. The resolution was: "*Resolved:* that the Senate approves and strongly endorses the action taken by the President in sending the diplomatic note of December 18 to the nations now engaged in war suggesting and recommending that those nations state the terms upon which peace might be discussed."
[83] *Ibid.*, p. 736.
[84] *Ibid.*, p. 739.
[85] *Ibid.*, pp. 792-797.

York Sun editorial which had already been placed there by Senator Gallinger.

When Senator Borah took up the discussion he went immediately, not to the resolution, but to that part of the President's note dealing with American coöperation for the establishment of peace. He called this a "stupendous proposition." It was not, he thought, a partisan question, because the President was in agreement with the League to Enforce Peace on this subject, and the league was supported by ex-President Taft. Senator Borah then quoted the platform of the league and President Wilson's endorsement of it in his May 27th address. This meant, he thought, that the United States would be obliged to make war upon nations, members of a league, who would not submit their disputes to an international tribunal and that the United States would authorize other nations to make war upon them if they refused "to submit some vital issue . . . to the decision of some European or Asiatic nation." "This," said Senator Borah, "approaches, to my mind, moral treason."

Since, in Senator Borah's view, Europe and Asia would always dominate the international court proposed by the League to Enforce Peace, the United States might actually be forced to make war on a Latin-American state—an obvious abandonment of the Monroe Doctrine. The league people, he said, had overlooked the fact that the government of the United States is still a government by the people, that the people are the ones who do the fighting and fortunately also the voting. He called upon the Senate to renounce any approval of the President's policy of entering into an agreement to guarantee the protection of small nations.[86]

The issue thus clearly raised by Senators Lodge and Borah was not brought to a vote. Senator Hitchcock declared that he had not intended to raise the issue of approving the President's whole note of December 18, but only that part of it calling upon the belligerents to state the terms upon which peace might be discussed. The resolution was amended to conform with that idea and was adopted.

The debate in the Senate was not more ominous for the

[86] *Ibid.*, pp. 892-897.

League to Enforce Peace than Theodore Roosevelt's attack upon it which appeared in the January *Metropolitan Magazine*. The former president abandoned his earlier position favorable to the enforcement of peace,[87] violently attacked President Wilson and Mr. Taft, and launched an avalanche of words against the league. Agitation for a league of nations was, in his opinion, infamous and immoral in general, and on the part of the President it was a "mean and odious hypocrisy." Mr. Roosevelt did not analyse and reason; he denounced, and it is his denunciation that is significant.[88]

Somewhat disturbed by the gathering opposition to the league and by newspaper reports that the President did not really believe in enforced peace,[89] Hamilton Holt and William Short secured a conference with Colonel House to find out about the President's position. Colonel House informed them that the President, far from abandoning the league idea, would go even farther than the League to Enforce Peace had gone; he would advocate a more complete program. Since Europe, in the opinion of House, was committed to the idea as the result of the replies to Wilson's peace note, it was up to the United States to see that the idea became a reality. He thought that an effort should be made, possibly through Secretary Daniels, to secure the support of Bryan, and that everything possible should be done to get senators and congressmen to commit themselves to the league idea; it was not a bit too soon for that.[90]

In the meantime, the President had already decided to deal once more with the subject of peace in his address to the Senate on January 22, 1917. He stated what he believed to be the fundamentals of a just peace, the conditions that would justify the adherence of the United States to a "League of Peace," and the association with other nations in enforcing peace and justice throughout the world. He believed that a

---

[87] Theodore Roosevelt, *America and the World War* (New York, Charles Scribner's Sons, 1915), pp. 220-243.

[88] For comment on Roosevelt's article see *The New Republic*, IX (Jan. 13, 1917), 281-283, and *The Independent*, LXXXIX (Jan. 15, 1917), 90. Also *Bulletin*, League to Enforce Peace, Jan. 11, 1917.

[89] *The New Republic*, IX (Jan. 6, 1917), 256.

[90] Memorandum of conversation, Jan. 13, 1917, *League Collection*.

league system was the way to avoid entangling alliances, for it would substitute for them a concert of power; that through a league of nations the Monroe Doctrine would be adopted as the doctrine of the world.[91]

The President's address drew immediate fire. In the Senate, Cummins of Iowa set himself the task, as he put it, of separating in the President's message the generalities which "mean nothing but pleasure to the ear" from the "startling announcement" of "a new and supreme government which is to command our resources in both blood and treasure." Adherence to a league of nations, he said, would be "sheer madness," for it would involve the United States in redividing the world in countless wars. He pictured American armed forces being used by the super-state to fight their own people in cases where the United States refused to accept the decisions of the world state.[92]

A few days later, Senator Lodge delivered a prepared address on the President's message. He first discussed the President's fundamentals of peace, setting up hypothetical cases that might arise under his own interpretation of the President's statements, and implying that in each the resultant situation would be unsatisfactory to the United States. Then he condemned the proposal that the United States join in a concert of nations and specifically repudiated his earlier support of the idea. He pictured a league of nations "veiled by glittering and glancing generalities," forcing the United States to abandon its sovereign right to exclude Mongolian and Asiatic immigration. American adherence to such a program would be, of course, an abandonment of the policies of Washington and Monroe. The true foreign policy for the United States, he said, was to observe its own promises, but to terminate all treaties of arbitration, for they too were war breeders, and to strengthen its military might beyond danger of attack from any source.[93]

In dealing with the Senate debate *The New Republic* declared

[91] Baker and Dodd, *op. cit.*, IV, 407-414.
[92] *Congressional Record*, 64 Congress, 2nd Session, Vol. 54, part 3, pp. 2230-2235.
[93] *Ibid.*, 2364 ff.

that with few exceptions the Republicans in the Senate intended "to obstruct and if possible to wreck" the policy of the President for world peace. It was absurd, it thought, for Roosevelt and Lodge and other pro-Allies who had been demanding that the United States face its responsibilities in the world, to join hands with Borah and Cummins who wished to commit the nation to permanent isolation. The indictment continued:

> For the Republican party to make itself the defender of American isolation is a confession of bankruptcy. From every platform and editorial desk it had been telling the country that it was the party of national responsibility and international purpose. The Democrats were negative, irresponsible, without policy, and blind to the facts of the modern world. Yet today it is a Democratic President who grasps the truth that isolation is over and strives to guide our entrance into world politics toward stability and safety. It is the Republican party that proposes to crouch at its fireside, build a high tariff wall, arm against the whole world, cultivate no friendships, take no step to forestall another war, and then let things rip. The party which was inspired by the idea of American union is becoming the party of secession and state's rights as against world union....[94]

The President's message of January 22 and the debate in the Senate contributed to the increasing tempo of discussion over the league issue. The arguments of the league's opponents tended to crystallize. "To all who are carried away by the seraphic beauty of President Wilson's concert of power," the *Washington Times* recommended a study of the Holy Alliance. It would be found that such schemes had failed. The league was exactly what Washington had warned against; it would be a departure from the Monroe Doctrine, would involve the United States in entangling alliances, would place it in a subordinate place in a foreign organization, would send its sons to die on foreign battle fields fighting for things in which the United States had no interest, and would open United States

---

[94] *The New Republic*, X (Feb. 3, 1917), 2.

gates to hordes of oriental laborers.[95] Ex-Secretary of War Garrison and Dr. S. T. Dutton, General Secretary of the World Court League, both issued statements against the league idea.

The strength of the opposition rested in its development of slogans and symbols. The statement that the Holy Alliance was a scheme for world organization similar to the plan of the League to Enforce Peace, that it was a complete failure, and that the United States should be guided by this experience of mankind, was an easy and simple statement of alleged fact with sinister overtones. To explain why the Holy Alliance offered no precedent whatsoever for the league program involved an elaborate recital of data and required sustained thought on the part of a listener or reader. What Washington warned against and what relevance his warning had to conditions a century later, and why American security might be greater as a part of a league than under a condition of world anarchy were also problems of complexity. The success of the league movement might well depend upon three factors: (1) the ability of its proponents in finding symbols and in explaining the defects in the arguments of its opponents in language understandable to all, (2) the self-restraint and sense of responsibility of league opponents in avoiding sophistries which they knew were unworthy of consideration, and (3) the avoidance of partisan political division over the issue.

The partisan danger was the greatest.[96] The league wanted its policies to become the policies of the government and therefore sought the support of the President. But the very moment that he expressed approval of its ideas, the issue could become political at the option of the opposition party. The league appeared to have triumphed over politics, since it had secured the President's endorsement of a movement previously espoused by ex-President Taft, Senator Lodge, Theodore Roosevelt, and

[95] *Literary Digest*, "Shall America Join a Peace League," LIV (Feb. 10, 1917), 324-325; *Current Opinion*, "Will the United States Fight to Preserve the Peace," LXII (Feb., 1917), 82-85; F. G. Stone, "An Illusion of Today," *19th Century*, LXXXI (Mar. 8, 1917), 700-705.

[96] While no issue is inherently political, any issue is political if politicians choose to make it so.

other prominent Republicans. In other words, President Wilson and the Democratic Party had an opportunity to make the league issue political in May, 1916, but chose rather to support its principles. This action, together with the subsequent endorsement of the idea by Mr. Hughes, kept the issue out of the political campaign of 1916.

From the beginning, however, the spectre of partisan politics, which every effort was made to dispel, haunted the fate of all league proposals. The secretary of the executive committee of the Massachusetts branch of the league observed that "in view of President Wilson's endorsement" he was afraid of the issue's "drifting into party politics with a strong faction of the Republican Party against us."[97] Republican Congressmen John J. Rogers and Augustus P. Gardner of Massachusetts, the latter a son-in-law of Henry Cabot Lodge, were among the ardent opponents of the league.[98] It has already been noted that Senator Lodge removed the league plank from the tentative draft of the Republican platform and that he subsequently repudiated his earlier support. "The more I have considered the question," he wrote to Dr. Lowell, *"and particularly since the utterance of the President in his address,* I am forced to the conclusion that the League of Peace as he proposes it would be a very dangerous thing. . . ."[99] The league's field secretaries noted that the German newspapers, which had been almost unanimously Republican in 1916,[100] were attempting to show that the league's purpose was to promote an Anglo-American alliance.[101]

Other political straws indicated the direction of the wind. In commenting upon a League to Enforce Peace dinner in Indianapolis on January 25, 1917, the *Indianapolis Times* noted that since the President's address of January 26, Henry Lane Wilson had resigned as state chairman of the league and that Senator-

[97] James M. Hallowell to Dr. Lowell, June 15, 1916, *Lowell MSS.*
[98] *Bulletin,* League to Enforce Peace, Feb. 2, 1917.
[99] Lodge to Lowell (italics mine), Jan. 30, 1917, *Lowell MSS.*
[100] The organized German-American influence was strongly against Wilson in 1916. See Clifton James Child, *The German Americans in Politics, 1914-1917* (Madison, University of Wisconsin Press, 1939).
[101] Report of Field Secretaries, Nov. 2, 1916, *League Collection.*

elect Harry S. New had remained away from the dinner for fear that he would appear to attend a Democratic rally.[102] In his interview with Mr. Holt, Colonel House observed that "Democratic senators" would support the league,[103] and both the league's secretary[104] and its Washington representative noted that the outspoken support among senators came from the Democrats and the opposition from the Republicans.[105] Elihu Root continued his silence on the issue,[106] and Mr. Hughes lapsed into silence, although privately he continued to support the league program with reservations.[107]

"If we go into this war," said Newton D. Baker, "it will be solely for the purpose and with the object of making the right kind of peace. It will be very important, therefore, that from the very beginning, we shall hold this fact before the eyes of the country."[108] "But the manner," said Senator Lodge, changing his tack somewhat, "in which the League was drawn into the question of the peace which was to terminate the war ... has caused me to withdraw from its support."[109] Thus political lines were obviously being drawn by April, 1917. Would the war unite the American people on the issue of world peace? Could the League to Enforce Peace survive both war and politics?

[102] *Bulletin,* League to Enforce Peace, Feb. 8, 1917.
[103] Memorandum of interview, Jan. 13, 1917, *League Collection.*
[104] William Short to Filene, Jan. 27, 1917, *Filene MSS.*
[105] Reports from Washington office, Mar. 5 and 15, 1917, *League Collection.* This, of course, was obvious in the Senate's debate over the message of Jan. 22, and was noted by most observers. *Bulletin,* League to Enforce Peace, Feb. 15, 1917.
[106] Dr. Lowell thought that Root would support the league, but Taft believed that Lowell missed the significance of the "Root cult." See William Howard Taft to Henry W. Taft, May 19, 1916 (copy), *Taft MSS.*
[107] Memorandum of interview with W. S. Drinker, Jan. 21, 1917, *League Collection.*
[108] Memorandum of interview with Secretary Baker, not dated, *League Collection.*
[109] H. C. Lodge to Dr. Lowell, Feb. 3, 1917, *Lowell MSS.*

CHAPTER FOUR

The League as a War Aim

PRESIDENT WILSON did not know, when he addressed the Senate on January 22, 1917, his last public effort to effect peace among the warring nations, that Germany had already elected to renew unrestricted submarine warfare. This decision was in reality a declaration of war against the United States. It demonstrated what the President had long understood and clearly stated, that a nation could not protect its independence and preserve its freedom and at the same time avoid war if its rights and freedom were violated by the aggression of another power. Neutrality did not protect a nation from attack; it only avoided giving just cause for attack. Germany's decision to renew submarine warfare was beyond American control.

The nearer the United States came to war, the greater was the President's realization that the hope for peace on the part of one nation depended upon the willingness of all nations to prevent aggression against any nation. He believed that the United States would support a war against German aggression, but he was far from certain that it would support a league of nations for the purpose of making such a war unnecessary. While the nation had, in his opinion "responded nobly" to his message of January 22, he had noticed the unfavorable European comment and the political trend of the debate over it in the Senate.[1] In his second inaugural address, March 5, 1917, he spoke, therefore, not only about the imminence of war but also about the future as well. He touched upon the forces beyond American control which had drawn the nation within their influence, about the injuries the United States had received upon the seas, about the reason for armed neutrality, and about

[1] Baker, *op. cit.*, VI, 431.

the high purpose of the United States to seek nothing by conquest. But the time had come, he said, for the United States to realize that the "greatest things that remain to be done must be done with the whole world for a stage and in coöperation with the wide and universal forces of mankind."[2]

In his war message of April 2, the President referred in several places to the problem of world peace. "Let us make it very clear," he said, "to all the world what our motives and our objects are." They were the same things that he had referred to in his message of January 22, the determination "to vindicate the principles of peace and justice," and "to set up amongst the really free and self-governed peoples of the world such a concert of purpose and of action as will henceforth insure the observance of those principles." Almost at the very end of the message he reasserted the objects for which the United States would fight: "for democracy, for the rights of those who submit to authority to have a voice in their own Governments, for the rights and liberties of small nations, and for a universal dominion of right by such a concert of free peoples as shall bring peace and safety to all nations and make the world itself at last free."[3]

In the President's speeches, there was an increasing note of confidence that the American people would support the idea of a concert of free peoples for the maintenance of peace. In May, 1916, he said he believed that he spoke for the people on that subject, but in his address of April 5, 1917, he spoke without qualifying terms about the principles for which the American people stood. "I need not," he said, "argue these principles to you, my fellow countrymen: they are your own, part and parcel of your own thinking and your own motive in affairs. They spring up native among us. Upon this as a platform of purpose and of action we can stand together."

It was altogether proper for the President to speak as he did about the united determination of the United States to support a league of nations. The President and the members of his party who had been returned to office in the election of 1916 were

[2] Baker and Dodd, *op. cit.*, V, 1-5.
[3] *Ibid.*, pp. 6-16.

clearly committed to the league principle. In a sense, too, the majority of the people were committed to support the policies which their chosen leaders had openly advocated in presenting themselves for office. In a strictly logical sense the President received from the people in 1916 a mandate on the league issue and had an obligation to them to carry forward his announced policies. The people too had an obligation to support the President in doing what they had authorized him to do. Logically, the relationship between the people and the President was contractual and involved reciprocal rights and duties. But the President knew that whatever might be the logic of the situation, the actual results might be uncontrolled by it. Many people who voted for him might reason to themselves that they had not done so on account of his league ideas, but for other reasons and therefore that they were not committed to all of his policies. Moreover, they reserved the right to change their minds at any time. Experience must have taught the President that the struggle for a league of nations was still to be won, for in a democracy a majority can always become a minority.

That there was not, even in well-informed circles, unanimity on the league issue, is well illustrated by a meeting of the American Academy of Political and Social Science. Immediately after the President's address of January 22, that academy changed earlier plans for its annual meeting and arranged a conference on American foreign policy. The entrance of the United States into the war gave added emphasis to the timeliness of the academy's program which was built around the subject: "America's Relation to the World Conflict and to the Coming Peace."[4] Some of the speakers at the meeting dealt with specific territorial or other problems that would arise at the end of the war, the disposition of Constantinople, the Bohemian question, and the like. The majority of the speakers, however, in one way or another touched upon the problem of world organization. Among these, with a few exceptions, there was general agreement that some sort of a concert of nations for the preservation of peace was essential.

[4] *The Annals,* American Academy of Political and Social Science, LXXII, July, 1917.

Walter Lippmann, in the opening address, sounded the keynote of the conference. He reviewed the history of the war and declared that Germany had abolished neutrality. Germany began, he declared, by refusing to permit a reference to Europe of a Balkan dispute, went on to destroy an international state, and ended by attacking the merchant shipping of all nations. She had carried the doctrine of exclusive nationalism to a war upon mankind. But the "terrible logic" of Germany's policy had had a stupendous result. "By striking at the bases of all international order, Germany convinced even the most isolated of neutrals that order must be preserved by common effort. By denying that a society of nations exists, a society of nations has been forced into existence. The very thing Germany challenged Germany has established." Before 1917 only a handful of visionaries talked about world federation. Now men had learned that they must coöperate in order to be free. They could now hope for things they dared not hope for in the past. It was the privilege of the United States to insure that the war would terminate in a "union of liberal people, pledged to coöperate in the settlement of all outstanding questions, sworn to turn against the aggressor, determined to enact a larger and more modern system of international law upon a federation of the world."

If Mr. Lippmann represented the majority opinion at the conference, there were present nevertheless, the pacifists, the imperialists, and the defeatists. The arguments of these groups were not new and have been noted elsewhere. The defeatists, in particular, were more difficult to deal with. They admitted that world organization was necessary but felt that proposed solutions for the problem were inadequate and that it was futile to seek more promising ones. Of this group, James M. Beck was the outstanding example. He referred to a conversation with Sir Edward Grey when the British statesman asked him what reasons he had to believe that the United States would assume its share of a joint obligation and really take an active part in enforcing whatever a league of nations thought to be just under given circumstances. Mr. Beck did not think the United States would consent to the submission of great questions of "national and racial destiny" to a supernational body. The League to Enforce Peace did not, in his opinion, offer any real solution to the problem of national self-interest. While the President's war message was one of the noblest utterances in American history, Mr. Beck doubted that the people were capable of understanding the destiny that was before them. They were interested in the price of cotton, in baseball, and the movies. "How," he asked, "are we going to make them feel that they are in the very heart of the world and that the Atlantic and the Pacific are nothing more than open highways over which hostile fleets could freely pass?" He had no answer.[5]

Thus Mr. Beck, as far as his own thought was concerned, appeared to be in harmony with the President and the league. But he did not believe that the people at large were capable of understanding that their own self-interests would be advanced by advancing the welfare of the people of other nations and that peace for the United States could be achieved by establishing world peace. The league advocates, on the other hand, had confidence in the capacity of the people to understand international affairs at least sufficiently to follow enlightened leadership. On this confidence President Wilson staked his hope for world peace. President Wilson had faith in democracy: Mr. Beck did not. And it is not without significance to note that in the final struggle for the League of Nations, Mr. Beck joined with those who opposed it.

After the entrance of the United States into the war, the League to Enforce Peace was faced with the difficulty that confronted the league movement in England and France, the possibility that many people would regard it as a pacifist organization, interested in an immediate peace. The executive committee dealt with this problem and decided to give the widest possible publicity to a "war program" which was adopted to create a war council to organize league assistance to war work, and to delete the word "peace" from league literature wherever it tended to lead to the conclusion that the organization was in any sense pacifist.[6] The league's war program was as follows:

[5] *Ibid.*, pp. 208-216.
[6] *Bulletin*, League to Enforce Peace, July 27, 1917.

In the words of the Secretary of War "our combined armies from now on will represent a League to Enforce Peace with Justice."

The war with which we are engaged is the case of an attack by an aggressive power before submitting any question to arbitration, a contingency against which our proposals provide.

The purpose of the war is to discourage aggression by such a defeat of the German autocracy that no nation will again undertake a war for self-aggrandizement.

This purpose requires that the war shall be vigorously prosecuted until it can be terminated in such a way that peace will be permanent.

The organization of permanent peace requires the continuance and extension of the League of Democratic Nations with which the United States is now coöperating to protect our own liberties during the war and safeguard them afterwards.

The League therefore urges its State and County branches to assist the Government actively in pushing the war to victory, and to help create such an overwhelming conviction that this is a righteous war that Congress and all officials, in the passage of bills and the carrying out of projects, will act with the speed and loyalty which the President, as Commander and Chief of the Army and Navy, must have to win the war for democracy and for such a "League of Honor" among nations as he has forecast in his great war messages.

The league's opportunity to identify itself with the war effort as well as with a program for world peace came with the request from the Secretary of the Treasury that the league lend its support to the Second Liberty Loan Campaign. The league fairly jumped at the offer. It set out to extend its efforts to reach every county of the nation, to provide speakers whenever and wherever needed, to distribute literature, to handle local press publicity, and in general to become so far as possible the chief agency in support of the loan. In this way the league managed to identify itself with patriotic endeavor, to extend its organization, and to associate its objective with war objectives. It was estimated that on "Liberty Day," October 24, 1917,

THE LEAGUE AS A WAR AIM

not less than 1,000 speakers, provided by the league, would speak for the loan—and incidentally for the league.⁷

During 1917, the league extended its influence in many ways. Lowell, Holt, and Taft made speaking tours, and some of their addresses attracted nation-wide attention.⁸ This was especially true of Taft's vigorous campaign against what he called a premature peace, one made before the military power of Germany was completely crushed. The league associated itself wherever possible with war preparedness committees, with councils of defense, with the National Security League, the Army and Navy League, as well as with the Church Peace Union and The World Alliance for Promoting Friendship Through the Churches.⁹ It continued its endeavors to secure resolutions of approval by state legislatures and by fraternal, business, educational, and religious organizations.

Through the influence of Louis J. Alber, general manager of the Coit Alber Chautauqua System, the league's program was presented to 3,878 Chautauqua audiences attended by an estimated number of 4,000,000 people. Similar arrangements were made to reach the Lyceum audiences during the winter months.¹⁰ Copies of the league's "War Reference Book," and the league's "Handbook" were distributed widely to councils of defense, libraries, "Four Minute Men," who spoke for the nation's war efforts, school principals, labor leaders and the like.¹¹ During the year 1917 more than two million pieces of league literature were distributed. The league's committee on information reported that a check-up on newspaper editorial comment during six weeks prior to September 8, 1917, revealed 152 editorial comments on the league with 149 of them favorable.¹²

League officials did not overestimate their success. They realized that a great amount of indifference regarding the

---

⁷ *Minutes*, Executive Committee, Sept. 20, 1917, *League Collection*; *Bulletin*, League to Enforce Peace, Oct. 12, 19, 1917.

⁸ *Report*, Committee on Information, Nov. 17, 1917, *League Collection*.

⁹ *Bulletin*, League to Enforce Peace, Sept. 17, Dec. 28, 1917.

¹⁰ *Ibid.*, Sept. 7, 1917; *Minutes*, Executive Committee, Nov. 24, 1917, *League Collection*.

¹¹ *Report*, Committee on Information, Dec. 27, 1917, *Filene MSS*.

¹² *Ibid.*, Sept. 8, 1917, *Filene MSS*.

league's aims still existed, that leaders of other organizations were more interested in their own problems, and that in many cases active league endeavor had slowed down because of the belief that the cause was already won.[13] In a stock-taking review of the league's successes and problems, Glenn Frank reported that there was a decline in interest in executive committee meetings, an increasing difficulty in raising money, an inclination for many people to believe that the league's great service to society was accomplished, since the governments of both the United States and Europe had accepted its main contention, and that there was an apparent reluctance on the part of the administration to approve further activity on the part of the league.[14]

This last assumption was not correct. The attitude of President Wilson toward the league was, of course, very important and also very clear. He believed that it would be unwise to formulate and advocate specific programs for world settlement or for a constitution of a league of nations in such a way that popular support would be aroused.[15] Conditions that would prevail at the end of the war could not be exactly foreseen, and the peace program would have to be worked out later in detail. Particularly the President had in mind that the details of a program would have to be reached through democratic processes if the necessary free concert of nations was to be secured. This inevitably meant that each nation would have to accommodate itself in some respects certainly to the general will. He was anxious therefore that the people should think about the problem, should understand the larger principles involved in it, but that they should avoid crystallizing their thoughts around specific blueprints of a world system. This view he expressed to his own party leaders, to representatives abroad, and to foreign representatives in the United States, as well as to representatives of the League to Enforce Peace.[16] In

[13] *Report*, Committee on Organization, Dec. 22, 1917, *Filene MSS*.
[14] Edward Cummings to A. Lawrence Lowell, Oct. 2, 1917, *Lowell MSS*.
[15] Baker, *op. cit.*, VII, 53.
[16] *Ibid.*, pp. 99, 129, 203.

general the administration was rather reluctant to associate officially with a private organization which was in no way under its control and which was dealing with foreign policy.[17] This did not constitute hostility to league activity. Colonel House explained to league representatives that the President would not be wise in giving his personal sanction to League to Enforce Peace projects. Informally the President would keep in touch with the league. Colonel House thought that it would be very valuable for the league to study problems that would probably arise at the peace conference and to continue its vigorous propaganda in behalf of the league of nations idea.[18] The league's secretary felt that Colonel House was modest and unpretentious, that the league was very fortunate to have his confidence, and that it was under obligation to be sincere and open in all relations with him.[19]

In the meantime, the President had continued his study of the problems of peace.[20] The result of this study and of the progress of world events was the address to Congress of January 8, 1918, the famous Fourteen Points speech. The well-known fourteenth point provided that "a general association of nations must be formed under specific covenants for the purpose of affording mutual guarantees of political independence and territorial integrity to great and small nations alike."

The address was well received throughout the nation. *The Independent*, in commenting upon it, believed that the United States had "come of age," that the President was the "foremost champion of liberalism" in the world, and that he "articulated ... the very conscience of the American people."[21] In considering the address in detail, however, rather small attention was given by the nation to the fourteenth point. *The Literary Digest* found the nation's press generally favorable but made

[17] *Memorandum*, on attitude of the government toward the league, July, 1917, *Filene MSS.*
[18] *Memorandum*, Aug. 25, 1917, *League Collection.*
[19] William Short to Taft, Oct. 2, 1917 (copy), *League Collection.*
[20] Baker, *op. cit.,* VII, 420, 451-456; Seymour, *op. cit.,* III, 325-329, 334-337.
[21] *The Independent,* XCIII (Jan. 19, 1918), 89-92.

virtually no reference to the league issue.[22] The Senate did not engage immediately in a discussion of the address, and resolutions of approval were referred to the Committee on Foreign Relations.[23]

In this situation, with the attention of the people turned more toward winning the war than to the organization of a peaceful world thereafter, the decision of the League to Enforce Peace to hold another national convention was undoubtedly timely. The purpose of the convention was to sustain the war effort of the nations until Prussian militarism was defeated, to oppose a premature peace, and to gain support for a guarantee of peace by a league of nations.[24] In an interview printed in the *New York World*, Secretary Short explained that the program would provide "discussions by leaders in thought and action of the things at stake in the war and the things that must come out of it if our sacrifice and the sacrifice of all the nations in it is to be justified." The convention, he said, would attempt to dramatize the fact that the United States was fighting for a peace that would last, "so that every soldier will go to the front with the crusader's spirit and every man and woman who remains behind will be consecrated to the task of seeing to it that their entire nation shall, when the war ends, demand with one voice that the men who settle their war shall create such effective guarantees that so far as is humanly possible such a war shall not be gone through without gain, and that the world in the future shall be builded upon the foundations of justice, freedom, and democracy."

Plans for the convention were made with even more care than had been the case with earlier conventions. The central office of the league had prepared a file of the most prominent leaders in American life. This file was carefully combed and almost 5,000 invitations to the meeting were sent. Invitations were sent, for example, to the governors of states and to other political leaders, to the heads of 185 advertising clubs, to 57

[22] *Literary Digest*, LVI (Jan. 19, 1918), 11-14.
[23] Resolutions were introduced by Senators Robert L. Owen and James H. Lewis, *Congressional Record*, 65 Congress, 2nd Session, Vol. 56, part I, pp. 817, 1506.
[24] *Bulletin*, League to Enforce Peace, Mar. 8, 1918.

agricultural leaders, to 285 Rotary Club presidents, to 500 college presidents, to 400 Catholic clergymen, and so on until it was believed that no important group or section in America had been overlooked.[25]

When information reached President Wilson regarding the convention, which he apparently thought was to be held in Washington, his first thought was that it would not be wise to hold such a meeting. The result was that Taft and Lowell arranged for an interview with the President, who explained to them his fear that the "framing of a plan for a League by men of prominence would embarrass him thereafter in dealing with the subject." The President had no objection to the meeting when he understood that it was not the intention of the League to Enforce Peace to discuss details of a world organization.[26]

Mr. Taft hoped that Charles E. Hughes and Cardinal Gibbons would speak at the Philadelphia meeting. Mr. Hughes, who was also invited to become a member of the executive committee of the league, said that he agreed with the league's general principles but that he did not see any "prospect of substantial progress" with regard to the idea until Germany was completely defeated.[27] Although he could not attend the meeting, Cardinal Gibbons said he hoped that principles of truth and justice would prevail at Philadelphia and elsewhere, and that militarism would be overthrown.[28]

Notwithstanding the inability of the league to secure the attendance of certain prominent men, this failure was apparently not noticed, and the convention which opened at the Academy of Music in Philadelphia, May 16, 1918, was as successful as its sponsors could reasonably have hoped. More than 3,500 delegates attended the Allied War Dinners held simultaneously at various hotels; ten state governors conferred at a meeting in Independence Hall, and the various speakers were, for the most part, people of national prominence.[29]

[25] *Memoranda*, Win the War for Permanent Peace Conference, *League Collection*.
[26] William H. Taft to A. Lawrence Lowell, Mar. 18, 1918, *Lowell MSS*.
[27] Charles E. Hughes to Taft, Mar. 30, 1918, *League Collection*.
[28] Cardinal Gibbons to Taft, May 15, 1918, *League Collection*.
[29] *Memorandum* of the Conference, *League Collection*.

The convention's slogan was "Win the War for Permanent Peace," but the first part was more characteristic of the time and the meeting than the second. Mr. Taft sounded the keynote in his address, "Victory with Power," when he said that the convention was called to "sound the trumpet of stern implacable war to the end." "We should set our faces," he continued, "stern and unbending, but for one purpose, war—war—war." Edward A. Filene declared that the United States was engaged "in the holiest war in history . . . a crusade of deepest spiritual meaning . . .; when war is for the commonweal, then war is worship, war is prayer." Nearly all the speakers placed special emphasis on the danger of a premature peace, one that would leave German militarism undefeated. They demanded complete victory. With one exception they advocated the formation of a league of nations to preserve peace once it had been established. Altogether forty-six addresses were given at the convention, and a new war platform of the League to Enforce Peace was adopted.[30]

The publicity, of course, was one of the chief purposes and values of the Philadelphia meeting. The league hoped that its existence and objectives would receive notice in hundreds of local newspapers. Plans were made to get such papers to discuss the purpose of the convention before it was held, to report on speeches and events of the meeting, and to print reports from and interviews with returning delegates. The hopes of the league in this regard were fully realized, and the emphasis in the press accounts was placed where it had been at the convention, upon the need for the complete defeat of Germany. News stories and editorials were carried under such headlines as the following: "Peace, but not without Victory,"[31] "War to Death Taft's Demand of Peace League,"[32] "Peace League to Urge Victory First,"[33] "No Peace by Compro-

---

[30] The addresses given at the convention were printed in a pamphlet, "Win the War for Permanent Peace," which was widely distributed by the league. For the war platform see Appendix II.
[31] *Albuquerque Journal,* May 17, 1918.
[32] *St. Louis Dispatch,* May 16, 1918.
[33] *Christian Science Monitor,* May 3, 1918.

mise,"[34] "Germany must be Whipped to a Standstill,"[35] "Carry on War till Victorious Peace is Forced on Huns."[36] Some editors used the convention merely as another opportunity to denounce Germany. One demanded that Germany be made to repay England and the United States their total war expenditure.[37] Another called for the complete crushing of Germany,[38] and still another declared that "any peace with an unwhipped Germany" would be a "wicked peace."[39]

The above examples serve to underline the success of the league in making it clear that it was not a pacifist organization. At the same time many papers gave adequate treatment to the desirability of a league of nations as a war objective, and some of them placed the major emphasis on that subject. *The Toledo Blade*, in referring to the convention, stated that "the proposed League of Nations is virtually a necessity. It will be the creation not of dreamers, but of practical statesmen. It will be the development not of idealism, but of cold, hard necessity."[40] "We doubt," commented the *Indianapolis Enquirer*, "if there has ever been a convention composed of uncommissioned and unofficial membership, summoned without other authority than that inherent in the course that impelled their presence, greater in character, more virile in expression, with clearer and less beclouded vision or purpose more resolute and significant."[41] "If we get the league of nations," stated the *Ohio State Journal*, "there will be no need for universal military training, and if we don't God pity us all, for there will be war from now to kingdom come..."[42]

A few journals used the opportunity to denounce the league movement. In any league of nations, declared the *Chicago Tribune*, some nation would assert leadership. Germany might

[34] *Indianapolis Star*, Mar. 18, 1918.
[35] *Auburn Advertiser*, Mar. 22, 1918.
[36] *Philadelphia Press*, May 16, 1918.
[37] *Glens Falls* (New York) *Times*, Mar. 24, 1918.
[38] *Scranton* (Pennsylvania) *Times*, May 18, 1918.
[39] *Grand Forks* (North Dakota) *Herald*, Apr. 27, 1918.
[40] May 8, 1918.
[41] May 23, 1918.
[42] Apr. 18, 1918.

well be the nation to do this, and since the United States would be trustful and credulous, it would be the principal victim of such an organization.[43] The *Wall Street Journal* did not think a league of nations could be contemplated if Germany were to be admitted,[44] and the *Milwaukee Leader* declared that the League to Enforce Peace was working for a "mechanical" world movement which could not succeed without the growth of world patriotism.[45] In an article on the League to Enforce Peace, written especially for the *Irish World*, R. E. Thompson declared that for a third of a century the Holy Alliance had crushed liberty, that a league of nations would probably assist Japan if Korea should revolt, and that the League to Enforce Peace advocated free trade which caused war.[46]

The Philadelphia meeting was intended as the spearhead of a renewed nation-wide campaign. State branches of the League to Enforce Peace were to organize state "Win the War for Permanent Peace" conventions, and these were to be followed by county conventions. Great efforts were to be made to secure resolutions by state legislatures endorsing the league idea, and to induce state governors to serve as vice-presidents of the League to Enforce Peace. Since 1918 was an election year, many of the state conventions were to be held after the first of November. The coming of the Armistice and the subsequent effort placed by the league upon a series of regional congresses disrupted, in many cases, the plans for state meetings. Several were held, however, during October,[47] and one of the most successful was held in Wisconsin on the eighth, ninth, and tenth of November.[48]

By August, 1918, thirty-four state governors had agreed to serve as vice-presidents of the League to Enforce Peace,[49] and

[43] May 18, 1918.
[44] Apr. 1, 1918.
[45] May 28, 1918.
[46] May 25, 1918.
[47] *Bulletin*, League to Enforce Peace, Oct. 12, 1918.
[48] This meeting was sponsored by the University of Wisconsin and was endorsed in a joint resolution of the Wisconsin Legislature: R. T. Ely to Lowell, Oct. 3, 1918, *Lowell MSS*.
[49] *Bulletin*, League to Enforce Peace, July 20, Aug. 10, 1918.

sixteen state legislatures either in concurrent or joint resolutions had endorsed the league of nations idea.[50] Typical of these resolutions was that passed by the Massachusetts House of Representatives on February 6, and by the Senate on February 11:

> Resolved: That the Commonwealth of Massachusetts favors the entrance of the United States, after the war, into a League of Nations to safeguard the peace that must be won by the joint military forces of the allied nations. . . .

Early in 1918 the league, together with the Church Peace Union and with the assistance of the World Alliance for International Friendship through the Churches, organized the Committee on the Churches and Moral Aims of the War. Hamilton Holt was chairman of the committee, and Taft, Lowell, Short, and Talcott Williams were prominent members. The policy of the committee was to conduct a "campaign of education through the churches in support of the President's policies in prosecuting the war for Democracy, International Justice, and a League of Nations." It arranged speaking tours for prominent churchmen, held institutes for clergymen, published literature written especially for religious organizations, and in so far as possible organized American religious leadership in support of the league. Over 33,000 ministers and 700,000 other people attended meetings sponsored by the committee.[51]

The activity of the central office of the league steadily increased during 1918. It built up an elaborate organization for the distribution of news and carefully investigated the most efficient methods of advertising its work. Its newspaper clipping department watched the press for the names of people who had expressed sympathy with the league's objectives. Personal letters were written to such people, and they were invited to join the local organization if such existed or to start a local branch. Any hostile editorial or item was sent to some friend of the

[50] *Ibid.*, Dec. 14, 1918.
[51] *Reports,* Committee on the Churches and Moral Aims of the War, May-October, 1918; Glenn Frank to Short, July 9, 1918; *Memoranda* on the Committee etc., *Filene MSS.*

league in the area indicated with the request that a reply should be attempted publicly. News releases were being sent to more than 200 papers by mid-summer of 1918, and it was not uncommon for the central office to mail 2,000 letters in a day. In October, thanks to the generosity of the Bush Terminal Sales Company, the league took over full charge of the twenty-third floor of the Bush Terminal building at 130 W. 42nd Street, and the new space was none too large.[52]

The League to Enforce Peace hoped that, as in 1916, in the congressional campaign of 1918 political partisanship over the league issue could be avoided by securing public statements of approval of the league idea from both major parties. Letters were sent to state and national chairmen and committeemen of the two groups asking them to put planks into their platforms favoring the participation of the United States in an international organization to preserve the future peace of the world.[53] This strategy was successful to the extent that no clear-cut cleavage on the league issue appeared in the state party platforms.[54] Chairman Vance C. McCormick of the Democratic National Committee was a member of the executive committee of the League to Enforce Peace and was quite willing to say that he approved of the league idea. But Chairman Will H. Hays of the Republican National Committee, while professing that he favored the league idea, declared that the United States should rely upon its own self-defense and should not substitute internationalism for "fervent American nationalism."[55]

This obvious attempt of Mr. Hays to straddle the issue was in all probability ascribable to his realization that some of the most influential members of his party did not accept Taft's leadership on the league question. One of the most vocal members of the party and one of the most ardent advocates of

[52] *Bulletin*, League to Enforce Peace, Oct. 19, 26, 1918: *Report* of the Committee on Information, Aug. 24, Oct. 19, 1918, *Filene MSS*.
[53] W. R. Boyd to Glenn Frank, July 15, 1918, *Filene MSS*; W. R. Short to Lowell, Aug. 27, 1918, *Lowell MSS*.
[54] In New York, for example, both parties approved of a League of Nations, the Republican Party platform being the more specific in its support. *Bulletin*, League to Enforce Peace, July 27, 1918.
[55] *Ibid.*, Aug. 31, 1918.

making opposition to a league of nations the central tenet of the Republican campaign was ex-Senator Albert J. Beveridge. In July he wrote to Roosevelt that President Wilson had "hoisted the motley flag of internationalism." "That," he said, "makes the issue, does it not? Straight Americanism for us."[56] Roosevelt promised to voice his and Beveridge's views on internationalism, and the latter replied, "Now we shall have an issue."[57] Beveridge, who began to denounce the idea of a league of nations as early as February, 1917, had renewed the fight in an attack upon the League to Enforce Peace in an address at Indianapolis on Memorial Day, 1918. He declared that under a league system the United States would be unable to protect the Panama Canal, would be deprived of the right to declare war, would have to take part in foreign wars, and would be united with an un-American organization.[58]

This address was answered by Booth Tarkington, who took up Beveridge's arguments *seriatim* and finally came to the conclusion that the ex-Senator had set up simply an imaginary league fashioned so that he could push it over. "Senator Beveridge," he said, "is not really attacking the 'League to Enforce Peace' that he believes he is attacking. What the Senator is so indignant with is really a league of his own construction. In his anxiety lest America plunge hot foot into the unknown, he makes up a constitution and a set of by-laws and house rules and a membership committee for a suppositious league, and then having built a club house for it, of the most inflammable materials, he proceeds to set it on fire with shells of incendiary oratory; beats up the members with a rhetorical club, and dances on the ashes with a combination of grace and grimness suitable to the devastated occasion."[59] But no answer, however logical, restrained the anti-league activities of Beveridge.

The Roosevelt-Beveridge agreement regarding the league issue tended to become more significant when, at Saratoga, New

---
[56] Bowers, *op. cit.*, p. 498.
[57] *Ibid.*
[58] *Bulletin*, League to Enforce Peace, June 22, 1918.
[59] Open letter to Beveridge, June 21, 1918, quoted in *Bulletin*, League to Enforce Peace, June 22, 1918.

York, on July 19 and 20, Taft united with Roosevelt, Hays, and Root in denouncing the Wilson administration and calling upon the country to elect a Republican Congress. Such a Congress, it was stated, could be relied upon to carry on the war, and it would not be subject to the "discipline of the Administration" in dealing with the problems that would arise later.[60] Some attempt was made by the Republicans, with the assistance of the National Security League, to show that Republican congressmen had been more vigorous than the Democrats in the support of the war. This conclusion was based upon the party alignment on certain selected war measures. The Democrats, however, made up another list of war measures to prove that the Democratic Party had been more consistent in supporting the war.[61]

Mere charge and counter-charge with respect to support of vigorous war measures were not the stuff of which an election victory could be won. The danger of an inconclusive peace, however, was a different matter. The idea that the Democratic Party, under the leadership of the President, favored a "Peace without Victory," a negotiated peace, possibly a league of nations with German membership, and in general a peace program that would leave Germany undestroyed, was well worth considering as campaign material. Some of the President's phrases unfortunately lent themselves to misinterpretation if anyone had the desire to distort or strain the meanings of words. Peace without victory, as the President used the term, meant a postwar settlement without injustice to the Central Powers, and an end of the war whenever they were willing to accept the terms offered to them by the Allies. But peace could be used to mean the end of the war and victory the defeat of Germany. Thus peace without victory might be interpreted to connote the end of the war without the military defeat of Germany. Since the popular mind was saturated with the idea of a knockout fight and the conquest of Germany, if the President's peace program could be presented to the people in such a way as to equate it with a compromise peace, their opposition to his program could be aroused.

[60] *The New York Times*, July 19, 20, 1918.
[61] *Ibid.*, Oct. 26, 1918.

No one understood this situation better than Senator Lodge, and no one was more capable of exploiting it to the full. In a prepared speech in the Senate on August 23, he launched a full-dress attack upon the President's peace program. Significantly emphasizing his position as a Republican leader in the Senate, he took up the President's phrase "peace without victory" and declared that he favored a dictated not a negotiated peace. He made it clear that he had no use for the preservation of democracy that the President talked about through a system of world peace, but that he believed in preserving American independence through the strength of its own armed might. Then, taking up the President's program in detail, he discounted every idea that in his opinion did not look toward the complete overthrow of German power.[62] In an interview with the press a few days later, he added his support to the statements that had been made by Taft, Root, Hays, and Roosevelt, that the election of a Republican Congress was necessary for carrying on the war to complete victory and for the proper kind of reconstruction policies later.

During the early days of the campaign President Wilson confined his political activity to the Democratic primaries. On several occasions he expressed the hope that certain congressmen who had opposed the policies of his administration would not be renominated. Some Republican papers denounced the President for this action, calling his attitude "intolerant," his act "prescriptive," and a "kind of moral terrorism."[63] The Democratic press and some independent papers defended his acts. "There is no reason," commented *The Springfield Republican*, "why the President should not seek openly to have Senators elected who would support his proclaimed policies. Especially when the war comes to an end, he will need friends and sympathizers in the Senate, if his ideas of a world-peace are to be given a chance to materialize."[64]

For a time after his address of January 22, President Wilson had been doubtful about the possibility of securing a league

[62] *Congressional Record*, 65 Congress, 2nd Session, Vol. 56, part IX, pp. 9394-95.
[63] *Literary Digest*, LVIII (Aug. 24, 1918), 10.
[64] *Ibid.*, p. 11.

of nations to enforce peace. He was discouraged by European comments concerning his address and by the attack upon the league idea by prominent Americans in and out of office. He was impressed, too, with the difficulties that had arisen when the attempt was made to secure unity of military command among the allied armies. The allies agreed that unity was needed but disagreed about the person who should be given the supreme command. The President expressed misgivings to Taft and Lowell when they talked with him in March about the Philadelphia meeting of the League to Enforce Peace and discussed them also with Colonel House.[65] He told Lowell and Taft that the common law had developed little by little in accordance with experience and that it might be better to start with guarantees of political independence and territorial integrity, enforced by whatever arrangements could be made at *ad hoc* conferences when the need arose. Experience would show what further steps could be taken.

The misgivings that the President had were not regarding the league idea but about gaining acceptance for a satisfactory league. Lowell and Taft assured him that it was possible to secure American support and that it was essential to create a well-organized international security system at the end of the war while the people of the world were more aware of its need than they would be after a period of peace. They urged him to continue his advocacy of the idea and indirectly, therefore, committed themselves to support his efforts. Later when Taft had joined the President's opponents he used this discussion as the basis for asserting that Wilson did not favor a league.

Whatever fears the President may have had about popular approval for the league, he did not permit them to deter his advocacy of the cause. When he referred again to the subject publicly, he spoke with all the conviction that he had expressed earlier. In an address delivered at Mount Vernon on July 4, he outlined once more the ends for which the war was being fought, one of which was the following:

---

[65] Charles Seymour, *The Intimate Papers of Colonel House* (Boston, Houghton Mifflin Company, 1926-28), IV, 12-19.

> The establishment of an organization of peace which shall make it certain that the combined power of free nations will check every invasion of right and serve to make peace and justice more secure by affording a definite tribunal of opinion to which all must submit and by which every international readjustment that cannot be amicably agreed upon by the peoples directly concerned shall be sanctioned.[66]

In opening the Fourth Liberty Loan campaign in New York on September 27, the President discussed what he called the practical implications of a peace settlement based upon the avowed principles for which the nation had been fighting. His remarks on the subject of a league of nations were as definite as any that he had made. If, he declared, the governments associated against Germany wanted, "in deed and in truth" a lasting peace, they would have to be willing "to create in some vital fashion the only instrumentality by which it can be made certain that agreements of the peace will be honored and fulfilled . . . that indispensable instrumentality is a League of Nations formed under covenants that will be efficacious. . . ." He believed that the constitution of a league had to be a part of the peace settlement, that it would not be formed before the peace without being merely an alliance of the nations associated against Germany, and that it was not likely that it could be formed later. Very significantly he declared that there should be no "economic combinations within the League" and no boycotts except those that the league itself might use.[67]

In surveying the reactions of the press to President Wilson's Liberty Loan speech, the *Literary Digest* declared that the President had brought "the dream of a league of nations into the realm of practical politics." Various papers were quoted as agreeing with this view. *The Philadelphia Public Ledger* asserted that he had "made permanent peace possible" and continued:

> He took the league of nations out of the toy-shop of speculative statecraft and presented it to us as a workable tool and weapon with which the police power of organized

[66] Baker and Dodd, *op. cit.*, VI, 231-235.
[67] *Ibid.*, pp. 253-261.

civilization can be put squarely behind the informed, impartial, and just judgment of civilization. He sees that to make peace without making simultaneously a league of nations to protect it would be like driving a band of bandits out of a village they were looting, without providing any police law or armed force to keep them from coming back again. He is no impractical visionary fondly fancying that the world can be ruled as yet without force. His slogan is, "force, force to the utmost," when force is needed. But he does believe—and this is where he leads the best thought of the world at this moment—that force can be recruited into the unselfish service of law, order, and justice, and employed to protect a peace based in every nation—even the weakest—on the content of the peaceful.[68]

Not all of the press was favorable to the President's program. The papers that had opposed the league of nations idea all along continued to do so. *The Boston Transcript* thought that the very universality of the league would split it into hostile groups, while *The New York Tribune* argued that if it should be organized with the Teutonic powers out, the world would be split into hostile camps, and if they were permitted to come in, security would rest "upon the word of criminal members who have no faith to pledge."[69]

The real attack upon the President's peace proposals, however, was launched by Senator Lodge in the Senate on October 7. The question, he said, was not the "14 points or the 4 points, or 8 points or whatever they are," but one of placing Germany where she could never again enter upon a war of conquest. Continuing, he said, "As for this league of nations to enforce peace it is caught up by Germany in order to divert attention. . . ." The real peace program should be no peace without the destruction of Germany and no league with Germany as a partner.[70]

"This is not the first time," said Senator Pittman replying to Senator Lodge, "that the Senator from Massachusetts has voiced

[68] *Literary Digest*, LIX (Oct. 12, 1918), 11-12.
[69] *Ibid.*
[70] *Congressional Record*, 65 Congress, 2nd Session, Vol. 56, part XI, p. 11160.

his disapproval of the principles, policies, and methods pronounced by the President for the conduct of the war, the negotiation of peace, and the settlement of post-war conditions looking to a lasting and permanent peace." Comparing the peace proposals of the President with those stated by Lodge on October 23, he said, "The spirit that the two programs breathe is as different as might is from justice. The program of the Senator from Massachusetts means one for victory, revenge, advantage, while the program of the President means one for victory, justice, and everlasting peace." Declaring that Lodge's opposition to the President's peace program was a grave concern, Senator Pittman asked this pointed question: "Would a Republican United States Senate, under the leadership of Senator Lodge, ratify treaties embracing the President's program, or would they substitute for it a program formulated by the senior Senator from Massachusetts?" The coming election, he said, would be inevitably a contest between the "policies of Woodrow Wilson and the policies of Henry Cabot Lodge."[71]

Senator Lodge met the challenge. Again specifically stating that he was speaking as a Republican and as a leader of the Republican Party, he declared that to put Germany "where she cannot again break out like an armed lunatic upon the world" would "do more than any league of peace." He made it clear that he would support the President's war measures but not his peace proposals. "The Republican Party," he said, "stands for unconditional surrender and complete victory, just as Grant stood. My own belief is that the American people mean to have an unconditional surrender. They mean to have a dictated, not a negotiated peace."[72]

Senator Lodge's proposals deserve analysis. He wanted to defeat Germany and to prevent her from becoming again an aggressor. That was what the President and the League to Enforce Peace wanted. They proposed a method through which their aims could be accomplished, international action against any aggressor state. Germany's unconditional surrender offered no security whatsoever against her future aggression. Thus

[71] *Ibid.*, pp. 11166-7.
[72] *Ibid.*, p. 11171.

Lodge advocated an objective but denounced the only method for its accomplishment.

This increasing opposition to the President's peace program was significant, for the war was rapidly drawing to a close by the end of October. Between October 3, when peace negotiations were initiated by the German Chancellor, Prince Max of Baden, and October 23, when President Wilson turned over to the allies his correspondence with the Chancellor, the President achieved one of the greatest diplomatic triumphs of his career. In the exchange of notes Germany not only agreed specifically to the Fourteen Points as a basis for peace but also accepted complete military defeat.[73] The problems that would soon face the country would be those of peace and reconstruction and not of war. It was on October 23, however, that Mr. Taft joined with Theodore Roosevelt in an appeal to the voters of Michigan to elect Truman H. Newberry to the Senate, although Henry Ford, Mr. Newberry's opponent, had noted as early as October 17, that powerful interests in the United States were being organized to oppose the League of Nations which he was pledged to support.[74]

The third of the Fourteen Points provided for the "removal, so far as possible, of economic barriers and the establishment of an equality of trade conditions among all the nations consenting to the peace and associating themselves for its maintenance." Chairman Fess and other Republican leaders began to attack this part of the President's peace program and to declare that the election of Democrats to Congress would bring about free trade.[75] At the same time, Republicans were appealing for re-election on the ground that since they had supported the war, President Wilson was quite willing to rely upon them for support of his policies at its conclusion.[76] Democratic can-

[73] See Charles Seymour, *American Diplomacy during the World War* (Baltimore, Johns Hopkins Press, 1934), pp. 298-331.
[74] *The New York Times*, Oct. 17, 1918.
[75] *Ibid.*, Oct. 22, 24, 25, 1918.
[76] Democratic leaders from Albuquerque, New Mexico, sent word to the President that Senator Fall's friends were claiming that the President was not opposed to Fall's re-election. The President answered that Senator Fall had given such repeated evidence of hostility to his whole administration that "no one who wishes to sustain me can intelligently

didates for re-election, who had supported the President's domestic as well as his war policies and who were willing to support his peace program, felt that they deserved some active help from the administration.[77]

Confronted with this situation, President Wilson, on October 25, appealed to the people to support the Democratic Party if they wished to support his policies both domestic and foreign. He did not doubt the patriotism of the Republican Party but felt that the "difficulties and delicacies of the present task" were such that divided leadership would be unfortunate. Although Republican spokesmen were urging the election of Republicans with the claim that they would support the President, really they wished to curtail his influence and to initiate policies of their own.

This appeal by the President was the signal and the excuse for a renewed attack upon his peace program. A statement signed by the official spokesmen of the Republican Party declared that the party was opposed to "negotiations and discussion carried on by diplomatic notes" and that it stood for "victorious peace" and "unconditional surrender."[78] Senator Poindexter asserted that the President wanted the election of Democratic senators because he wanted a league of nations with Germany as an equal member. He hoped that Great Britain and France would insist upon the defeat of Germany before there was any discussion of the "humanities," a "peace based upon justice," a "lasting peace," and "all that sort of thing." This issue in the election, he continued, was whether we would "compromise the war with a weak peace." The President would simply serve German designs if he granted her an armistice on any terms.[79]

---

vote for him." Fall answered that he would "support no Bolsheviki-German peace." *Congressional Record*, 65 Congress, 2nd Session, Vol. 56, part XI, pp. 11524-11525.

[77] Statement of Vance McCormick to the author. McCormick was chairman in 1918 of the Democratic National Committee.

[78] Signed by Senators Smoot and Lodge, and Congressmen F. H. Gillett and S. D. Fess. See *Congressional Record*, 65 Congress, 2nd Session, Vol. 56, part XI, p. 11502.

[79] *Ibid.*, p. 11501.

While Senator Lodge continued to attack the President's peace program as vigorously as Poindexter, Roosevelt, or Beveridge, he was a little less certain than they were that a frontal assault would be successful. He offered to Beveridge some sage advice:

> I think it would be a mistake to admit that the League would be a good thing, but I think we should make a mistake if we met the proposition with a flat denial. The purpose of the League—that is, the preservation of world peace—we are all anxious to see, but what we oppose is the method. Now the strength of our position is to show up the impossibility of *any of the methods proposed* and invite them, when they desire our support, to produce their terms. They cannot do it. My own judgment is that the whole thing will break up in conference. There may be some vague declarations of the beauties of peace, but *any practical League* that involves control of our legislation, of our armies and navies, or the Monroe Doctrine, or an international police, and that sort of thing, *then our issue is made up, and we shall win.* We can begin by pointing out these dangers, and that I am sure will be done.[80]

This statement is worthy of the most careful reading, for it is a proposal that fraud should be practiced upon the American people. They should pretend to favor world peace but should oppose any method of achieving it. Thus they could avoid a split in the Republican Party on the league issue. Their policy would be successful unless the pro-league Republicans were able to see through the deception.

Officially the League to Enforce Peace took no part in the political campaign, but it was soon involved indirectly through the activity of its president, Mr. Taft. On October 23 he issued a ringing denunciation of President Wilson and called again for the election of a Republican Congress.[81] In doing this he inescapably allied himself with Roosevelt and Lodge who were denouncing the President's peace program.[82] Various members

---

[80] Henry C. Lodge to A. J. Beveridge, Dec. 3, 1918, quoted in Bowers, *op. cit.*, p. 500. Italics mine.
[81] *The New York Times*, Oct. 26, 1918.
[82] *Ibid.*, Oct. 28.

of the league protested vigorously against Mr. Taft's activity. It was reported that funds for the League to Enforce Peace could not be raised while Taft was coöperating with the enemies of the league program,[83] and many people who had given considerable sums to the league felt that Mr. Taft had betrayed the cause.[84]

In reply to a telegram from Governor T. W. Bickett, state chairman of the league in North Carolina, requesting him to counteract Roosevelt's denunciation of the Fourteen Points,[85] Mr. Taft stated that Wilson did not favor the League to Enforce Peace while Roosevelt did, and that as far as the Fourteen Points were concerned he agreed with Roosevelt and not with Wilson. "I think," said Taft, "those fourteen points cannot be made the safe bases of a treaty of peace. They are too vague and too indefinite. They will give rise to as many disputes as the present war." He hoped that a Republican congress would be elected.[86] Later he was overjoyed when his hopes were fulfilled.[87]

Taft's actions during this campaign were consonant with his previous political conduct on the league issue and were a forecast of his later acts. It can scarcely be doubted that he was sincerely and honestly devoted to the league of nations cause. For two years he had advocated it with unstinting effort. He could not have been blind, however, to the fact that the most active leaders of his party, men like Roosevelt, Poindexter, Borah, and Lodge, were denouncing the league idea at every opportunity. His statement that Wilson did not favor the league might possibly have resulted from his conversation with the President in March, had the President said nothing on the subject thereafter. But it is inconceivable that he was unaware

[83] Bolton Smith to Percy M. Gordon, Financial Agent of the League to Enforce Peace, Nov. 4, 1918, *League Collection*.
[84] James M. Moore to Herbert S. Houston, Nov. 2, 1918; B. F. McLeod to W. M. Gardner, Nov. 2, 1918; M. Fairchild to William Short, Nov. 5, 1918; Mrs. Augustus Hemingway to P. M. Gordon, Nov. 5, 1918, *League Collection*.
[85] Governor Bickett to Taft, Oct. 25, 1918 (copy), *League Collection*.
[86] Taft to Governor Bickett, Oct. 30, 1918 (copy), *League Collection*.
[87] Pringle, *op. cit.*, II, 913.

of the President's addresses of July 4 and September 27. As mentioned previously, the President did not tell Taft and Lowell that he had lost faith in the league idea but that he feared the strength of the league opposition. Taft had urged the President to go ahead with his league program, and the President had done so. Now Taft joined with the opponents of the league and explained his actions on the unwarranted allegation that the President had abandoned the league cause. Within two months after the election, Taft was denouncing the "selfishness," the "littleness," and the "blindness" to the interests of the United States and of the world of many of the Republican leaders with whom he had joined in the political campaign.

After the election which resulted in a Republican majority in the Senate, Taft apparently did not think that his coöperation with the isolationists, the Hearst press, and the other anti-league forces, had in any way weakened the influence of the League to Enforce Peace or had damaged the league cause. He reasserted his entire loyalty to the cause and expressed his belief that the leaders of the Republican Party would have too much political insight to array themselves in the future against it.[88] Speaking before a small group of newspaper men and editors, Taft took sharp issue with his former Secretary of State Knox and with Lodge in their advocacy of postponing the consideration of a league system until after a treaty of peace had been made. He believed that the solution of problems involving disarmament, colonies, small new nations, and international economic affairs all depended upon having a league of nations as a part of the peace treaty. "This treaty at Paris," he said, "is going to be worth nothing but the paper it is written on, unless you have a League to Enforce Peace. . . . Gentlemen, the Lord has delivered the foes of a league of nations into your hands. You cannot escape it. Unless you have such a league, your war is a failure, your treaty is a failure, and your peace is a failure."[89]

Notwithstanding the importance given to the league issue

[88] *Minutes*, Executive Committee, Nov. 23, 1918, *League Collection*.
[89] *The New York Times*, Dec. 6, 1918.

and the obvious direction in which the Republican leaders were tending, it is doubtful that the election could be considered as a repudiation by the people of the league idea. The political situation was too complicated and the relation of the parties to programs for world peace was too indistinct for a conclusion of that sort. The leading journals of neither party interpreted the election as a repudiation of the President's peace program,[90] and very probably Democratic candidates received as many votes because they supported the league idea as Republicans did because they opposed it. Moreover, Lodge's tactics already noted and Taft's vigorous support of the Republican cause may well have kept doubting pro-league Republicans within the fold.

Meanwhile a new society, the League of Free Nations Association, was established in New York. During the summer of 1918 a group of about sixty editors, publicists, lawyers, and others held weekly meetings in New York to consider the problem of a postwar league of nations. Among other members of the group were Charles A. Beard, Herbert Croly, John Dewey, Stephen P. Duggan, Felix Frankfurter, and Hamilton Holt. They soon discovered that their discussions led them virtually to the same ideas that were being advocated by the League to Enforce Peace. As soon as the Armistice was declared, these two societies formulated a declaration of principles which they called the Victory Program.

This Victory Program became, therefore, the official platform of the League to Enforce Peace and supplanted the earlier program without abandoning its objectives. The former platform advocated the establishment of an international league designed to prevent war primarily through judicial processes and was therefore rather narrowly juridical in character. The new platform declared that a league of nations should be created at the time of the treaty of peace and "should aim at promoting the liberty, progress, and fair economic opportunity of all nations, and the orderly development of the world." Thus security would be sought not only by the settle-

[90] *Literary Digest*, LIX (Nov. 16, 1918), 14-15.

ment of disputes but also by the elimination of their causes.[91] This was in keeping with the development of thought on the subject since the League to Enforce Peace was formed, and, as it turned out, was in keeping with the character of the League of Nations that was created at Versailles.

[91] Appendix III.

CHAPTER FIVE

The Crucial Test

THE PRE-ARMISTICE AGREEMENT, which led shortly to the end of hostilities against Germany on November 11, 1918, contained the program on which the United States and the Allies promised to construct world peace.[1] This program, with two exceptions, was the one laid down by President Wilson in his message to Congress of January 8, 1918, and in subsequent addresses, and included, therefore, several statements concerning a league of nations. In his message of January 8, the President stated as the fourteenth point that an "association of nations" must be created "for the purpose of affording mutual guarantees of political independence and territorial integrity to great and small states alike." Subsequently he referred to the league idea several times, but his most extensive discussion of it was his New York address of September 27. On that occasion he asserted that a "League of Nations" was the "indispensable instrumentality" by which the peace of the world could be guaranteed and that the construction of such a league should be a part, "in a sense the most essential part," of the peace settlement.

While the President's program of peace was broad and far-reaching, it certainly contained three fundamental stipulations. The first was the establishment in Germany of a responsible government. The second was the evacuation by Germany of invaded territory, and the third was the creation of a league of nations. The first of these was required of Germany as a condition of the Pre-Armistice Agreement. The second was a part of the terms of Germany's military capitulation, the so-called Armistice. But the third stipulation imposed an obligation

[1] See below, Chapter VII.

on the United States and the Allies. In effect, they made a contract with Germany and pledged their honor and good faith to carry out their part of it. Nothing in this pledge was more precise than their obligation to create a league of nations.

In view of this situation, the leaders of the League to Enforce Peace might have assumed that their work was done as soon as the Pre-Armistice Agreement was signed, but they knew that it would be necessary to crystallize American public opinion back of the Pre-Armistice pledge and to bring the weight of their opinion to bear upon the Senate when the time came to ratify a treaty of peace including a league. The executive committee decided, therefore, to hold regional, state, and local conventions, to initiate a series of paid advertisements in the press, and to expand the speakers bureau. The need to secure the passage of resolutions at meetings, and the need for letters to the press, letters to senators, and other forms of expression favorable to the league idea was to be stressed, and special effort was to be made to secure the support of the Roman Catholic Church. The whole program was to be directed by an Emergency Campaign Committee.[2]

The first major project in the new campaign to arouse public opinion was the holding of ten regional congresses during the month of February, 1919. Large cities were selected for the meetings, each as near as possible to the center of a designated region. Through field secretaries, the national office of the league coöperated with local branches in securing newspaper advertisements and other publicity, in getting organizations to send delegates, and in searching for local speakers of the greatest possible political and civic prominence and influence. In order to allow one group of speakers to attend all the congresses, arrangements were made to hold them in a series beginning February 5 and ending February 28.[3] Among the speakers sent out by the national office to speak at all or many of the

[2] *Minutes*, Executive Committee, Nov. 16, 1918, and Dec. 7, 1918, *League Collection*.

[3] Beginning at New York, congresses were held in order at Boston, Chicago, Minneapolis, Portland, Oregon, San Francisco, Salt Lake City, St. Louis, and Atlanta.

congresses were William Howard Taft, A. Lawrence Lowell, Frank P. Walsh, Henry Van Dyke, Henry Morgenthau, George Grafton Wilson, James W. Gerard, Herbert S. Houston, and Edward A. Filene. The party that left New York travelled 8,000 miles and addressed 175 audiences attended by some 300,000 people.

The congresses were unquestionably successful. Meetings were everywhere attended by overflow audiences; funds were easily raised by private subscription to pay the considerable expenses; prominent people attended as delegates and speakers; and front page attention was given to the meetings by the press. Quite naturally Taft received the greatest amount of attention, both at the congresses and during brief stops at other cities along the route. The journey from one place to another was, in fact, almost a triumphal tour on his part. But other speakers received attention too, and some of the papers printed summaries of all the speeches, descriptions of the events connected with the congresses, and the complete text of the league's Victory Program.

All the congresses passed resolutions supporting the league idea. Typical among such resolutions are the following:

> Resolved: That in the formation of a League of Nations with adequate economic and military sanctions to guarantee the peace we see the triumph of American ideals, the realization of American hopes and aspirations, the next step forward in human progress, the beginning of a new era in material, moral, industrial and political well-being for ourselves and for all mankind.[4]
>
> We pledge our unrestricted support to the President of the United States in his advocacy of a League of Free Nations for the purpose of securing and maintaining enduring peace.[5]
>
> We are convinced that the public opinion of the United States is in favor of a League of Nations to maintain the peace of the world....[6]

It was the general practice for each congress to send copies of

[4] Adopted by the New England Congress, Boston, Feb. 8, 1919.
[5] Adopted by the Great Lakes Congress, Chicago, Feb. 10, 1919.
[6] Adopted by the Atlantic Congress, New York, Feb. 6, 1919.

its resolutions to President Wilson and to the senators from the states within the region of the congress.

While some members of the League to Enforce Peace were campaigning in the United States for a league of nations, other members were in Paris doing what they could to assist President Wilson in his struggle for a league. Oscar Straus and Hamilton Holt were the principal agents sent to Paris for this latter purpose. They were instructed: (1) to coöperate with the British League of Nations Union, the French Society for a League of Nations, and other similar societies, in order to harmonize their several programs and to provide united support for a league at the Paris Conference; (2) to demonstrate to the whole conference that the American people were back of the President in demanding that a league should be "the most important part of the peace treaty"; and (3) to provide the league workers at home with information concerning the progress of events at Paris in order to guide them in their campaign of education and in order to prevent the President's work at Paris from being destroyed from the rear.[7]

In his struggle for a league of nations President Wilson had four successive tasks. The first was to secure from the Allies a promise that they would establish a league. The second was to gain the recognition of that promise by the Paris Conference. The third was to draft a covenant acceptable to all the nations represented at Paris. And the fourth was to secure the approval of the United States Senate.

The President accomplished his first task when he secured the Pre-Armistice Agreement, and he succeeded in his second task with comparative ease. In a significant address at the second plenary session of the conference, January 25, 1919, he stated the case for a world league. The conference had met, he said, not only to make peace but also to secure peace. They could not hope to make permanent decisions which would never need to be altered, but they could establish "permanent processes" through which changes could be peacefully effected. For these reasons a league of nations was the keystone of the whole American purpose and ideal in the war, he declared. If

[7] Press release, Dec. 31, 1918, *League Collection.*

the American delegates should return home without having made every effort to realize their program, they would meet with the merited scorn of their fellow citizens.[8] A resolution was quickly passed calling for the formation of a league "to promote international coöperation, to insure the fulfillment of accepted international obligations, and to provide safeguards against war."

The President's third task was complex and difficult. The Anglo-American concept of a league based upon the widest possible diffusion of authority was in fundamental conflict with the French concept based upon the centralization of authority. The French, conscious of their past, feared invasion and thought in terms of security which would be achieved through the military might of a super-state. To please President Wilson the super-state might be called the League of Nations, but in reality it would be the Allied and Associated Powers permanently united into a military alliance, with conscript armies if necessary and with the ready authority of the sword. But President Wilson, conscious of America's past, feared both concentration of authority and militarism, and thought in terms of voluntary agreements wrought out of free political institutions. He would rely upon the moral force of enlightened world opinion, upon established peaceful methods of settling disputes, upon solemn pledges given by each member of the society of nations to respect its own obligations and to unite with other members in applying sanctions against a law-breaking state. He would balance liberty and order. He was anxious that the league should be strong enough to preserve peace but not powerful enough to destroy freedom. And most of all, he knew that he had to secure a league which the United States would accept.[9]

In his struggle with the French, the President had two

[8] D. H. Miller, *My Diary at the Conference af Paris*, twenty volumes, privately printed, IV, Document 230, pp. 53-56.
[9] This problem is brilliantly treated in Paul Birdsall, *Versailles Twenty Years After* (New York, Reynal and Hitchcock, 1941). It should not be inferred from this brief analysis that President Wilson favored a league too weak to perform its functions. The League had ample powers, particularly under Article 16.

further difficulties to surmount. One was the complexity of affairs in Paris which enabled the French to intrigue, to form alliances, and to demand concessions either to their point of view on the League or on other parts of the treaty. The other was the use that could be made of the opposition to the President in the United States. In the hands of France this latter difficulty was a double-barrelled gun. It could be used to undermine his prestige at Paris and at the same time to force him to cater to American anti-league forces.

It was with reference to this second difficulty that the League to Enforce Peace rendered its most positive assistance to President Wilson at Paris. This was done both directly and indirectly. The indirect assistance was the great national campaign, the ten regional congresses already referred to. The vigorous pro-league opinion aroused by these congresses tended to weaken the anti-league forces at home and to encourage the President in Paris. Time and again both the President and Colonel House expressed their appreciation of this work of the League to Enforce Peace.[10] Indeed Lowell and Taft were so confident of success and so certain that American opinion was back of the league idea that they urged the President to work for a league that would provide for tribunals with compulsory jurisdiction backed by both economic and military sanctions.[11]

The League to Enforce Peace exercised direct influence through its agents in Paris. Oscar Straus arrived in Paris on February 9, 1919, on the eve of one of the several crises in the conflict between President Wilson and the French. Hamilton Holt had already reached Paris and had been in touch with Colonel House. On February 11, Colonel House told Straus and Holt that the League was on the rocks because of French demands that at the conclusion of the peace an international police force, with American troops included, should be ready to defend the Franco-German border, and that the League

---

[10] For example, House to William Short, Feb. 8, 1919 (cable), and Wilson to Taft, Feb. 15, 1919 (cable, copy), *League Collection*.

[11] Messrs. Lowell and Taft to Wilson, Feb. 8, 1919 (cable, copy), *League Collection*.

should have internal control of armaments and preparedness in the member countries.[12] Straus and Holt agreed to confer with Léon Bourgeois, French member of the League of Nations Commission and mouthpiece of Clemenceau.

At a three-hour conference with Bourgeois and Baron d'Estournelles de Constant, Straus and Holt discovered that the insistence of the French was based partly, possibly primarily, upon the growing belief that President Wilson did not represent the American people, and that the Republican Party leaders who opposed a league of nations were the real representatives. Straus and Holt sought to dispel this impression, and rested their main argument upon the activity of the League to Enforce Peace. They described its widespread organization, its non-partisan character, its activity at the moment, and its great influence. They declared that their great organization would support a league of nations "above anything else," and that like Straus himself, who was chairman of its Overseas Committee, the league's president, Taft, and its executive committee chairman, Lowell, were both Republicans. In this way, they sought to convince Bourgeois that Senators Lodge, Borah, Poindexter, and other Republican opponents of Wilson were the ones who did not represent either the Republican Party or the American people.[13] Straus was greatly pleased with the results of the conference and wrote, doubtless with some exaggeration, that the league was "off the rocks." President Wilson took particular pains to thank Straus for his assistance.[14]

Whether a league such as the French advocated would have

[12] Oscar Straus to William Short, Feb. 21, 1919, *League Collection*. See also Birdsall, *op. cit.*, p. 127, and David Hunter Miller, *The Drafting of the Covenant* (New York, G. P. Putnams Sons, 1928), II, 292 ff.

[13] Straus to Short, Feb. 21, 1919, *League Collection*.

[14] Oscar S. Straus, *Under Four Administrations* (Boston, Houghton Mifflin Company, 1923), pp. 424-426. In conversations with the author, Mr. Holt was inclined to doubt that he and Mr. Straus greatly influenced the outcome of events in Paris. He confirmed, however, the accuracy of the account given by Straus of their conference with Bourgeois. In any event, in view of the statements that Mr. Straus made in Paris, his later collaboration with Republican opponents of the League, throws an interesting light upon the reasons for the failure of the League in the United States.

been more successful in establishing permanent peace than the League of Nations would have been if the United States had adhered to it and member states had utilized its possibilities to their full extent is a question that need not be considered here. None of the principal opponents of the League in the United States advocated a stronger league and none of the amendments to the Covenant suggested by the Senate was patterned after French ideas. The irreconcilable opponents of the League did not oppose it because they thought it was too weak and would fail, but because they thought it was strong and would succeed. They opposed the league idea, not the specific provisions of the Covenant. If President Wilson could not secure the acceptance by the United States of the Covenant as it was amended in accordance with the suggestions of Taft, Root, Hughes, and others, none of the suggestions being designed to increase the commitments of states under an international government, it is fatuous to suppose that he would have secured American approval of a stronger league.

As soon as the Covenant of the League of Nations had been accepted by the conference, the President returned to the United States to attend to various matters of pressing importance prior to the adjournment of Congress. He took this opportunity to discuss the Covenant although the treaty could not be presented since it was as yet unfinished.

Already the bitter, planned, and partisan opposition to the Covenant had begun, and in spite of the President's conciliatory attitude, it continued to grow during the month of February.[15] The famous round robin, signed by thirty-nine Republican senators and senators-elect and read to the Senate just before midnight on March 3, declared that the Covenant, as adopted at Paris, "should not be accepted by the United States" and that further consideration of a proposal for a league of nations should be postponed until peace had been made with Germany. This was a direct challenge to the supporters of the Covenant. But it was more than that, for it opposed the President's funda-

[15] It does not seem necessary to relate here the details of the origin and development of opposition to the Covenant. The history of that opposition has been well surveyed by Fleming, *op. cit.*, and Holt, *op. cit.*

mental idea of connecting a league of nations with the treaties of peace. This lifted the discussion out of the realm of debate over specific provisions of the Covenant and into the realm of fundamental policies. The challenge was understood and squarely met by both Mr. Taft and President Wilson in their speeches in New York on March 4.

The position of the League to Enforce Peace with respect to the Covenant was as clear as anything could be. The league had sent to Paris agents instructed to support President Wilson. While the President was on his way home with the Covenant and while he was discussing it with congressional leaders, the League to Enforce Peace was carrying on its nation-wide series of congresses. On February 16, two days after the Covenant was submitted to the Paris Conference and one day after its text was published in the United States, Mr. Taft analyzed its provisions in an address at Portland, Oregon. He called it the "great covenant of Paris," and thanked God that such an important advance had been made "toward the suppression of war and the promotion of permanent peace." He did not believe that the Senate would reject "such a vital feature" of the treaty. He believed that the nation was pledged to the league idea and that good faith required the United States to support the program that other nations had accepted.[16] Later in February, Taft spoke at San Francisco, Salt Lake City, and St. Louis, and in each case he spoke unreservedly for the Covenant.

Whatever might have been the status of American public opinion, the influence of the President, and the strength of the League to Enforce Peace, all favorable to the Covenant, it was obvious to most observers that its opponents had won an initial victory by their round robin maneuver. Taft was easily convinced that the Covenant needed to be amended to meet the criticisms of at least some of the round robin group in order to secure its acceptance by two-thirds of the Senate. Senator Hitchcock, Colonel House, and other advisers of the President

[16] Theodore Marburg and Horace E. Flack, editors, *The Taft Papers on the League of Nations* (New York, The Macmillan Company, 1920), pp. 228-241.

agreed with Taft, and Wilson reluctantly accepted their conclusions. It was one thing, however, to agree that amendments should be made in order to satisfy the American Senate and quite another thing to secure the acceptance of such amendments by the nations at Paris without agreeing in turn to their demands for other changes which would make the Covenant even less acceptable to the Senate than the original document. If the President's task in securing a covenant which he believed would be acceptable to the Senate had been difficult in the first instance, this new problem was one to test the skill of the most consummate diplomat. But this was his task, and he set about it.

First of all, he must find out exactly what amendments were needed. Through Henry White, Senator Lodge was asked to state what amendments should be made in order to satisfy the Senate. Upon the advice of two bitter opponents of the Covenant, however, Senators Brandegee and Knox, and also of Elihu Root, Lodge refused the request. He reported to Root that his refusal was worded exactly as Root had framed it and that "Wilson's whole performance" was "intolerable."[17] Root himself, when called upon, did not hesitate to recommend changes. Suggestions were secured also from Mr. Taft, William Jennings Bryan, and Senator Hitchcock. Through the efforts of Oscar Straus, a survey was made of American press opinion regarding the Covenant, and information was collected on speeches made concerning it by Charles Evans Hughes, Senator Arthur Capper, and others.[18]

Mr. Taft's suggestions for changes in the Covenant were, indirectly at least, representative of the League to Enforce Peace. Changes were suggested also, however, by the chairman of the league's executive committee, by Dr. Lowell, and by the executive committee itself. Dr. Lowell's recommendations were formulated in connection with his joint debate on the Covenant with Henry Cabot Lodge, held in Boston on March 19, 1919.

---

[17] Elihu Root to Henry Cabot Lodge, Mar. 13, 1919 (copy), and Lodge to Root, Mar. 14, 1919, *Root MSS*.

[18] This data may be found in Miller, *The Drafting of the Covenant*, I, 354-419. See also Miller, *My Diary at the Peace Conference*, VI and VII.

In the course of his address, Lowell presented a masterly analysis of the Covenant, made constructive suggestions for its improvement, and offered a few remarks concerning its opponents. He had heard very little constructive criticism, he said, but a good deal of destructive criticism from those who professed to believe in *a* league of nations but not in this particular League. "I agree fully with Senator Lodge," said Dr. Lowell, "that if you see a burglar entering your house you shoot him, but you shoot him not for the purpose of improving the burglar—it is because you do not wish to improve the burglar. Of course, if you look on this treaty as a burglar, shoot it; but, for goodness' sake, say you are trying to shoot it and not that you are trying to improve it by constructive criticism."

Dr. Lowell conceded that the Covenant was rather poorly drawn and that improvements in it should undoubtedly be made. With improvements it would probably still be imperfect, since nothing human was perfect, but it could never be drawn so as to satisfy everybody. Compromise was the life blood of all legislation, and the evil had to be taken with the good for the sake of the greater good. He believed that some of the objections to the Covenant were the result of "overheated imagination," and that most of them stemmed from a "misunderstanding of the nature of the League proposed and of the functions of its organs." He went on to declare that "the opponents of the League set up an imaginary scarecrow of their own creation, and then fire at it with great satisfaction to themselves. Their shots do not touch the real mark, although the noise may confuse the public."

He offered, however, several constructive suggestions for changes in the charter, not because he thought they all were needed but because they would satisfy the fears of some people and would not damage the effectiveness of the League. Clauses might be added (1) permitting a member to withdraw on reasonable notice, providing all its obligations were fulfilled up to the time of its withdrawal, (2) excluding matters of vital national interest, such as tariffs and immigration, from consideration by the League, and (3) stating that "no foreign power shall hereafter acquire by conquest, purchase, or in any other way, any possessions on the American continents or the islands adjacent thereto."

One of the notable features of the Lowell-Lodge debate was the challenge offered to Senator Lodge to give categorical answers to two questions. Would he vote in the Senate for the Covenant of Paris provided it should be amended as he desired, and what amendments did he desire? Dr. Lowell asked the audience to notice carefully whether Senator Lodge answered these questions, and stated his belief that if Lodge would formulate the amendments he wanted and send them to Paris with the promise to vote for the Covenant if his amendments were accepted, they would be adopted at the conference. In answer, Senator Lodge said that he would support a league, he *supposed* the present one, if it were changed to suit his specifications, *but he absolutely refused to say what his specifications were.*

Mr. Taft's suggestions for amendments to the Covenant covered the Monroe Doctrine, the withdrawal of members from the League, a term for the limitation of armament, unanimity of action of the executive council and body of delegates, and the exclusion of domestic policies from League control. Regarding the latter proposal, Mr. Taft noted in a memorandum that Republican senators were trying to stir up anxiety over the tariff issue. Although he thought the President had already met that issue, a specific reservation would cut the ground from under senatorial objection. He believed that a reservation on the Monroe Doctrine would probably permit the ratification of the treaty but that the other amendments would make its acceptance certain.[19]

Officially the League to Enforce Peace confined its suggestions for amendments to one point, the Monroe Doctrine. Its executive committee sent word to President Wilson that in its opinion Republican senators would be able to defeat the treaty unless the Monroe Doctrine was specifically safeguarded, and that with such a safeguard in the treaty it would be "promptly ratified."

President Wilson and his advisers in Paris, particularly those

[19] Marburg and Flack, *op. cit.*, pp. 321-329.

connected with the Drafting Committee of the League of Nations Commission, were fully apprised of the difficulties that would be encountered when they proposed substantial changes in the Covenant in order to meet American criticisms. Verbal changes might be effected without much difficulty, and, as Dr. Lowell had noted, improvements of that sort were desirable. But substantial changes were a different matter, and once the bars were down the field would be open to France and to other nations for proposals that would more than nullify, as far as the American Senate was concerned, the changes that the President had to secure to appease the Senate. Since there was no other way to meet the problem, a meeting of the commission was called for March 22. Four other meetings were held including the final one on April 11.

Most of the American amendments and many verbal changes that improved the Covenant were adopted by the commission without serious controversy. The former included provisions for withdrawal, the exclusion of domestic questions, unanimity in the Council and Assembly, and an amendment providing that the acceptance of a mandate would be optional.[20] The amendment on the Monroe Doctrine was the most important from the American standpoint and also the most vulnerable. All the skill, persuasion, and influence that President Wilson could command, all the aid that could be rendered by the agents of the League to Enforce Peace,[21] and by other friends of the proposed League, and all the prestige that the United States had were necessary to secure this amendment. The successful struggle that President Wilson waged for the American amendment during some of the most trying days of the Peace Conference, when the French and the Japanese, and at times even the British, were trying to make capital out of his necessity of appeasing the Senate, was nothing less than heroic.[22] He succeeded in securing amendments which covered six of the

---

[20] Miller, *The Drafting of the Covenant*, I, 418.
[21] Straus to Taft, Apr. 15, 1919, *Taft MSS*.
[22] Birdsall, *op. cit.*, pp. 132-147; Miller, *The Drafting of the Covenant*, I, 336-536; Miller, *Diary*, I, 234-238; Baker, *Wilson and World Settlement*, I, 324-333.

seven proposals made by Charles E. Hughes, the majority of Root's suggestions, and *all* of the recommendations of Taft, Lowell, and the League to Enforce Peace. Moreover these changes covered most of the objections that had been raised in speeches by Senator Lodge, and *all* the six changes which Senator Hitchcock had recommended to insure, "beyond doubt," the Senate's approval.

The leaders of the League to Enforce Peace were overjoyed with the revised Covenant. Taft wrote to Lowell: "The news of this morning is very good. The adoption of the Monroe Doctrine in the League insures its passage...."[23] The Emergency Campaign Committee called a meeting for April 30, to formulate a public statement of policy and to plan a campaign of action. The statement of policy was as follows:

> The Covenant for a League of Nations, in the amended form adopted by the Paris Peace Conference, should satisfy all except those who oppose any League whatever. It is now a thoroughly American instrument—thoroughly American and thoroughly non-partisan. Recent amendments include the more important changes proposed by the leaders of the Republican Party.
>
> Opponents must now show their true colors. The old argument—"we are for *a* League, but not *the* League"—will no longer serve. This issue now is—*The* League or none.
>
> The fate of the Covenant rests with the American people. While the Senate has power to ratify, to amend, or to reject it, to amend it is to require a reconsideration by all the nations parties to it and *to postpone peace indefinitely*.[24]

The committee resolved: "that the reception given the revised text of the Covenant and especially the obligations resting upon the League to Enforce Peace to support Senators

[23] Apr. 11, 1919 (copy), *Taft MSS*.

[24] *Minutes* of the Committee, Apr. 30, 1919, *League Collection*. Holt, Lowell, Taft, Short, and Glenn Frank were among the members present at this meeting. The presence of Taft and Lowell at this meeting is noteworthy, for the statement of policy adopted with their approval contained the slogan "*The* League or none." Later both of them accused President Wilson of holding to that policy although he neither originated the idea nor held to it.

who may be disposed to act independently of partisan considerations in dealing with the Covenant, make it essential that a far-reaching campaign be conducted." Plans were made, therefore, for a series of state "Ratifying Conventions," for coördinating the efforts of all pro-League organizations and for nation-wide activity of league workers. The strategy of the campaign was to concentrate the league's great effort upon fifteen states including New York, New Jersey, the New England states, Pennsylvania, and the Middle West as far as Nebraska. League activity in the South and the far West would be confined to whatever could be done by local authorities.

Following the procedure worked out for the regional congresses, held in February, the Ratifying Conventions were held in a series so that some of the most prominent leaders of the League to Enforce Peace could attend many or all of the meetings. The first convention was held in Burlington, Vermont, on May 21, and the last one in Albany, New York, on July 7. The conventions were financed locally wherever possible, and great effort was made to secure the most important political people in each state as speakers, and the greatest possible newspaper publicity. Among the league's national leaders who attended many of the conventions were Taft, Lowell, Holt, Herbert S. Houston, Stephen S. Wise, Dwight W. Morrow, Gilbert M. Hitchcock, Frank Crane, President William O. Thompson of the Ohio State University, and Dr. Anna Howard Shaw, the foremost leader of woman suffrage in America.[25] Everywhere the conventions were attended by overflow audiences and were regarded as highly successful.

While these conventions were being held, the League to Enforce Peace extended its efforts in many other ways, and reached, during May and June of 1919, the peak of its activity. Its headquarters staff of 115 employees occupied two entire floors of the Bush Terminal Sales Building. It had state organizations in all the states, and county organizations in at least one-third of the counties of the nation. Ten thousand people

[25] This campaign was the last work of Mrs. Shaw's life. Her last message to America, written on her death bed, was a plea for the League of Nations, *Philadelphia Public Ledger*, July 4, 1919.

had official positions in the various branch offices of the league, 50,000 people were enrolled as volunteer workers, and its list of available speakers reached 36,333 persons. It was estimated that during May, 1919, 12,000 addresses per day were being given by league speakers. Its mailing list contained the names of approximately 300,000 enrolled members. It was not considered unusual for the New York office to send out a half million copies of a particular publication.

This activity was frankly devoted to the creation of public opinion favorable to the Covenant of the League of Nations, and to the conversion of that opinion into political pressure upon senators. Through the activity of league speakers and workers, through the influence of league literature, and through the efforts of other organizations, it was hoped and believed that the pressure of public opinion favorable to the league would be so great that the Senate could not ignore it. While it is very difficult to estimate quantitatively the success of the league's activity, the response to its appeal was surprisingly great. Thousands of resolutions favorable to the ratification of the Covenant without complicating, delaying, or invalidating reservations were passed by college faculties, educational associations, state and local bar associations, farm, labor, and fraternal organizations, associations of Protestant clergymen, chambers of commerce, clubs and societies, public meetings, and by many other groups.

One of the most constructive efforts of the League to Enforce Peace to inform the public about the exact nature of the Covenant was a series of twenty-seven articles to be distributed as widely as possible to the newspapers. The whole series, patterned after the Federalist Papers, was to be called "The Covenanter," and one article was to appear daily beginning May 21. As they appeared in the press, the articles were unsigned, but later they were printed in pamphlet form with their various authors noted. Dr. Lowell, who suggested the series of articles, wrote thirteen of them, including an introduction and a conclusion. He explained the objectives of the league, the machinery and procedures of government provided for by the Covenant, and concluded that the objections raised in the United States to the original draft agreed upon by the conference were "adequately covered by provisions whose meaning could not reasonably be doubted by anyone who believes sincerely in such a League." Henry W. Taft wrote five of the articles dealing with the question of American sovereignty under the League, the constitutionality of the Covenant, and the Monroe Doctrine. He effectively demonstrated that the United States had made many treaties which limited its freedom of action, such as the Rush-Bagot Treaty regarding naval armament on the Great Lakes, and had made treaties guaranteeing the independence of states. The real question regarding sovereignty was not its restriction but whether its restriction would be justified by the expected result for which it would be imposed. He defended Article 10 and declared that the United States could not "with national honor" escape international responsibilities. George W. Wickersham wrote five of the articles dealing with arbitration, mandates, and labor.

When William H. Taft was approached regarding "The Covenanter" he said that he would like to write an article on the general character of the Covenant and one on Article 10. In the end he wrote four articles, two of them dealing with the first, and two with the latter subject. He analyzed the significance of Article 10, discussed the various arguments that had been raised against it, and stated that it was in effect an expansion of the Monroe Doctrine, the "embodiment" of the principle which the United States had fought the war to maintain, and one of the "great steps forward" toward world peace.

"The Covenanter" letters were sent to about eighty selected papers, were printed in full in about thirty of them, and in part or in summary in at least thirty more. An official summary was sent to a thousand smaller journals. In pamphlet form "The Covenanter" was distributed by the league and by the World Peace Foundation. Other pamphlets, about forty or more, explaining the Covenant were prepared and distributed, and many members of the League to Enforce Peace, including George G. Wilson, Everett Colby, and Leo S. Rowe sent signed articles to the press endeavoring to explain the meaning of the Covenant to the people. The New York office made a survey of the editorials of the nation's press for the week ending June 3, 1919, and found that out of approximately 1,200 editorials, 1,100 favored its adoption and 100 opposed.[26]

It is as certain as anything in the realm of public opinion can be that in May, 1919, the majority of the American people favored the ratification by the Senate of the Treaty of Versailles with the Covenant as it was. A *Literary Digest* poll of the nation's press, taken in April, confirmed the surveys made by the League to Enforce Peace. The questionnaire sent by the *Literary Digest* asked editors of all daily newspapers in the United States for their views toward joining the proposed League of Nations and for the attitudes of their respective communities. The *Digest* reported that the response "broke all records" and that 1,377 editors replied "losing no time about it." Of the 1,377 editors, 718 unconditionally favored the league, 181 opposed, and 478 favored it conditionally. Breaking down the figures, the *Digest* found that if the issue were left to the Democrats, *the* League would win, if left to the Republicans, *the* League or *a* league would win, and if left to the Independents, *the* League would win. The replies, taken geographically, showed that in each clearly defined region, the sentiment was for the League. Moreover, in no one state was there an opposing majority.[27]

Evidences of public opinion gathered from other sources confirmed the conclusions reached by the *Literary Digest* and the league. For example, organized labor and farm organizations were almost solidly behind the League. Sixty-four of the nation's sixty-eight farm papers supported the League unconditionally, and only one paper clearly opposed it.[28] Thirty-two state legislatures had passed resolutions favoring the entrance of the United States into a league of nations, and similar

[26] "The Covenanter" articles are conveniently found in the pamphlet entitled "The League of Nations," World Peace Foundation, II, June, 1919. See also Lowell to Taft, Apr. 11, 1919, *League Collection*. Report of Committee on Information, June 13, 1919, *League Collection. Bulletin*, League to Enforce Peace, May 24, 1919.
[27] *Literary Digest*, LXI (Apr. 5, 1919), 13-14.
[28] League to Enforce Peace *Bulletin*, May 10, 1919.

resolutions had passed one branch of some other legislatures. In only a very few states had legislatures shown opposition to the idea.[29] The majority of the Protestant clergy and educational leaders favored the League. In fact, clear opposition to the Covenant was confined to the radical opponents in the Senate, a fairly small minority of violently partisan Republicans, the Hearst following, and certain national groups, notably the Irish. Answering a letter from Adelbert Moot of Buffalo, Elihu Root agreed that the great majority of the American people wanted the treaty ratified "*at once*." He justified his opposition to it on the ground that the people had not read the treaty and believed that the Senate should not be guided by ignorant popular sentiment.[30] A year later Root mentioned the fact that in 1919 the League opponents in the Senate had been "in danger of being overwhelmed by a demand for some sort of a league of nations."[31]

While no further evidence is necessary concerning the favorable attitude of the majority of the people toward the acceptance of the Covenant as it was drawn at Paris, such evidence, if desired, can be found in the admissions of Senator Lodge himself. Writing in 1925, he declared that in May, 1919, the "great mass of the people, the man in the street, to use a common expression, the farmers, the shop keepers, the men in small businesses, clerks and the like, in short the people generally" wanted the treaty ratified "as quickly as possible."[32] He declared also that the majority of the clergymen, university professors, newspaper editors, and the men and women who were in "the habit of writing and speaking for publication" advocated the League "as it stood."[33]

The leaders of the League to Enforce Peace well understood that popular approval of the treaty did not guarantee its

[29] *Ibid.*, May 3, 1919; *Current History*, X (June, 1919), 509.
[30] Root to Adelbert Moot, July 11, 1919 (copy), *Root MSS*. (italics mine).
[31] Root to Lodge, May 14, 1920 (copy), *Root MSS*.
[32] Henry Cabot Lodge, *The Senate and the League of Nations* (New York, Charles Scribners Sons, 1925), p. 146.
[33] *Ibid.*, p. 147. For further evidence see the analysis given in Fleming, *op. cit.*, pp. 205-206.

ratification by the Senate. Their analysis of the situation in May, 1919, shows their awareness of the strategy that would be employed by the League's opponents:

> The opponents of the Covenant in the Senate probably will stake everything upon amendment. While amendments probably will defeat the plan just as effectively as absolute rejection, they offer a means to knife the Covenant without standing openly before the people as its assassins. But if the opposition senators cannot amend, it is almost certain that all but a few irreconcilables will vote for ratification on the final show-down.[84]

Although the tactics of the opposition were revealed by their acts at the time, any doubts about their intentions were dispelled by Lodge himself when he later reviewed the events. He revealed that he had discussed with Senator Borah the hopelessness of defeating the treaty by "a straight vote in the Senate," and that he had proposed that the way to proceed was by "amendments and reservations."[85] Senator Borah agreed with Lodge's analysis of the situation and made a bargain with him to support amendments and reservations. Borah made it clear, however, that even after the treaty was amended he would still vote against it.[86]

The task of the League to Enforce Peace was to prevent, if it could, the success of the scheme thus agreed upon. And the method of prevention was to persuade other Republican leaders to abandon the Lodge-Borah program. Taft came out with a pamphlet published by the League to Enforce Peace and entitled "Ratify the Covenant." He stated that while the Senate could ratify the treaty conditionally, reservations which constituted the elimination of any article or a change in its meaning would force the President to resubmit the treaty to the powers that had signed it. "Upon those," said Taft, "who insist that substantial amendments must be made to the treaty will therefore fall the responsibility for the indefinite postponement of peace which unconditional ratification of the treaty will

[84] League to Enforce Peace *Bulletin*, May 10, 1919.
[85] Lodge, *op. cit.*, p. 147.
[86] *Ibid.*

at once bring about." Taft asserted again that Article 10 was the "heart of the League" and that it represented "the effort of the world of law-abiding nations to defeat forever the greedy purposes of militarism, whether of Germany or any other nation."

In a League to Enforce Peace pamphlet entitled "Attention, Republicans," George W. Wickersham made a direct appeal to Republicans to abandon the leadership of Senators Borah, Knox, Lodge, and Johnson, who, in his opinion, were "not willing to recognize any responsibility in America for the future preservation of the peace of the world." Mr. Wickersham declared that Republicans who were afraid to support the treaty for fear of aiding the Democrats should look at the facts. He then took up the objections that had been made by Taft, Lowell, Knox, Root, and Hughes to the first draft of the Covenant and showed point by point and article by article how completely the objections had been met in the revised Covenant. He argued that the objections of the Republicans had been fairly met by the Paris Conference, and he reached this conclusion:

> The question before the Republican party today is whether it shall allow a few senators blinded by passion and resentment at the President and his administration to commit the party of great national and international ideas to the reversal of its principles, the abandonment of its high mission and a position of opposition to the only practicable, attainable plan before the world to avert from posterity the recurrence of the horror, the misery and the tragedy of future wars.[37]

While Taft, Wickersham, Holt, Houston, and other officials of the League to Enforce Peace were striving to influence public opinion against the Lodge-Borah faction, Dr. Lowell perceived the exact nature of the problem and attempted personally and directly to deal with it. He observed clearly that the opposition to the treaty was not based to any large extent upon *bona fide* defects in the Covenant as it stood, and that

[37] This pamphlet and a large number of other League to Enforce Peace pamphlets are in the League collection at the Harvard University Library.

public opinion was in favor of the league idea. The hope of success of the Lodge-Borah group rested almost exclusively upon their ability to make the League the symbol of Republican opposition to the Democrats. What was needed, therefore, was for some Republican, with great party prestige, to take a public stand for the treaty and therefore to lift the issue out of partisan politics. In Lowell's opinion this needed person was Elihu Root, and to him Lowell appealed.

Dr. Lowell attested in his appeal to Root that the original movement in the United States for a league was supported by Republicans more than by Democrats. There was no reason, therefore, why the League should not be a vital element of Republican policy. He analyzed the situation in the Republican Party as follows:

> The lesser Republicans over the country are holding back, waiting for direction; and if you, who have more influence than any other man, were to come out and say that the Covenant as amended is now satisfactory, they would fall in behind you in crowds, for they are timid and waiting for direction.
>
> The revised draft contains, I should think satisfactorily, *all the amendments you asked for*, except the one requiring that justiciable questions should go to a permanent court that would have authority to determine its own jurisdiction, and I think there is a reason why this was difficult. . . .[38]

While all of Dr. Lowell's letter is important, no part is more significant than the expression of opinion that all but one of Root's suggested amendments to the first draft of the Covenant had been included in its final form. Lowell's opinion was significant on account of his unquestioned competence to deal with a problem of this kind. But Root disregarded Lowell's advice and opinion and cast his lot with the Lodge-Borah side. In view of this fact it is essential to examine more closely the conditions under which he wrote his original recommendation.

Root's suggestions for amendments to the first draft of the Covenant had been made partly on account of appeals from Henry White to the effect that President Wilson "was not in

[38] Lowell to Root, May 1, 1919, *Root MSS* (italics mine).

the least adverse to amending the Covenant."[39] Particularly, however, they resulted from the special insistence of Republican Party leaders. Senator Lodge appealed to Root "to show the public what ought to be done" regarding the establishment of a union of nations. Will H. Hays, chairman of the Republican National Committee, realized too that the country favored a league of nations, that some confusion existed in the public mind about just what kind of league was needed, and that Root should make a statement. Root was in close touch with Henry L. Stimson, who believed that it would be very unfortunate for the Republican Party to oppose a league of nations, because in his opinion the time had come when an act of aggression by one nation upon another should be regarded as an offense against the community of nations. Stimson felt that the Republicans should act constructively or not at all since "to offer criticisms of detail after they are too late to be adopted is as bad as opposing the entire program."[40]

The result of this situation was that Stimson, Root, Hays, and George Harvey conferred, drafted a letter from Hays to Root asking for an opinion, and drafted a reply to Hays in which Root analyzed the draft Covenant and suggested amendments.[41] Stimson, Hays, and Harvey all were enthusiastic about the Root letter, which was published March 29, 1919. Dr. Lowell, congratulating Root on the letter, said that when Wilson had secured the amendments, "the Senate would be compelled to ratify the Covenant."[42]

Dr. Lowell did not in the least underestimate the compelling force of Wilson's success in securing the amendments demanded or suggested by the Republican critics of the original draft of the Covenant. If the President had refused to consider the suggested changes that were made by Taft, Lowell, the League to Enforce Peace, the Root-Stimson-Hays-Harvey group, and others, or if he had half-heartedly pressed for their acceptance at Paris and had been unsuccessful in securing their

---

[39] Henry White to Root, Paris, Mar. 19, 1919, *Root MSS.*
[40] Henry L. Stimson to Will Hays (copy), *Root MSS.*
[41] Jessup, *op. cit.*, II, 390.
[42] Lowell to Root, Apr. 2, 1919, *Root MSS.*

incorporation into a revised Covenant, the situation would have been entirely different. But the fact was that he had accepted suggestions, had successfully championed them at Paris under trying conditions, and had, therefore, presented to the Senate not his Covenant exactly, or a Paris Covenant, but in a real sense, Root's and Taft's and Stimson's and Hughes' also. Thus for the moment it appeared that the Lodge group would be obliged either to accept Lowell's view and support the League or the Borah-Knox-Brandegee view and oppose it outright. But for Lodge to choose the latter alternative was to invite defeat, for he did not believe that the Senate would dare to fly directly into the face of public opinion.

This was the desperate situation in which Lodge found himself when he made his bargain with Borah to advocate new and additional amendments to the Covenant. Obviously, however, he had to have assistance beyond that of the "death battalion." His chief difficulty was that the situation in May was different from what it had been in April, for in the interim the Covenant had been revised. If Lodge was to succeed he simply had to secure the support of some of the Republicans whose suggestions had been accepted by the President in revising the Covenant. It is a compliment to Lodge's political sagacity that he immediately addressed himself to the person who Lowell had said had more influence than any other man, Elihu Root.

It cannot be said that Senator Lodge did not bestir himself. The revised Covenant was published in the United States on April 29, 1919. Before the day was over Lodge talked with Root on the telephone and wrote him a letter. In the letter he told Root that very little improvement had been made in the Covenant and that the Senate should make further amendments to it. He explained, however, that Root's help would be "vitally necessary" if the Lodge forces were to control the Senate for purposes of dealing with the treaty.[43] Lodge next hurried off to various Republican Senators telegrams in which he revealed his state of mind as well as his necessity. He stated that the Covenant needed to be amended, that he could not make a statement about it because he had not studied it, and that they

[43] Jessup, *op. cit.*, II, 397.

THE CRUCIAL TEST

should not comment on it until they had held a conference to decide what they should do.[44]

How "vitally necessary" for Lodge the aid of Root was is shown by the dispatches printed in the *New York Times* on the days that Lodge sent his letter to Root and his telegrams to Republican senators. A dispatch from Washington on April 29 stated that "nearly all senators" agreed that the people of the country wanted a league, and the following day Senator McNary, whose support Lodge also needed, was quoted as having said: "In my opinion the Covenant has been amended to correct *all the legitimate objections raised against it*." Taft was exerting, at this time, the very peak of the pro-League effort. His "Covenanter" discussion supporting Article 10 was printed on June 7, and he repeated again his belief that Article 10 was the heart of the League in an address at Albany on the same day. Secretary of War Newton D. Baker had already announced that the returning soldiers favored the League.[45] Thus it appeared that the people at home and the returning soldiers favored the League, that Taft was still strongly supporting it, that at least one prominent Republican senator had committed himself unreservedly for it, and that only a few senators, the Borah-Knox group, were willing to oppose it.[46]

Elihu Root was confronted, therefore, with a problem upon his solution of which, according to both Lowell and Lodge, rested the fate of the League of Nations. Root could take the position of Lowell, Taft, and all the Republican leaders of the League to Enforce Peace and recognize that the revised Covenant contained the essential changes which they had requested, and that the interests of world peace required that it should be supported by the Republican Party in the Senate. Or he could take the position of Lodge that the revised Covenant was not essentially improved and that further changes should be undertaken. He chose the latter course, and, having made up his mind, he did not act independently or without con-

---

[44] *New York Times*, Apr. 30, 1919.

[45] *Ibid.*, Apr. 6, 1919.

[46] Borah said that it would be treason to ratify the treaty as it was. *New York Times*, Apr. 30, 1919.

sulting the people with whom he had decided to cast his lot. He went to Washington and conferred with Lodge, Knox, and Brandegee, showed them a draft of his statement calling for amendments to the Covenant, changed his draft somewhat to meet their views, and published the result in the form of a letter to Senator Lodge, dated June 21, 1919.[47]

At the beginning of his letter Root allied himself on the side of Borah and Knox by stating that the Covenant should have been separated from the treaty. Since, however, it would be difficult to do that under the existing circumstances, and since, in his opinion, the Covenant had not been revised in the ways that he had suggested, it would be necessary for the Senate to amend the Covenant in a resolution of ratification. He denied that the revision had adequately provided for peace procedures in the form of arbitration and judicial action or that adequate provision had been made for the development of international law. He thought the withdrawal clause was vague, that the Monroe Doctrine statement was erroneous in its description and ambiguous in meaning, and that Article 10 should have been limited to a term of years.

Root now proposed that Article 10 should be excluded entirely from the Covenant, that the United States should be allowed to withdraw from the League and to decide for itself whether its obligations had been fulfilled, and that nothing in the Covenant should be construed so as to interfere with American freedom of action with regard to "purely American questions." He virtually denied that the United States had any international responsibilities, repeated Washington's advice about keeping out of European controversies, and advised against permitting Europe to have any share in the settlement of western hemisphere affairs. Both the tone and the content of the letter were isolationist in character, and the fact that it was written with the approval of Senators Knox, Brandegee, and Lodge should have been obvious to everyone.

There is no reason to believe that Mr. Root had any trouble in making up his mind about which side of the controversy he would take. As early as May 7, Henry W. Taft reported that

[47] Jessup, *op. cit.*, II, 401.

Wickersham asked Root if he did not think that most of his objections to the Covenant had been overcome in the revised edition. Root replied "with some asperity in the negative."[48] Henry Taft believed that Root would take Lodge's side, and that since there was a "Root cult" in the country, and what Root said would be of assistance to the Lodge group, steps should be taken to counteract his influence.[49] Once Root had taken his position with the Lodge side, he took the arrogant view that President Wilson could either accept an amended treaty or be responsible for its failure.[50]

Root's reservations were hailed as showing the Republicans a way out of their dilemma. The opponents of the treaty who were finding their views very unpopular in the country could support the Root formula and then say that they were not against an amended treaty.[51] Charles E. Hughes immediately adopted Root's proposed amendments,[52] Lodge believed that forty-nine senators would support them,[53] and Will Hays declared that Root had shown the way for the Republicans to ratify the treaty and thus to convert "what threatened to be a Republican liability into a Republican achievement."[54]

Thus Root became the attorney for the League's opponents. Mr. Hays probably exaggerated when he said that Root had shown the way which the opponents should take. The way was already known. More precisely, Root stepped vigorously along the way and provided the example as well as the intellectual leadership for those who followed him. It was Root rather than Lodge who chose the particular reservation which neither the League to Enforce Peace nor President Wilson could logically accept. Mr. Root held that Article 10 of the Covenant was not an "essential or even an appropriate part" of a league of nations and that it should be eliminated from the Covenant.[55] He as-

[48] Henry W. Taft to Lowell, May 7, 1919, *Lowell MSS.*
[49] Henry W. Taft to Lowell, May 16, 1919, *Lowell MSS.*
[50] Root to Lodge, Dec. 1, 1919 (copy), *Root MSS.*
[51] *Philadelphia Public Ledger*, editorial entitled "Root to the Rescue," June 25, 1919.
[52] Root to Will Hays, July 5, 1919 (copy), *Root MSS.*
[53] Will Hays to Root, July 1, 1919, *Root MSS.*
[54] Charles D. Hilles to Taft, July 11, 1919, *Taft MSS.*
[55] Root to Lodge, June 19, 1919 (copy), *Root MSS.*

serted that "no nation in Europe would have had the effrontery to propose such an agreement" and that a rejection of it would "impose no obstacle whatever to the making of peace."[56] When he later agreed to the Senate's reservation on Article 10, he did so not because he had changed his mind but because he believed that the reservation completely nullified the Article. "The Senate," he said, "instead of dropping the Article, chose to adopt another course, and to agree to the Article with reservations which would make it innocuous."[57]

In contrast to Root's position, President Wilson, The League to Enforce Peace, Taft, and all those who thought as they did, believed that Article 10 was so essential to the whole program of world peace embraced in the Covenant that they could not consent to its removal by reservation or otherwise without abandoning their principles and abdicating to the League's enemies. For if Article 10 was the heart of the League, then to eliminate the Article was to destroy the League. To the League's friends, no difference existed between the rejection of the League and the elimination from it of its vital part. Root's proposals therefore offered a challenge to the League to Enforce Peace no less direct than the challenge of the "round robin" proposal to separate the treaty from the League, or the challenge of the irreconcilables.

The league quickly took up this challenge. The first public reply to Root of a prominent league member was that of Oscar S. Straus. He noted immediately, as others did, the differences between Root's statement of March 31 in which he favored Article 10 for a limited time and his later vehement indictment of it. Straus presented reasons for the view that Article 10 was the key article in the League structure, and that to eliminate it was to amend the treaty and to require its resubmission to the contracting powers. While he believed that Root's proposals might serve the purpose of some senators who preferred a "negative acceptance to an affirmative rejection" of the treaty, the formula only would be different; the result

[56] Root to Adelbert Moot, July 11, 1919 (copy), *Root MSS.*
[57] Root to Senator Kellogg, Mar. 13, 1920 (copy), *Root MSS.*

would be the same.⁵⁸ Henry W. Taft explained Root's stand as simply the result of his desire to discredit the President. "But," said Taft, "such glaring inconsistency as that displayed in his two letters is a high price to pay for the satisfaction of getting back at Wilson."⁵⁹

The League to Enforce Peace contained many other prominent men among its members, but none of them was known nationally as well as William Howard Taft, and none had as much personal prestige or influence. How Taft would meet the challenge of reservations was, therefore, of great importance. During the early part of the debate over the Covenant, no person in the whole country supported it more firmly than he did. His opinions were expressed in letters to his friends, in the public press, and in public speeches. He asserted that President Wilson should be adamant against further changes in the Covenant, that no "real distinction in principle" existed between reservations and amendments, and that all attempts to modify the Covenant should be voted down by its friends so that the partisan opponents would be shown for what they were. The issue should be clear cut, for the Covenant or against it.⁶⁰ He placed particular emphasis on his support of Article 10 of the Covenant. "It really is," he said, "the heart of the League. It is the embodiment of what we fought for, and on it as a foundation rest the other provisions in the League to secure peace. It contains the primal essence of the League, which is the union of force in the world to suppress lawless force...."⁶¹

Taft was sharp in his criticism of Republican opposition to the treaty and extremely sharp in denunciation of the report of the Senate's Committee on Foreign Relations putting forward the first draft of the so-called Lodge reservations. He noted that the committee had been organized by the Republican Party leadership in the Senate in such a way as to exclude pro-

⁵⁸ Statement entitled "Mr. Root and Article 10: His Conflicting Views," released to the press, June 22, 1919.
⁵⁹ Henry W. Taft to William H. Taft, July 2, 1919, *Taft MSS.*
⁶⁰ Taft to Oscar Straus, May 5, 1919 (copy), *Taft MSS; Philadelphia Public Ledger*, July 14, 1919; Taft to Horace D. Taft, May 5, 1919 (copy), *Taft MSS.*
⁶¹ Taft to Caspar S. Yost, May 22, 1919 (copy), *Taft MSS.*

league Republicans,[62] and he characterized "Lodge's report" as "insulting and utterly oblivious to any sense of responsibility to the world."[63] "When I read the report of Lodge for the Foreign Relations Committee," wrote Taft to a friend, "with his sneers, his cheap sarcasm, it makes me ashamed that a man of his antecedents and predecessors should have descended to such a point...."[64] He believed that the Republican opposition to the Covenant was the result of an "obsession of hatred" against Wilson, that it stemmed mainly from "personal spite,"[65] that the arguments used against the treaty were absurd, and that if they succeeded in defeating the treaty they would be making it possible for an aggressive Germany to rise again.[66] Although Taft particularly denounced Lodge, Knox, and Borah, he was equally disappointed at what he termed Elihu Root's "indefensible" change of front on the League issue and his surrender to Lodge and Knox.[67] For a time, therefore, neither Wilson nor anyone else more firmly supported the treaty than did Taft.

Beginning, however, probably as early as May, 1919, while he was still vigorously defending the Covenant as it stood, Taft entered upon a course of action which little by little entangled him in such a web of compromises and contradictions that eventually he found himself in the camp of the League's outright opponents. It is reasonable to suppose, and in justice to Taft it may be assumed, that he did not foresee the consequences of his initial acts, and indeed that he never perceived either the direction of his policies or their ultimate results. He disregarded the character of the Lodge opposition to the League, misjudged people to whom he gave his confidence, voluntarily abandoned his own non-partisan position, and irreparably damaged the influence of the League to Enforce Peace

[62] Taft to Gus Karger, May 31, 1919 (copy), *Taft MSS.*
[63] Taft to I. M. Ullman, Sept. 13, 1919 (copy), *Taft MSS.*
[64] Taft to Harlow Fiske, Sept. 13, 1919 (copy), *Taft MSS.*
[65] Taft to Horace Taft, May 10, 1919 (copy), *Taft MSS;* Taft to Caspar Yost, May 22, 1919 (copy), *Taft MSS.*
[66] *Philadelphia Public Ledger,* June 6, 1919.
[67] Taft to Gus Karger, May 31, 1919; Taft to Herbert Parsons, July 8, 1919; Taft to Henry W. Taft, July 10, 1919 (copies), *Taft MSS. Philadelphia Public Ledger,* July 14, 1919.

which he had helped so much to build. Taft's tortuous path led not only to the failure of the League to Enforce Peace but also to the defeat of the League of Nations, and that path must be retraced by anyone who wishes to understand fully either of these two events.

The exact moment when Taft began to lose his way cannot be determined, but the first incident that marked his divergent course was his consultation with Will Hays regarding the advisability of devising reservations to the Covenant.[68] Mr. Hays was chairman of the Republican National Committee and as such was a functionary whose job was not to unite the world but to unite the Party. He was in close touch with Root, Borah, Lodge, and all others who might be said to lead factions and to have influence in the Party. How much Taft was led by Hays in reaching his decision to support further amendments to the Covenant by senatorial action is unknown, but as soon as he arrived at that decision and informed Hays about it, he indirectly informed Lodge and Borah too, placed himself among the reservationists, and abandoned the position of the League to Enforce Peace. He drafted a set of amendments to the Covenant, including one on Article 10, and sent them to Hays in Washington to be privately circulated among selected senators.[69] Taft's amendment to Article 10 effectively nullified it, although Taft did not think so, for it limited the article to a term of five years and stipulated that the consent of Congress would be necessary for any American action under it.

At the very moment that Taft proposed his amendment to Article 10 he denounced the attitude of Root and Lodge on the article, which attitude he declared "is German, is domineering, is bullying, is offensive, and is wholly unwarranted by any precedent."[70] He said that if he were Wilson he certainly would not concede to the opposition anything beyond the amendment which he, Taft, had drawn, for in his opinion Wilson could go to the country and secure the support of the

[68] Taft to Lowell, July 27, 1919, *Lowell MSS.*
[69] Taft to Gus Karger, July 10, 1919 (copy), *Taft MSS.*
[70] *Ibid.*

people "in refusing anything more."[71] Notwithstanding this attitude, Taft sent his amendments to Hays who was working closely with Root and Lodge both of whom had vigorously denounced Article 10. Although Hays had agreed not to show Taft's proposals to Root or to Lodge,[72] he immediately sent a copy to Root with a statement that Taft had agreed for Root to see them.[73] Root commented in a letter to Lodge that Taft's amendments lacked precision, and Lodge replied by inquiring whether Root had ever "seen anything of Taft's that had precision."[74]

Thus Taft took the path that led away from the League, and strangely enough he thought that he was taking it in order to bring other members of his party back to the League. His motives were undoubtedly good, but his action was characterized by confusion of thought and ingenuous hopefulness. His confusion is obvious, for within the space of eight days, July 10-18, 1919, he stated that France would object to any modification of Article 10,[75] that France would not object,[76] and that his amendment to the article was[77] and was not[78] an interpretative reservation. His ingenuous hopefulness is shown by his confidence in Hays, his apparent belief that Republican "mild reservationists" would rally around his standard and not Lodge's, and that he could draft an amendment to Article 10 which would weaken it sufficiently to satisfy its opponents without alienating its friends.

Taft realized of course that his actions if known would involve the League to Enforce Peace. He sent, therefore, a copy of his proposed amendments to the league's secretary together with an explanatory and to some extent an apologetic statement. He stated that Hays had agreed to keep the Taft amendments confidential until the amendments proposed by the Committee

[71] *Ibid.*
[72] Taft to Charles D. Hilles, July 20, 1919 (copy), *Taft MSS.*
[73] Hays to Root, July 17, 1919, *Root MSS.*
[74] Lodge to Root, July 28, 1919, *Root MSS.*
[75] Taft to Gus Karger, July 13, 1919 (copy), *Taft MSS.*
[76] Taft to Short, July 18, 1919 (copy), *Taft MSS.*
[77] Taft to Gus Karger, July 10, 1919 (copy), *Taft MSS.*
[78] Taft to Short, July 18, 1919 (copy), *Taft MSS.*

on Foreign Relations had been rejected and until Hays had secured an agreement between "Borah and the more extreme crowd of Republicans," and those "more anxious for a League." He was afraid that Senator McCumber would make concessions to the Borah group. Taft did not explain what the agreement could be between those who wished to defeat and those who wished to sustain the League, nor did he give any reason for supposing that Senator McCumber would make concessions to the League's opponents.

Taft's reservations were discussed at a meeting of the executive committee of the League to Enforce Peace, which Taft did not attend. The sentiment of the committee was that the league should not support any reservations because they believed that to do so would be to show signs of weakening in their support of unqualified ratification. This conclusion represented the unanimous opinion of the executive committee. Secretary Short's letter to Taft informing him of the committee's action contained the following significant paragraph:

> Your action in requesting Mr. Hays and the Senator with whom you conferred by letter not to make your suggestions public until a much later stage of the Senate debate was fully approved and, indeed, considered most important. Considerable fear was expressed that they might get out prematurely and do harm. It was the unanimous feeling, after conference, that any suggestions from the League or its leading members at this time, suggesting reservations, would be used to convince the country that we were weakening and were ready to compromise at a point much further in their territory than we have any idea of going.[79]

The next event was one of great importance in the history of the League to Enforce Peace, and possibly in the history of the contest for the treaty. Will Hays, unauthorized by Taft, published Taft's letter suggesting reservations.[80] This left Taft with two options as to his future policy. One was to denounce Hays for publishing his confidential correspondence and then to abandon his attempt to appease the Lodge-Borah group. The

[79] Short to Taft, July 22, 1919 (copy), *League Collection.*
[80] Taft to A. H. Vandenberg, Sept. 21, 1919 (copy), *Taft MSS.*

other was to take the position that reservations were necessary and hold that the treaty would be defeated unless the friends of the treaty agreed to reservations, thus allying himself with the Lodge-Borah group. He chose the latter course and adhered to it with increasing vigor.

It is possibly true that the senators who formed the Lodge and the Borah groups did not think of themselves as members of groups or of a Lodge-Borah coalition. Yet the inner necessity of Lodge's political objective forced him to secure amendments to the Covenant, whether they be called reservations or not, which he knew the President would not accept. Any reservation the President would accept was politically useless to Lodge, for if the President accepted a reservation it became at that moment a part of "Wilson's League." Lodge had to be prepared, and apparently he boasted privately that he was prepared to devise new reservations if the President showed any signs of accepting those that had been suggested. Lodge's great hurdle was to prevent his followers from admitting that the Covenant needed no substantial revision. Once he had persuaded them to say that the Covenant needed *some* revision, then he was in a position to make *killing* revisions without appearing to do so. Taft's great opportunity was to expose the whole political "plot" and thus prevent the success of Lodge's scheme.

Taft did not abandon his great opportunity because he wished to defeat the League, and there can be no certainty that he would have prevented its defeat if he had chosen another course. It is probable also that Root did not devise his idea of reservations for the purpose of defeating the League, and certainly some of the senators who followed in the leadership of Lodge did not think that they were opponents of the League. All of these people who were advocating reservations, Taft, Root, Lodge, and Borah and their followers wanted to defeat the Democratic Party, and some of them wanted to defeat the League. The only certain way to prevent the latter was to prevent the League issue from becoming a football of politics. This was what Lowell tried to do when he appealed to Root. But that appeal failed. Now Taft had the chance to put his influence and that of the League to Enforce Peace into the balance against the whole plan of Lodge to use the League issue for political purposes. He either did not see his chance, or did not understand the logic of Lodge's scheme, or he thought that notwithstanding the pitfalls that were in the way he could outmaneuver both Lodge and Borah.

Taft thought, in view of his stand for reservations, and the opposing unanimous view of the executive committee of the League to Enforce Peace, that the committee would ask for his resignation as president of the organization. He authorized Lowell to submit his resignation. When the committee met to consider the dilemma with which it was confronted it had before it a report from its Washington representative which clearly indicated that Taft's offer should be accepted. The report contained the following conclusions:

> In conclusion I wish to emphasize my opinion that the League to Enforce Peace should stand steadfast for ratification of the treaty as it stands, without amendment, without reservation, without declaratory or other qualifications. To do less would weaken our position, would have a tendency to cause some of our supporters to vacillate between conflicting positions, would serve to postpone the getting together of all favorable forces. The country in general now understands that we favor the Covenant, *just as it is*, with any amendments to come through action by the League itself. My judgment is that we weaken our position if we agree to anything less.[81]

On the other side Lowell strongly opposed the acceptance of Taft's resignation. Lowell's action appears to have been based not on his agreement with Taft's reservations but upon his belief that some reservations should be agreed to by the friends of the League. The fact was that he had a scheme of his own to satisfy the "mild reservationists."[82] Thus Lowell placed the weight of his great prestige on the side of Taft and the reservationists. The executive committee which was loath to break with Taft and Lowell resolved its dilemma by taking what amounted to a contradictory stand. It retained Taft as

[81] Report of W. R. Boyd to the League to Enforce Peace, *Filene MSS.*
[82] Lowell to Taft, Aug. 7, 1919, *Taft MSS.*

President but issued a strong statement against reservations. The statement reaffirmed the league's earlier position favoring "unconditional ratification" of the Covenant and opposing "any amendment or reservation."[83]

During the next three months, August, September, and October, the League to Enforce Peace continued officially to work for ratification without reservations. The Washington bureau of the league, under the direction of Harry N. Rickey, was gradually expanded until its personnel included Guy Mason, Talcott Williams, Charles D. Warner, Denys P. Myers, and Frank Lamb. The bureau provided the channel through which the league distributed to senators the publications of the league, resolutions adopted at public meetings, and petitions for the treaty. The league continued to send out requests for money in order to organize support for the treaty without amendments or reservations,[84] and to secure letters to senators favoring unqualified ratification.[85] One circular letter addressed to members of the league ran in part as follows:

> The crisis is at hand which will determine whether America joins the League of Nations or forsakes her allies and negotiates a separate peace with Germany. A vote for any reservations may require re-submission and endanger the Treaty....[86]

As time went on, the situation regarding the ratification of the treaty became one of almost utter confusion both among the senators in Washington and within the League to Enforce Peace. Filene asked the secretary of the league for enlightenment. He had received, he said, a letter from one of the league's officials urging him to renew effort to bring pressure to bear upon the Senate to ratify the treaty without reservations, and at the same time he learned that other officials of the league, Lowell and Straus, had been in Washington urging the President to accept reservations. Mr. Short answered that Mr.

[83] July 31, 1919.
[84] For example, telegram sent to selected people on Oct. 22, 1919, signed by the members of the finance committee.
[85] Circular letters dated Sept. 12 and Sept. 16, 1919, *League Collection*.
[86] Sept. 29, 1919, *League Collection*.

Filene's information about the league's work in Washington was not quite accurate, that while officially the league "talked in the direction of no reservations, confidentially we shall not object to harmless reservations . . . which promise to get a two-thirds majority in the Senate." [87] Short enclosed in his letter a copy of the statement of July 31 in which the executive committee opposed any reservations.

Within a week after this confused statement was made by Mr. Short, he was engaged in an attempt to secure a large number of signatures of prominent men to a manifesto calling for immediate and unqualified ratification of the treaty. He appealed to Taft to sign the manifesto on the ground that without his signature many people might believe that the League to Enforce Peace was divided and that some signatures were dependent upon Taft's.[88] Short asked Taft to revise the statement if he did not like the one drawn mainly by Lowell.[89] Taft refused either to sign or to write a declaration that he would sign. He said that he believed in reservations and that the league could act without him unless it would advocate reservations too.[90] Through a misunderstanding on Short's part, Taft's name was included on the manifesto which was signed by more than 200 men including Alfred E. Smith, Daniel Willard, and Thomas W. Lamont. This whole episode demonstrated the growing cleavage between factions in the League to Enforce Peace. Taft soon became unwilling for the league to use his name in requesting funds,[91] was disgruntled because Bernard Baruch had contributed to the support of the league's Washington bureau which in Taft's opinion was advising with Democrats,[92] and early in November came out with a published statement demanding reservations to the treaty.[93] Taft went to

[87] Short to Filene, Aug. 13, 1919, *Filene MSS.*
[88] Short to Taft, Aug. 21, 1919 (copy), *League Collection.*
[89] Short to Taft, Aug. 22, and also Aug. 23, 1919 (copies), *League Collection.*
[90] Taft to Short (telegram), Aug. 21, and letter Aug. 24, 1919, *League Collection.*
[91] Taft to Short, Sept. 25, 1919, *League Collection.*
[92] Taft to Short, Aug. 29, 1919, *League Collection.*
[93] *Philadelphia Public Ledger,* Nov. 8, 1919.

Washington early in October to see if he could unite the so-called "mild reservationist Republicans" in a program. His report on the situation that existed there revealed that Senator Kellogg, who was supposed to favor the treaty, was in a highly nervous state in which he alternately damned the President and the treaty, that every senator favored his own brand of reservations, and that almost no one agreed with anyone else regarding what would or could be done.[94] Taft urged Lowell to support the "mild reservationists," and by the end of October, Lowell was ready to do so.[95] Lowell believed that the "mild reservationists" had committed themselves in agreements with the "irreconcilables," and that while "we do not want" the reservations, it would be impossible to ratify the treaty without them.[96]

During the days of confusion, officially the League to Enforce Peace stood firmly against compromise. The league's Washington bureau repeatedly advised that if the league committed itself to reservations it would thereafter be the servant of the Lodge group.[97] Senator McCumber, the Republican Senator who most consistently opposed drastic reservations, repeatedly appealed to the League to Enforce Peace not to yield to the reservationists.[98] On these premises and in keeping with its original position, the league did stand firm throughout September and October. At the meeting of the executive committee of October 28, Lowell was convinced of the need for reservations, but Herbert Hoover, a new member, was not convinced. Hoover had taken a strong stand against reservations, saying that he was certain that if "we attempt now to revise the Treaty we shall tread a road through European chaos."[99]

[94] Taft to Lowell, Oct. 5, 1919, *Lowell MSS.*
[95] Lowell to Short, Oct. 22, Nov. 1, 3, 1919, *League Collection.*
[96] Lowell to Short, Nov. 4, 1919 (copy), *Lowell MSS.*
[97] Talcott Williams to Lowell, Nov. 11, 1919, *Lowell MSS.*
[98] McCumber to Taft, July 18, 1918, *Taft MSS;* McCumber to Lowell, Nov. 1, 1919, *Lowell MSS.*
[99] *Minutes,* Executive Committee meeting, Oct. 28, 1919, *Filene MSS;* Speech by Hoover at Palo Alto, Oct. 2, 1919. In several minutes of the executive committee, Hoover is noted as a "guest," and therefore not a member, but these notations are undoubtedly inaccurate, for Hoover had

Some of the members of the committee were convinced, however, of the Taft-Lowell viewpoint, and on November 6 a small group of the committee met and decided to call a meeting for November 13 to discuss again the problems of reservations.[100] A call was sent out to the members of the committee in the following form:

> Very important meeting Executive Committtee League Enforce Peace Thursday evening November thirteenth six thirty at dinner League headquarters stop All agree reservations of Foreign Relations Committee except last reservation excluding questions effecting honor and vital interests will be adopted with possible slight alterations stop Even President Wilson and Senator Hitchcock concede that ratification without reservations is impossible. Under these conditions Treaty faces these alternatives.
>
> First ratification with present reservations by Republican and Democratic votes Second compromise between Democrats and Republicans on new and milder reservations which Washington representatives of League claim highly improbable. Third present rejection of the Treaty and appeal to country on the issue in next Presidential election.
>
> Thursday meeting will consider whether League shall continue to hold its present attitude or urge ratification with present resolutions as amended as preferable to rejection and further delay. If unable to attend please telegraph your view.

The committee duly met on November 13 with nineteen members present. Dr. Lowell reviewed the situation regarding reservations to the treaty, and Talcott Williams, Harry N. Rickey, and Herbert S. Houston presented their views regarding the situation in Washington, and the views of those favoring support for the Lodge reservations. Some members, however, opposed the policy of approving reservations, and representing that group, Hamilton Holt moved the following resolutions:

> That the Committee prefers the rejection of the Peace Treaty and League of Nations Covenant as altered by the

---

become a member of the committee. See Taft to Robert A. Taft (copy), Nov. 25, 1919, *Taft MSS.*
[100] Short to Lowell, Nov. 6, 1919, *Lowell MSS.*

reservations of the Foreign Relations Committee, exclusive of No. 15, called the Reed Resolution, with the hope of getting something better later on, rather than its adoption now with these reservations.

This motion was lost by a vote of ten to five, four members not voting. The chairman then said: "The opinion of this committee is that we had better accept the Treaty with such reservations as the majority pass rather than have it rejected by this present session of the Senate."

The minutes do not show whether a vote was taken on this statement, nor do they record the names of the people voting on the Holt resolution.[101] Short later reported that the "vote" was strongly opposed by some members of the committee who he thought might issue a minority statement.[102] Four of the five people, however, who voted for the Holt resolution, were Holt, Theodore Marburg, Vance McCormick, and William G. McAdoo, and probably the fifth vote was cast by Herbert Hoover.[103]

In the notice sent to the executive committee announcing the meeting of November 13, members who could not attend were asked to indicate by telegraph their opinions on the issues indicated. It will be noted that the statement of the issue to be voted upon was prefaced by an explanation that was virtually advisory in character. The preface stated that "all" agreed that the Senate would vote for reservations, and that "even President Wilson" conceded that the treaty could not be ratified without reservations. The committee was then asked to vote on three proposals: (1) ratification with present reservations by "Republican and Democratic votes," (2) compromise later on milder reservations, (3) rejection of treaty and reference of the question to the next presidential election. As the questions were framed, therefore, an affirmative vote on the first proposal was clearly called for.

[101] *Minutes*, Executive Committee meeting, Nov. 13, 1919, *League Collection*.
[102] Short to Filene, Nov. 15, 1919, *Filene MSS*.
[103] Short to McAdoo, Nov. 14, 1919, *League Collection;* statements of Holt, Marburg, and McCormick to the author.

THE CRUCIAL TEST

The votes sent in by mail or by wire before the meeting of November 13 showed that eight members favored an expression of the League to Enforce Peace supporting the Senate's reservations. Six members either opposed ratification with the Senate's reservations, or opposed any action on the part of the League to Enforce Peace at that time. Among this group were Henry W. Taft, Alton B. Parker, George W. Wickersham, and Henry Van Dyke. Of those who sent votes after the meeting of November 13, expressing approval or disapproval of the majority action, nine approved and six opposed.

Some of the comments that were made by members of the committee who voted by mail or by wire or expressed their opinions after the meeting of the committee throw light upon the diversity of opinion that existed. Henry W. Taft changed his opinion between November 12, when he opposed supporting the Lodge reservations, and November 15 when he accepted the decision of the committee.[104] Leo S. Rowe felt "very strongly that the League to Enforce Peace should stand by its principles in this matter," and not create the impression throughout the country that "we are prepared to accept an emasculated treaty."[105] Alton B. Parker thought that the Lodge reservations represented the purpose of the majority of the Senate to "scuttle" the treaty and that the league would have no future usefulness if it supported such a decision.[106] Edward W. Frost favored the committee's action because he thought the treaty would be ratified "even with these unwise, and almost, if not quite, vicious reservations. . . ."[107] George W. Wickersham believed on November 13 that the league should take no action because eight of the fourteen proposed reservations were "simply amendments," that the Committee on Foreign Relations intended them to be such, and that if adopted the treaty would have to be resubmitted to all parties to the treaty. On November 17, however, Wickersham was willing to favor the action of the executive committee.[108] Henry Van

[104] Henry W. Taft to Short, Nov. 12 and 15, 1919, *League Collection*.
[105] Leo S. Rowe to Short, Nov. 18, 1919, *League Collection*.
[106] Alton B. Parker to Short, Nov. 13, 1919, *League Collection*.
[107] Edward W. Frost to Short, Nov. 17, 1919, *League Collection*.
[108] Wickersham to Short, Nov. 13 and 17, 1919, *League Collection*.

Dyke believed that reservations "emasculated" the treaty, left the Covenant useless, and represented a "plot" to defeat the treaty.[109] Later, after Van Dyke had received the minutes of the meeting of November 13, he complained that they did not make clear what had been done. Had the committee, he inquired, voted on a written resolution, or approved of a statement by Dr. Lowell, or what?[110]

As far as the public and the Senate were concerned, the details of the vote in the committee were of no importance and were in fact unknown. The committee's action put the League to Enforce Peace back of the Lodge reservations, and a public statement, published November 18, 1919, notified the nation as well as the Senate of that action. This public statement was read into the *Congressional Record* and was as follows:

> The League to Enforce Peace, through the action of its executive committee, urged that the reservation to the treaty introduced by Senator Reed, known as reservation 15, be defeated as nullifying the treaty. This reservation has been defeated. The Senate voted it down 56 to 36. Those remaining have their objections, and some are harmful: yet they leave a covenant which will create an efficient league equal to the task of preserving the peace of the world. A league of nations which will enforce and make more secure the peace of the world is the object for which "the League to Enforce Peace" was organized, for which it has labored through four and one-half years, and for which alone it exists. The treaty, even with the reservations now adopted, can accomplish this purpose and should be ratified. There is no adequate reason why it should not be. The world waits. Delay is perilous. Any action which casts the covenant for a league of nations for peace into the partisan politics of a presidential election will delay peace and halt political reorganization and economic rehabilitation of nations sorely smitten by war, by winter, and by famine.
>
> The League to Enforce Peace, speaking for the great multitude which has labored for this supreme end, sensible of its responsibility, calls for the immediate ratification of the

---

[109] Van Dyke to Short, Nov. 13, 1919, *League Collection*.
[110] Van Dyke to Short, Nov. 17, 1919, *League Collection*.

treaty, even with its reservations, but it is most important that the preamble be changed by removing the necessity for positive action on the reservations by nations definitely named and contenting ourselves by acceptance in the ordinary way by silent acquiescence within a time limited.

Failure to ratify the treaty now would defeat the world's hopes for peace now and always. Such a failure would throw the world back into worse than prewar conditions by re-establishing a balance or hostile grouping of powers with an increasing burden of armaments. If the league be once established and permitted to function with our country as a member the foundations of a new world order would continue to grow in beneficent stability, securing for all nations great and small peace with justice.[111]

In so far as the action of the executive committee was designed to influence Democratic senators to accept the Lodge reservations, the committee failed, for it secured no votes. Indeed it was a double failure, for the Lodge reservations, which some advocates claimed were designed to win the votes of the Borah group, missed their alleged—and somewhat incredible—objective also. The Borah group voted against the treaty after they had assisted Lodge in making the reservations unacceptable to the friends of the treaty. The League to Enforce Peace, therefore, contributed to the defeat of the League of Nations almost as effectively as if it had been in outright opposition.

The majority of the executive committee, led by Dr. Lowell and Mr. Taft, now urged that the League to Enforce Peace initiate a campaign to bring about a compromise among the "friends of the Treaty." They had committed themselves to the view that the Lodge reservations were not important, that the Covenant was virtually as good with them as it was without them, and in short that pressure should be brought to bear upon the Democrats to accept reservations.[112] In conformity to this line of thought, the committee passed resolutions calling upon the Senate to "forget prejudice and partisanship and agree upon a resolution of ratification couched in terms that will permit

[111] *Congressional Record*, 66th Congress, 1st Session, Vol. 58, part IX, pp. 8773-4.
[112] Taft to Horace D. Taft, Nov. 26, 1919 (copy), *Taft MSS.*

the other signatories of the Treaty to acquiesce in the conditions of our ratification."[113] Although this resolution was stated in general terms, the League to Enforce Peace made its position clear through other published materials and through letters from its officers. "We are advocating," said Secretary Short, "ratification on the basis of the Lodge resolution with the change only of the preamble."[114] Thus the senators who were now being accused of partisanship and who were being called upon to forget prejudices were the Democrats. The "compromise" called for did not relate to the reservations proper but to the preamble, and the statement put the league behind the belief that the Lodge reservations would be accepted by the signatory powers. The league held that the differences between Lodge and Wilson were minor differences,[115] but certainly neither Lodge nor Wilson thought so.

The official view of the League to Enforce Peace, therefore, after the vote on the treaty in the Senate, was a continuation of the view expressed in the resolution adopted at the meeting of the executive committee on November 13. This view was based upon four interdependent assumptions: (1) that the treaty could not be ratified without substantial reservations, (2) that the Lodge group were in fact "friends of the Covenant," (3) that the Lodge reservations did not damage the Covenant as a constitution for a feasible world organization for the preservation of peace, (4) that the nations signatory to the treaty would not object to the reservations.[116] If any one of these proposi-

[113] Circular dated Nov. 23, 1919.
[114] Short to George E. Roberts, Dec. 12, 1919, *League Collection*.
[115] Circular letter sent to 500 League to Enforce Peace speakers, Nov. 23, 1919.
[116] Although this statement is an analysis of a point of view, it is so well substantiated by repeated statements of such people as Lowell and Taft that no conflict can exist regarding its accuracy. For example, Dr. Lowell believed that Lodge was "evidently anxious to ratify" the treaty and that he had made concessions for the purpose. Lowell to Short, Mar. 15, 1920, *League Collection*. He believed that Article 10 was damaging to the Covenant, that no difficulties would arise over securing other nations' approval of reservations, and that simply the "stubbornness" of Wilson had prevented ratification. Lowell to Carl Joslyn, Nov. 11, 1920 (copy), Lowell to Mrs. Ward Banister, Sept. 6, 1919 (copy), *Lowell MSS*.

tions was invalid, the executive committee should, in strict logic, have been compelled to reach a different decision. It is true, of course, that each assumption was founded on a complicated and at least somewhat controversial set of conditions and value-judgments. It is equally true that decisions had to be reached by men whose party associations and personal friendships were inescapably involved and who could not be expected to have prophetic foresight regarding the future conduct of Lodge, Harding, and Hughes. Granting these truths, it is nevertheless the proper function of the historian to examine the validity of the four assumptions on the evidence that existed at the time they were accepted by the committee, and to inquire whether a more rigorous and objective consideration of them would have led to their rejection. In making this analysis it must be remembered that a minority of the committee did reject them and that some other members who did not attend the meeting on November 13 either rejected them or expressed no opinion at all.

The first assumption, the necessity for reservations in order to secure the approval of the Republican "mild reservationists" is one that has to be considered in relation to time. It is by no means certain that the minds of some of those senators were crystallized in favor of reservations at the time that Taft began to work with Hays and others in support of them. Senator McCumber, the only Republican who voted for the treaty in November, was not certain in July that reservations were needed. He strongly disapproved of some of Taft's proposed reservations, thought that they were damaging to the Covenant, and did not feel that any reservations would appease Senator Knox.[117] Subsequently McCumber appealed again and again to the league to stand fast against reservations.[118] He was not the only Republican who saw the situation in this light. Senator Colt was both disturbed and dissatisfied with the attitude of Republican leaders. "May I say," he concluded in a letter to Root, "that I do not like the attitude of our Republican leaders in the Senate. They seem to be determined to kill the whole

[117] McCumber to Taft, July 18, 1919, *Taft MSS.*
[118] McCumber to Edward Cummings, Sept. 25, 1919 (copy), *Lowell MSS.*

Treaty. As I view it, their position is unwise both as respects our national honor and the future of our party."[119] Perhaps, however, the best evidence on this subject comes from Senator Lodge himself. Lodge appealed to Root for aid in securing the support of some Republican senators for the Lodge reservations. Especially he asked assistance in dealing with Senators Colt and Kellogg, declaring that only through Root's efforts had they been won over to the support of any reservations at all. But further efforts were needed.[120] Root answered that he had written to Kellogg, who apparently had been won over, that he had some difficulty in thinking of a way to approach Colt but that he had done what he could.[121] As late as the first of October, therefore, it was by no means certain that some of the so-called "mild reservationists" were reservationists. Some of them distrusted Lodge and the irreconcilable opponents of the treaty almost as much as they disliked the prospects of an alliance with their Democratic opponents.[122] When the struggle was over and the issue was settled to his satisfaction, Lodge confessed how difficult it had been to get some Republican senators to support any reservations.[123]

Taft went to Washington early in October to work for reservations, talked with the Democratic leader, Senator Underwood, and reported later that Underwood was "as level-headed" as anyone he saw in Washington. Underwood told Taft that forty Democratic senators would support the treaty without amendments or reservations. The real difficulty in getting the Democratic forces to agree to reservations of any kind arose from the fact that once the principle of the need for reservations was admitted, Democratic senators would assert their right to try their hands at devising them.[124] The whole logic of the situation, therefore, was on the side of the earlier official position of the League to Enforce Peace, namely the support of ratification without reservations. The major weak-

[119] Colt to Root, Sept. 2, 1919, *Root MSS*.
[120] Lodge to Root, Aug. 15, 1919, *Root MSS*.
[121] Root to Lodge, Aug. 28, 1919 (copy), *Root MSS*.
[122] Taft to Lowell, Oct. 5, 1919, *Lowell MSS*.
[123] See below, page 161.
[124] Taft to Lowell, Oct. 5, 1919, *Lowell MSS*.

ness in the league's position was that as soon as Taft began to support reservations, the league no longer spoke with one voice. In the minds of many people Taft was the symbol of the League to Enforce Peace, and as soon as he began to support reservations much of the effectiveness of the league's official position was lost, not only on the public but upon the senators who were sensitive to public opinion.[125] Soon the league's authorized agents in Washington began to work for reservations, some for one and some for another without concerted action,[126] and, as has been noted, the league's secretary admitted that the league talked in one direction and acted in another.[127] Much of the weight of the league's influence was actually thrown to the Lodge side long before November 13, when it took an official position favoring reservations. In view of these various signs, it was an assumption and not a fact that the "mild reservationists" could not have been brought to the unqualified support of the treaty if the League to Enforce Peace had stood its ground and brought its full strength to the treaty's support. While the league certainly had less strength the more it equivocated, it was never too late to act vigorously if it had possessed the will to act.

The second assumption was that the members of the Lodge group were in fact "friends of the Treaty." This assumption raises two important questions: (1) Did Lodge really seek to destroy the treaty through reservations that he knew would be rejected by the President? And (2) did the Senators who followed Lodge's leadership think that Lodge wished to defeat the treaty? As to the first question, the testimony of contemporary observers is significant. "The evidence," said the secretary of the league, "that Senator Lodge wishes to prevent agreement and defeat the Treaty is very strong. In addition to his public statements, which would lead to this inference, is the significant fact that near the close of the last session of Congress he gave Senator Hitchcock to understand that after the defeat of the several ratifying resolutions he would probably

[125] Leo S. Rowe to Lowell, July 28, 1919, *Lowell MSS.*
[126] Senator Frank B. Kellogg to Lowell, Oct. 31, 1919, *Lowell MSS.*
[127] See above, page 149.

agree to a recess for a day or two in order to give opportunity for a compromise that would result in ratification. Instead of doing this the Senator resorted to every parliamentary expedient to force adjournment and kill the treaty."[128] Senator McCumber, unquestionably a sincere friend of the Covenant, analyzed the Lodge reservations and ended with this query: "Is it [the attachment of the reservations] not a rather unfair way to attempt to secure the final defeat of the Treaty?"[129] The testimony of Taft is enlightening as well as amazing in view of his own conduct. "I feel confident," he wrote early in 1920, "that the truculence, selfishness, partisanship, and personal spite of the vociferous Republican Senators who have been opposed to the Treaty openly or have sought to kill it by amendment have shocked the moral sense of enough of our community, and humiliated them before the world so deeply that their feeling will find substantial expression in the ballot box unless the League is ratified." Horace D. Taft, in a letter to William Howard Taft, noted that the latter's anger turned on Wilson and Hitchcock. "There is nothing, however," he continued, "in all that they have done to excuse Lodge and his mates for their contemptible conduct, or the mild reservationists for simply giving up their principles. I feel much more savage against the Republicans for letting mere personal and party spite sway them than I do against Wilson for his constitutional cussedness. . . ." He said that he would bolt the Republican Party and thought that his brother should head the revolt.[130]

These various comments are, however, opinions and interpretations. Their significance rests upon the character of the people who expressed them and the fact that they are the comments of Republicans: the Democrats were virtually unanimous in their belief that Lodge simply wanted to kill the treaty.

More conclusive evidence regarding Lodge's intentions must be sought in his own acts and words. Note has already been

[128] Report of Short to the League to Enforce Peace, Dec. 17, 1919, *League Collection*.
[129] McCumber to Lowell, Nov. 1, 1919, *Lowell MSS*.
[130] Taft to George M. Wrong, Jan. 30, 1920 (copy), *Taft MSS;* Horace D. Taft to W. H. Taft, Nov. 20, 1919, *Taft MSS*.

taken of his assertion that he meant to kill Article 10 or kill the treaty.[131] This statement was made after President Wilson, and Taft as well, had said repeatedly that Article 10 was the heart of the League. Both Root and Lodge agreed that the Lodge reservations on Article 10 effectively nullified it. For Lodge to say, therefore, that he would kill Article 10 or kill the treaty, was virtually to say that he would do the latter once he was certain that the President would not accept the reservation on Article 10. Lodge explained to Root that in getting that reservation accepted by the Republicans he had to move very carefully. "If I had not moved in this way," he wrote, "there is a considerable body of men on our side who would have voted with the Democrats for pretty much any reservation of a milder type than the one existing. They would have put it in and the situation would have been embarrassing. I wanted to keep the matter in our own control as long as I could and I particularly wanted to avoid a position which would compel the Republicans practically alone to kill the Treaty...."[132] Lodge hoped that Wilson would refuse to make a treaty. "What I should like best," he said, "is to have him refuse to make the treaty and then come before the people next year as a candidate for the presidency. He would be the worst beaten man that ever lived...."[133] Lodge informed Root that no conflict existed between the irreconcilable opponents of the treaty and the mild reservationists regarding the Republican Party platform in 1920. What they wanted to do, he said, was to make no commitments "to ratification with reservations," but to leave the future course of action undefined. His major interest was to get the party to fight together, "every man fighting along the line he preferred providing he fight against Wilson's league."[134] Richard Henry Dana reported that Lodge had affirmed that he

[131] Quoted in Taft to Short, Sept. 14, 1919 (copy), *League Collection*. Lodge stated privately that he had devised reservations which he was confident the President would reject, and that he was prepared to propose others if the President showed signs of accepting the ones already devised. See Charles P. Howland, *Survey of American Foreign Relations* (New Haven, Yale University Press, 1928), p. 272.
[132] Lodge to Root, Mar. 13, 1920, *Root MSS.*
[133] Lodge to Root, Sept. 29, 1919, *Root MSS.*
[134] Lodge to Root, May 17, 1920, *Root MSS.*

"was opposed to the creation of any League whatsoever."[135]

From all this evidence it would seem to be clear that Senator Lodge was not a "friend" of the Covenant. The second question involved in the assumption is more difficult to answer because the *group* that followed Lodge's leadership was diverse. The Borah-Knox following, who assisted Lodge in securing the reservations, certainly did not think that they were contributing to the ratification of the Covenant, and yet up to a certain point they were members of the Lodge group. Some senators, for example Colt and McNary, were friends of *a* league of nations but were drawn for various reasons into Lodge's political web. Still other members of the Lodge group, for example Senator Harding, made remarks about the Covenant which were so contradictory that they simply cancelled themselves out. It is difficult to see, therefore, how the term "friends of the Covenant" could properly be used to indicate the Lodge group.

The third assumption was that the Lodge reservations did not damage the Covenant as a constitution for a feasible world organization, that is to say that the reservations were either explanatory in character and not major changes in the document or that they really changed the Covenant into something substantially different which was as good as or better than the original. But to hold the view that the reservations were unimportant, that they simply stated in a different way what was already stated or implied in the Covenant, was to cut the ground completely from under all the arguments that could be amassed to justify the action of the senators who pretended to favor the treaty but who voted against it on the grounds that the reservations were essential. On the other hand, to hold that the reservations were important, that they provided substantial changes in the Covenant, was to nullify the basis for the assumption that the signatory nations would not object to the reservations.

The Lodge reservations as they were voted on in November, again excluding the preamble, stated:

[135] Memorandum of conversations between Short and Dana, Dec. 13, 1920, *Vance McCormick MSS.*

1. that the United States should be the sole judge as to whether it had fulfilled its obligations under the Covenant in case it wished to withdraw;

2. that the United States assumed no obligation "to preserve the territorial integrity or political independence" of any other country;

3. that no mandate could be accepted by the United States without the consent of Congress;

4. that the United States could decide what questions were domestic in character and that such questions were beyond the consideration of the League;

5. that any question which in the judgment of the United States depended upon or related to the Monroe Doctrine should be outside the jurisdiction of the League and unaffected by any provision of the treaty;

6. that the United States should not be bound by Articles 156, 157, 158 of the treaty, commonly referred to as the Shantung settlement;

7. that the appointment and activity of American representatives to the League or to any of its agencies should be controlled by Congress;

8. that the powers of the Reparations Commission to regulate German-American trade should be subject to congressional control;

9. that the United States should not be obligated to contribute to league expense until such contribution had been appropriated by Congress;

10. that the United States could disregard disarmament plans of the League of Nations if the United States were "threatened" with invasion or engaged in war;

11. that the United States reserved the right to disregard Article 16 in so far as it related to specified nationals of a Covenant-breaking state;

12. Articles 296 and 297 of the treaty should not be construed so as to damage American rights;

13. that the United States withold its assent to the part of the treaty establishing an international labor organization;

14. that the United States should not be bound by any act of the League in which any member of the League "and its self-governing dominions, colonies, or parts of empire" in the aggregate cast more than one vote.

In addition to the fourteen reservations, the Lodge resolution of ratification contained a preamble stating that the resolution of ratification should not take effect until the resolutions had been accepted by "at least three of the four principal allied and associated powers, to wit, Great Britain, France, Italy, and Japan." The statement approving the Lodge reservations authorized by the executive committee of the League to Enforce Peace on November 13 and read in the Senate on November 19, called for the adoption of the treaty with the Lodge reservations with one exception. "It is most important," the statement read, "that the preamble be changed by removing the necessity for positive action on the reservations by nations definitely named. . . ." The Senate majority paid no attention to this recommendation but voted for the preamble as well as for the reservations. A consideration, therefore, of the probable effect of the reservations on the Covenant and the possibility of their acceptance by the signatory nations must take into account the preamble.

The inclusion of the preamble in the resolution of ratification is a fact of considerable importance because it removes all logical grounds for the fourth assumption on which the action of the League to Enforce Peace was based, namely that the reservations would have been accepted by the signatory powers. This subject was considered by Senator McCumber in the Senate on November 15. "I am certain," said Senator McCumber, "that every Senator must agree with me that if the reservation adopted by the Senate on the Shantung feature is equivalent to a rejection of the Shantung articles, then Great Britain, France, and Italy cannot honorably assent to it."[136] When Senator Pomerene asked McCumber if in his opinion the Lodge reservation in question was equivalent to a rejection, McCumber answered, "I do and I expect to show it." He immediately proceeded to show that if Great Britain, France, and Italy assented to the American rejection of the Shantung articles, their assent became in fact "an agreement of all four

[136] *Congressional Record*, 66 Congress, 1st Session, Vol. 58, part IX, p. 8562.

powers to the rejection."[137] No one attempted to disprove Senator McCumber's argument.

A detailed discussion of the other reservations would seem to be unnecessary here. The fourth reservation vitiated the Covenant, for it was so inclusive in its wording that the United States could have declared any question a "domestic" question and thereby could have excluded it from League consideration. The Latin-American nations could not have been expected to accept the Monroe Doctrine reservation; the British Dominions certainly would have objected to the fourteenth reservation;[138] and the armament reservation simply left the United States free from any commitment on that question. The eleventh reservation was a blanket provision that the rights of American citizens were not affected by the treaty. These various considerations, and no mention has been made of the second reservation on Article 10 which President Wilson thought simply nullified the Covenant, would seem to be conclusive in regard to the problem of submission of the reservations to the signatory powers.

The contemporary views of a keen observer who had just returned to the United States from Europe are worth quoting:

> I am absolutely convinced by a careful investigation since my return home that there is a very large body of public opinion in this country that has absolutely no appreciation whatsoever of the nature of the proposed reservations to the Peace Treaty. They have been shrewdly drawn to give the appearance of promoting American rights but as a matter of fact, their scope goes enormously beyond that point.
>
> Hidden in them are possibilities of the utmost danger, which I firmly believe very few people have yet sensed. At the same time some of them are contradictory, some obviously damaging to the country, some extremely confused. They very decidedly give the impression of rough and careless drafting. From the European point of view the reserva-

[137] *Ibid.*
[138] Professor George M. Wrong, of Toronto, told Taft that Canada would resent the reservation concerning the British Empire and would either force Great Britain to oppose that reservation or would withdraw from the treaty herself. Taft to Horace D. Taft, Mar. 1, 1920, *Taft MSS.*

tions are utterly disastrous. I can hardly believe that any nation over-seas will accept them, will indeed enter into a League of such wholly one-sided nature.[139]

With the exception of a few bits of evidence regarding Lodge's intention, these several facts regarding the assumptions upon which the majority group in the League to Enforce Peace based their action in supporting the Lodge reservations were available in November, 1919. The least that can be said about them is that they all lead in the direction of a conclusion that the assumptions do not stand up under examination.

[139] Arthur Sweetser to Short, Nov. 7, 1919, *League Collection*.

CHAPTER SIX

Confusion and Failure

THE ATTEMPTS of the League to Enforce Peace to bring about the ratification of the treaty on the basis of compromise over the Lodge reservations were foredoomed to failure. The fundamental difficulty was that the Lodge reservations did not represent a compromise between the Democratic friends of the treaty and the Republican mild reservationists, but a "compromise" among three groups of Republicans, namely the irreconcilable opponents of the treaty, the so-called party regulars, and the mild reservationists. This compromise was in no sense *bona fide*; it was not designed to secure a unified Republican vote for the treaty with the reservations, but only to secure the support of the irreconcilables for the reservations. Since the irreconcilables would not vote for reservations acceptable to the Democrats, for to do so would secure the ratification of the treaty, the so-called compromise simply made it possible to insure the defeat of the treaty. This fact was recognized at the time the reservations were being drawn,[1] and it is shown conclusively in the record of votes in the Senate. The irreconcilables openly stated that they would vote against ratification with or without reservations. Senator Lodge misrepresented the facts, therefore, when he presented his reservations as representing a compromise among the friends of the treaty, and he further misrepresented the facts when he stated that the Democrats who opposed the reservations were opposing compromise. If it was Senator Lodge's intention to confuse the public with his ruse regarding compromise, he succeeded to a marked

[1] Talcott Williams wrote to Short on Nov. 4, 1919, pointing out this fact, and Lowell had become convinced of it earlier. Lowell to Short, Nov. 1 and 4, 1919, *League Collection*.

degree. Even persons who had ample opportunity to know better were taken in. Taft, for example, who should have been able to see a straight path through the labyrinth of compromise, took the position that Wilson refused "all reservations."[2] Lowell, however, unwound the truth from the welter of rumors and ruses more carefully. He pointed out that the President had "practically said that he would accept any reservation that Senator Hitchcock and his followers approve."[3]

Senator Pittman tried to correct the misrepresentations. On the day of the Senate's vote on the treaty he stated emphatically that the Democratic senators had been willing to agree to what might be called clarifying resolutions. They had, for example, been willing to support and had voted for Senator McCumber's resolution on the Monroe Doctrine. Pittman continued: "That is not all. All the way through, from the very beginning to the end, there were offered on the other side by the Senator from North Dakota [Mr. McCumber], or there were offered on this side by the Senator from Nebraska [Mr. Hitchcock], or other Democratic Senators, substitute resolutions for practically every reservation offered by the majority, and in nearly every case, *these reservations that were offered as substitutes were the reservations that had been prepared by the so-called mild reservationists on the Republican side.* . . . The Democrats voted for them in every case and the Republicans voted against them in every case."[4] The Senator listed the reservations proposed by the "mild reservationists" and supported by the Democrats. Other Democratic senators followed Senator Pittman, offering to agree to interpretative resolutions, and Senator Hitchcock finally proposed a set of five resolutions. These were defeated by a strict party vote.[5]

During the final day of debate in November, Senator Harding expressed himself on the league question in a way which could leave no real doubt regarding his thoughts on the subject.

---

[2] Taft to Short, Sept. 14, 1919, *League Collection.*
[3] Lowell to Short, Nov. 8, 1919, *League Collection.*
[4] *Congressional Record,* 66 Congress, 1st Session, Vol. 58, part IX, p. 8794. (Italics mine.)
[5] *Ibid.,* p. 8800.

He said that he did not like the treaty but that he recognized the desire of the people to "do something" toward international coöperation. He continued:

> I could, however, no more vote to ratify this treaty without reservations which make sure America's independence of action, which make sure and certain our freedom in choosing our course of action, than I could participate in a knowing betrayal of this Republic.
>
> . . . .
>
> We are content to give you your league of nations, doubtful as we are about the wisdom of the great experiment. We realize that we are not giving it to you in the fullness of the ambitions of the Chief Executive who negotiated it; we realize and regret that it must be reported to the nations of the world with something very much akin to humiliation. That is not the fault of the Senate; that is the fault of him who negotiated it without recognizing that there is a Senate. It is a very great misfortune, and I am sorry about it; but I tell you, Senators, the independence of action and the preserved inheritance of this Republic are infinitely more important than the wounded feelings of the Senate. So we of the majority are agreed to preserve American freedom of action and to enter upon a league of nations, a league with such reservations that leave us our choice of action, the exercise of American conscience, the determination to do that which we think is our part in the promotion and preservation of civilization and peace without the surrender of things essentially American.
>
> If this ratification is made with the reservations which have been adopted, *there remains the skeleton of a league*, on which the United States can, if it deems it prudent, proceed in deliberation and calm reflection toward the building of an international relationship which shall be effective in the future.[6]

While Senator Harding had not been in any direct way an important figure in drafting the Lodge reservations, it was clear enough in his mind what purpose the resolutions were designed to accomplish. He accepted all the Lodge reservations.

[6] *Ibid.*, p. 8792 (italics mine).

The United States was to be relieved from any commitment to assist in preserving the independence or territorial integrity of League members,[7] to be free of League interference in any matter which it chose to call a domestic question, to be free to disregard League plans for disarmament, and to assume no obligations regarding mandates or reparations. In addition, the United States sought to impose amendments to the treaty regarding the Shantung settlement and the position of the British Empire in world affairs. It was clear also that the Senate majority had reached an agreement on the matter, that they would not change their position or consider compromise, and that they would defeat the treaty unless their demands were accepted.

The difference between such people as Senator Harding and the Lodge group, on the one side, and Senator Borah and the "irreconcilable" group on the other was that the latter opposed the assumption by the United States of any obligations to coöperate with the rest of the world to prevent war and aggression and therefore opposed the League of Nations, while the former agreed to the entrance of the United States into *a* league of nations whose members were not obliged to coöperate in the prevention of war and aggression. President Wilson and his followers were in perfect agreement with the Senate majority in one regard, that in the application of a specific policy of coöperation, the imposition of a boycott, or the use of armed forces, the consent of Congress would be necessary, but he held that the whole foundation of world organization for the preservation of peace rested upon the willingness of nations to agree to act in certain specified circumstances. The contest over the Lodge reservations, therefore, was not fundamentally a contest over wording, for to the very end of the controversy the Democrats were willing to accept changes in phrasing.[8] It was not a contest over amendments to the treaty, however disastrous

---

[7] This is not a controversial matter. "The word 'unless'," said Taft, "therein introduced [into the reservation on Article 10], and the word 'provide', mean *merely* that there is *no obligation* of the United States to respond to the provision of Article 10." Taft to Short, Dec. 24, 1919, *League Collection*. (Italics mine.)

[8] See Wilson's statement of Jan. 8 and Mar. 8, 1920.

an attempt to amend the treaty might have been.[9] It was not a question of the position of the British Empire in the League, however fantastic it was for the Senate to demand in one reservation that the British dominions should not be allowed a vote in the League under certain circumstances and in another to demand that Ireland be given a vote. The real issue was stated by Senator Harding. "We demand," he said, "independence of action." His group would agree to the creation of a "skeleton of a league" under which America can act "if it deems it prudent." President Wilson, on the other hand, wanted the United States to limit its freedom of action in specified ways, and to join a League of Nations which would "guarantee as a matter of incontestable right the political independence and integrity of its members." Senator Harding favored the Lodge reservations because they would permit the United States and other nations to do what they had been doing; President Wilson opposed the reservations precisely because he saw that the world must not continue to do what it had been doing.

During the early days of the League to Enforce Peace, various people and groups in the United States had suggested that the league should remove from its program the use of force in world organization, and advocate only voluntary conciliation and arbitration. A proposal of this sort had been made at the Philadelphia meeting which launched the league. At that time, Dr. Lowell made it very clear that the central idea of the league's program was that nations should commit themselves to use force against nations who refused to submit their disputes to peaceful settlement. He pointed out that a mere agreement to consult whenever a case arose, an agreement which allowed each nation to do what it pleased in each case, was not the sort of international organization the league was designed to advocate. Later Dr. Lowell re-affirmed this position. "We cannot leave out," he said, "the one thing in our program that is dis-

[9] Very few amendments were made to the Covenant between 1920 and 1940, and if change was needed it was to make the Covenant stronger rather than weaker. Suggestion for amending other parts of the treaty met with strong disapproval at the First Assembly in 1920. See Waldo E. Stephens, *Revision of the Treaty of Versailles* (New York, Columbia University Press, 1939.)

tinctive and essential, in order to bring in people who do not agree with it."[10] The principle that President Wilson advocated in 1919 was precisely the principle for which the League to Enforce Peace had stood. If the United States proposed to act only when "it deemed it prudent," it had not agreed to act at all.

Notwithstanding the fundamental conflict between the opponents and proponents of the Lodge reservations, the League to Enforce Peace launched its drive to secure a compromise agreement. In one sense the drive produced results. Petitions, resolutions passed by meetings of various organized groups of people, and personal appeals reached Washington in great numbers. Acting jointly with the American Federation of Labor, the League to Enforce Peace sponsored a conference at Washington on January 13, 1920. The meeting was attended by representatives of thirty-three organizations including the International Association of Rotary Clubs, the National Educational Association, and the National W. C. T. U. The conference declared that the treaty of peace should be ratified immediately "on a basis that will not require re-negotiation," and "with such reservations as may secure in the Senate the necessary two-thirds vote."[11] A committee was appointed to give to Senators Lodge and Hitchcock a copy of the conference's statement and to have power to reconvene the conference. The conference was reconvened on February 9. In the meantime, President Wilson had written a second letter offering to agree to reasonable reservations, going as far as to agree to Senator Hitchcock's resolutions on Article 10. In the meantime also Senator Owen of Oklahoma had proposed a resolution on Article 10 that was agreeable to the Democratic senators, and Senator Simmons had proposed a substitute acceptable to them. The conference declared that the differences between the opposing factions were not great enough to prevent a reasonable compromise.[12]

For a brief moment, the President's offer of compromise and

[10] Lowell to Short, Feb. 9, 1917, *League Collection*.
[11] *Minutes* of the conference, *Filene MSS*.
[12] *Ibid*.

the pressure from public opinion appeared to weaken Lodge's chances of holding together all factions of his following. But appearances were misleading. Lodge could put his finger on every pulse beat in his senatorial following. In November, 1919, he had secured a pledge from the "mild reservationists" that all Democratic proposals for change should be made through him.[13] The "Death Battalion" stood its ground during the crisis in February, 1920. If Lodge had made any concession to which they could expect Wilson to agree, they would have deserted Lodge and the result, ironically enough, would have been the ratification of the treaty. Actually Senator Lodge had the situation well in hand. He told Root that there would be no change, for change, he said, "would weaken our position in regard to the Treaty and also our party position. . . ."[14] When the treaty was called up for reconsideration, the Democrats rallied sufficient strength to remove the preamble to the Lodge reservations, but the Lodge forces re-wrote the reservation on Article 10 making it a more specific and complete negation of the article than the original reservation had been. Thus the treaty was again defeated, and the issue of the League of Nations went over to the political campaign of 1920.

The League to Enforce Peace was now split wide open on the issue of reservations. Secretary Short believed that the executive committee should hold a meeting and consider future policy. In his opinion the objections that had been raised to Article 10 were not sincere, for the Lodge reservations had simply been devised for the purpose of "putting up something to the President which he [Lodge] knew the President would not accept."[15] Dr. Lowell, however, seems to have assumed that Lodge was sincere, that he really wanted the treaty ratified, and he now considered that Article 10 was unimportant if indeed it was not harmful. The fact was that ever since Taft had joined the reservationists, the league had been rapidly falling apart. "While I have not said anything about it," wrote Short

[13] Lodge to Root, Dec. 3, 1919, *Root MSS*.
[14] *Ibid*.
[15] Short to Lowell, Mar. 22, 1920, *Lowell MSS*. See page 161 on this subject.

in December, 1919, "the facts are that the action taken at our Executive Committee Meeting on November the 13th, when we decided to issue a statement that we gave out from Washington on November the 18th, knocked us to pieces pretty badly. The Republican members of our organization throughout the country had already deserted us to a considerable degree because of the partisan opposition of the Republican machine. We had, therefore, rebuilt our organization largely out of Democrats. This alienated a great many of those. As an illustration of the results, I had a meeting here in my office with the Executive Committee of the New York State Branch and, in spite of my utmost efforts—and I never fought more desperately in my life—they absolutely refused to do a blessed thing, directly and avowedly because of that vote."[16]

Short's judgment was well founded. He had gone to Washington on December 16, 1919, had canvassed opinion there and had written an illuminating report. "Information," he said, "is to the effect that the President is not well disposed toward the League to Enforce Peace, that he feels that we parted company with him at a critical moment when we recommended ratification at the close of the last session. It is probable that our influence with him is something less than zero, that he would be inclined to disregard and oppose rather than follow suggestions that might come from our officers or committees."[17] Talcott Williams of the Washington bureau reached the same conclusion. "As you will remember," he wrote to Short, "I said at the conference which we held in Washington, which had to do with issuing the statement in regard to compromise that if it were sent out the League would have shot its last bolt and be out of the fight, except for personal work and canvass at Washington. I felt less certain about it at that time than I had earlier and said so. I do not think the League ought to be disbanded on any account, but I think it must await developments, hard at best, and doubly so under present conditions. The President, of course, will have no further use for us. . . ."[18]

[16] Short to Lowell, Dec. 29, 1919, *Lowell MSS.*
[17] Dec. 18, 1919, *Filene MSS.*
[18] Talcott Williams to Short, Dec. 25, 1919, *League Collection.*

For two months after the rejection of the treaty in March, 1920, the league drifted rather aimlessly. On May 6, however, a small group of the executive committee met at Taft's office in New Haven and considered what the policy of the league should be during the political campaign. They decided that the following things should be done:

> 1. That the league should give out information of an exact and non-partisan character regarding the attitude toward the League of Nations of candidates for office, especially of United States senators standing for re-election.
> 2. That it should give out information concerning the League of Nations Covenant and regarding the activity of the League of Nations, which was by that time, an active international organization.[19]

The party conventions met the following month. The first, the Republican, opened in Chicago on June 8, and Senator Lodge delivered what was really the "key-note" speech. He declared that in opposing the treaty and the League, Republican senators had fulfilled a high and patriotic duty, that they had revealed to the people what the league threatened. In Lodge's opinion the people understood the following:

> They saw that it was an alliance and not a league for peace. They saw that it did not mention the Hague conventions which we all desired to have restored as foundations for further extensions, did nothing for the development of international law, nothing for a world court and judicial decisions, and nothing looking toward an agreement as to dealing with non-justiciable questions. These real advances toward promoting peace, these constructive measures, were all disregarded, and the only court mentioned was pushed into an obscure corner.
>
> The people began to perceive with an intense clearness that this alliance, silent as to real peace agreements, contained clauses which threatened the very existence of the United States as an independent power—threatened its sovereignty, threatened its peace, threatened its life. . . .

[19] Taft, Lowell, Straus, Williams, Holt, and Short were the members present at this meeting.

Lodge went on to say that President Wilson was determined to have the treaty just as he brought it back or nothing, that adherence to Article 10 might cause American soldiers and sailors to "give their lives for quarrels not their own, at the bidding of foreign Governments."[20]

One group of delegates to the convention favored placing a plank in the platform specifically advocating the ratification of the treaty with the Lodge reservations, but the "Death Battalion" immediately threatened to bolt the party if any indorsement of any kind was given to the League. As a result, Lodge formulated a plank, written largely by Elihu Root, which managed to make no promise to ratify the treaty in any form.[21] The platform declared that the foreign policy of the Democratic administration had been founded upon "no principle and directed by no conception of our national rights and obligations" with the result that "our motives are suspected, our moral influence is impaired and our Government stands discredited and friendless among the nations of the world." The Republican Party, however, stood for a foreign policy founded upon moral and political principles, which would adequately protect the life, liberty, and property of American citizens. With regard to the League of Nations, the party stood for the following policy:

> The Republican Party stands for agreement among the nations to preserve the peace of the world. We believe that such an international association must be based upon international justice, and must provide methods which shall maintain the rule of public right by development of law and the decision of impartial courts, and which shall secure instant and general international conference whenever peace shall be threatened by political action, so that the nations pledged to do and insist upon what is just and fair may exercise their influence and power for the prevention of war. We believe that all this can be done without the compromise of national independence, without depriving the people of the United States in advance of the right to determine for themselves what is just and fair, when the occasion arises, and without involving them as participants and not as peacemakers in a

[20] *Current History*, XII (July, 1920), 551.
[21] See above, page 161.

multitude of quarrels, the merits of which they are unable to judge.

The covenant signed by the President at Paris failed signally to accomplish this purpose and contained stipulations not only intolerable for an independent people but certain to produce the injustice, hostility and controversy among nations which it proposed to prevent.

That covenant repudiated, to a degree wholly unnecessary and unjustifiable, the time-honored policy in favor of peace declared by Washington and Jefferson and Monroe and pursued by all American administrators for more than a century, and it ignored the universal sentiments of America for generations past in favor of international law and arbitration, and it rested the hope of the future upon mere expediency and negotiation.

The unfortunate insistence of the President upon having his own way, without any change and without any regard to the opinion of the majority of the Senate, which shares with him in the treaty-making power, and the President's demand that the treaty should be ratified without any modification, created a situation in which Senators were required to vote upon their consciences and upon the treaty as it was presented or submit to the commands of a dictator in a matter where the authority, under the Constitution, was theirs, and not his.

The Senators performed their duty faithfully. We approve their conduct and honor their courage and fidelity, and we pledge the coming Republican Administration to such agreement with the other nations of the world as shall meet the full duty of America to civilization and humanity in accordance with American ideals and without surrendering the right of the American people to exercise its judgment and its power in favor of justice and peace.

Phrased so, as an attack on Wilson and without a pledge to support the treaty with the Lodge reservations or in any fashion, the statement was acceptable to the Death Battalion. As an apparent promise of *some sort* of international association for the promotion of peace it was acceptable to the rest of the party also. Time was to show, what may not have been seen by some members of the convention, that it was not a promise of anything which could be accomplished.

The Democrats met in San Francisco on June 28, under many disadvantages. Not the least of these was Wilson's breakdown, which was a crippling blow. The opening address was delivered by Homer S. Cummings. Practically the entire address was devoted to the League of Nations. Cummings traced the history of the movement in the United States for a league and explained the efforts of President Wilson to meet Republican criticism. Many of the criticisms of the Covenant were considered, and the charge that President Wilson demanded that the treaty should be ratified without any change whatever was dealt with at some length. The convention adopted the following statement on the League issue:

> The Democratic Party favors the League of Nations as the surest, if not the only, practicable means of maintaining the permanent peace of the world and terminating the insufferable burden of great military and naval establishments. It was for this that America broke away from traditional isolation and spent her blood and treasure to crush a colossal scheme of conquest. It was upon this basis that the President of the United States, in prearrangement with our allies, consented to a suspension of hostilities against the Imperial German Government; the armistice was granted and a treaty of peace negotiated upon the definite assurance to Germany, as well as to the powers pitted against Germany, that "a general association of nations must be formed, under specific covenants, for the purpose of affording mutual guarantees of political independence and territorial integrity to great and small states alike." Hence, we not only congratulate the President on the vision manifested and the vigor exhibited in the prosecution of the war, but we felicitate him and his associates on the exceptional achievements at Paris involved in the adoption of a league and treaty so near akin to previously expressed American ideals and so intimately related to the aspirations of civilized peoples everywhere.
>
> We commend the President for his courage and his high conception of good faith in steadfastly standing for the covenant agreed to by all the associated and allied nations at war with Germany, and we condemn the Republican Senate for its refusal to ratify the treaty merely because it was the product of Democratic statesmanship, thus interposing partisan

envy and personal hatred in the way of peace and renewed prosperity of the world.

By every accepted standard of international morality the President is justified in asserting that the honor of the country is involved in this business; and we point to the accusing fact that before it was determined to initiate political antagonism to the treaty, the new Republican Chairman of the Senate Foreign Relations Committee himself publicly proclaimed that any proposition for a separate peace with Germany, such as he and his party associates thereafter reported to the Senate, would make us "guilty of the blackest crime."

On May 15, last, the Knox substitute for the Versailles Treaty was passed by the Republican Senate; and this convention can contrive no more fitting characterization of its obloquy than that made in the Forum Magazine of December, 1918, by Henry Cabot Lodge, when he said:

> "If we sent our armies and young men abroad to be killed and wounded in Northern France and Flanders with no result but this, our entrance into war with such an intention was a crime which nothing can justify."

The intent of Congress and the intent of the President was that there could be no peace until we could create a situation where no such war as this could recur. We cannot make peace except in company with our allies. It would brand us with everlasting dishonor and bring ruin to us also if we undertook to make separate peace.

Thus to that which Mr. Lodge in saner moments, considered "the blackest crime" he and his party in madness sought to give the sanctity of law; that which eighteen months ago was of "everlasting dishonor" the Republican Party and its candidates today accept as the essence of faith.

We indorse the President's view of our international obligations and his firm stand against reservations designed to cut to pieces the vital provisions of the Versailles Treaty, and we commend the Democrats in Congress for voting against resolutions for separate peace which would disgrace the nation. We advocate the immediate ratification of the treaty without reservations which would impair its essential integrity, but do not oppose the acceptance of any reservations making clearer or more specific the obligations of the United States to the League associates.

Only by doing this may we retrieve the reputation of this nation among the powers of the earth and recover the moral leadership which President Wilson won and which Republican politicians at Washington sacrificed. Only by doing this may we hope to aid effectively in the restoration of order throughout the world and to take the place which we should assume in the front rank of spiritual, commercial and industrial advancement.

We reject as utterly vain, if not vicious, the Republican assumption that ratification of the treaty and membership in the League of Nations would in any way impair the integrity or independence of our country. The fact that the Covenant has been entered into by twenty-nine nations, all as jealous of their independence as we are of ours, is a sufficient refutation of such charge. The President repeatedly has declared, and this convention reaffirms, that all our duties and obligations as a member of the League must be fulfilled in strict conformity with the Constitution of the United States, embodied in which is the fundamental requirement of declaratory action by the Congress before this nation may become a participant in any war.

Senator Harding was formally notified of his nomination for the presidency at Marion, Ohio, on July 22. Senator Lodge gave the notification address, in the course of which he denounced the League of Nations, abjured all alliances and "internationalism," but said again that he favored the extension of the Hague conventions, the codification of international law, the establishment of a world court, and the building of international conferences. His gloss of the party platform was clearly away from *the* League or *any* league.

In accepting the nomination for the presidency, Senator Harding dealt with the League issue at length. He upheld the Republican senators for halting "the barter of independent American eminence and influence" for an "obscure and unequal place in this merged government of the world." The Republicans in the Senate did not seek to "defeat a world aspiration" but to preserve a "free and independent" America. He declared, however, that the Republican Party was committed to the establishment of an "association of nations" based on justice rather than force, which would provide security through international law "so clarified that no misconstruction can be possible without affronting national honor." He promised that after dealing with pressing domestic problems he would approach the nations of the world for the purpose of establishing this new international organization, with the clear understanding that the United States would be left "free, independent, and self-reliant."[22]

Speaking at Des Moines on October 7, Senator Harding amplified his position fully. His political opponents wanted to know, he said, whether if elected he would "scrap" the League. He answered the question by saying that the League had already been "scrapped" and explained his point thus:

> Whether President Wilson is to be blamed or thanked for the result, the fact remains that the Paris League has been "scrapped" by the hand of its chief architect. The stubborn insistence that it must be ratified without dotting an "i" or crossing a "t," the refusal to advise—that is to consult—with the Senate, in accordance with the mandate of the Constitution, is wholly responsible for that condition.

He admitted that the Democratic Party was willing to attach to the Covenant reservations of a clarifying nature. "But," he continued, "there is no need of reservations of this character. The obligations are clear and specific enough." He said that he did not oppose the League because he did not understand the Covenant but because he did understand it. "I do not want," he continued, "to clarify the obligations; I want to turn my back on them. It is not interpretation but rejection that I am seeking." He said that there should be no misunderstanding about his position; it was simply this; Cox and the Democrats favored going into the League and he favored "staying out." What he did favor was this; an association of nations which would not place the sovereign power of the United States under any "compulsion or restraint," one that would recognize American

[22] *New York Times*, July 23, 1920.

"ultimate and unmortgaged freedom of action." He would consult with the "best minds" of the United States and find out how to organize such an association.[23]

Referring again to the League in an address at Kansas City on October 8, Harding declared that Article 10 of the Covenant was the "most dangerous proposition ever presented to the American people." The reason for this was that it pledged the good faith of the United States to assist the other members of the League in "preserving the territorial integrity and political independence" of member states. He favored an association of nations in which the United States would assume no obligations, one in which "the test of righteousness" could be applied in each case before any action was taken.[24] In answer to the criticism that it would be difficult to secure the agreement of other nations to his new association, Senator Harding said that the contrary was the case. "Why, my countrymen," he explained, "France is asking; France has sent her spokesman to me informally, asking America in its new realization of the situation to lead the way for an association of nations."[25]

President Wilson publicly asked Harding if he had been quoted correctly in the press on this point. The President pointed out that it would be very extraordinary for France, a member of the League of Nations, to approach a private citizen of the United States and request him to form a new international organization. Senator Harding could only admit that France had sent no one to him, but that a private citizen of France had expressed his own opinions regarding the views of private citizens of France.[26]

Governor Cox delivered his address accepting the Democratic nomination on August 7, and devoted much of his time to the League of Nations. He discussed the general ideal of a league and the specific League provided for in the Covenant and gave his unqualified approval to both. Harding, he said,

[23] *Ibid.*, Oct. 8, 1920. Earlier Harding had promised not only to take the advice of the "best minds," but also to consult all the people of the United States. Speech at Marion, Ohio, Aug. 28.
[24] *Ibid.*, Oct. 9, 1920.
[25] *Ibid.*, Oct. 19, 1920.
[26] *Ibid.*

favored staying out of the League, and he favored going into it. Harding favored a separate peace with Germany; he favored American adherence to the peace that the United States and her war allies had already made with Germany. Harding's proposals for an association of nations were, in his opinion, futile, would bring dissensions, and in the end would produce a world situation that would be more damaging than the war had been. He was not opposed to changes in the Covenant that would not destroy it, changes that would clarify and strengthen the Covenant, that would make American obligations more specific.[27] In subsequent discussions of the league issue, Governor Cox did not change his position. He denounced as false the statements of Harding, Root, and many other Republican spokesmen that Wilson had demanded the ratification of the treaty "without dotting an 'i' or crossing a 't.'" Moreover he specified what particular changes he would agree to, offered to accept other changes which would not annul the United States' responsibilities under the Covenant or weaken the League as an effective international organization.[28]

The irreconcilable opponents of the treaty, such as Senators Borah and Johnson, were quite satisfied with Harding's complete rejection of the League in his Des Moines speech. The Republican *Philadelphia Public Ledger* admitted that the irreconcilables were supporting Harding with a "whoop" after having placed "a pistol to the head of the Republican candidate with so little secrecy that it might as well have been done on the front porch at Marion."[29] That journal, however, reacted to this circumstance in a way which was typical of many leading Republicans who claimed to favor a league of nations. It excused Harding by explaining that Johnson and Borah were of no significance and by arguing in a curious twist of reasoning, that if the party had desired to abandon the League it would have nominated Johnson for the presidency. The irreconcilables, for their part, openly denounced the attempts to cover Harding with pro-League whitewash. They stated their views

[27] *Ibid.*, Aug. 8, 1920.
[28] See *Literary Digest*, Oct. 23 and Oct 30, 1920.
[29] *Ibid.*, Oct. 23, 1920, p. 12.

clearly and frankly. Borah, for example, made it clear that he was "opposed to any political alliance, co-partnership, or league with Europe or the old world," that individuals within the Republican Party who favored a league were in the minority. He denounced the idea of harmonizing the views of Republicans on the league issue because he said the majority of the party stood united against any international league, association, combination, or alliance of any kind.[30]

Taft's decision to support Harding was a foregone conclusion. As early as November, 1919, he had written to H. M. Daugherty that he regarded Harding as a warm friend and that he was glad Harding was to be a candidate.[31] He had been a little afraid that the strategy of Lodge would be to minimize the League issue in the election and to concentrate on other items. He had, therefore, sought Root's support in getting a clarifying plank in the platform. Any attempt, he thought, to submerge the League issue would be a mistake.[32] After Harding's nomination, he immediately came out for him, and while Taft admitted that the Republican Party platform was not as direct as it could be on the League of Nations, he thought that it was satisfactory to the "practical supporters" of the League.[33] As the campaign advanced, Taft grew more vigorous in support of Harding and seemed to be confident that he could have a Republican president and the League too. He assured Lowell, without stating the facts on which he based his conclusions, that Harding would make Root Secretary of State, that with Root's assistance Lodge would secure the ratification of the treaty with the League, and that Root could then retire and Lodge would be made Secretary of State.[34]

Later on in the campaign when Harding's position on the League became more uncertain, Taft managed to accommodate his reasoning to the drift of political expediency. He somehow convinced himself and endeavored to convince others that the

[30] *New York Times*, Oct. 16, 1920.
[31] Taft to Daugherty, Nov. 26, 1919 (copy), *Taft MSS*.
[32] Taft to Lowell, June 7, 1920, *Lowell MSS*.
[33] Taft to John L. Spurgeon, June 14, 1920 (copy), *Taft MSS*.
[34] Taft to Lowell, June 22, 1920, *Lowell MSS*.

League issue was not important in the campaign. "I think," he wrote in flat defiance of the facts and of his own earlier affirmations, "that it [the League issue] has been forced in by Mr. Wilson, and that the issue he seeks to make is whether the whole League should have been sacrificed to the rejection of Article 10." He acted on this theory and rejected the League because he could not get Article 10. By formal action, the League to Enforce Peace differed with this view and sought earnestly to have the League ratified with the Lodge reservations, especially as to Article 10. The Democratic Convention by its platform adhered to the position of the President, and Mr. Cox in his acceptance speech took the same ground.[35] Since, in Taft's opinion, the Senate would not ratify the treaty without reservations, the hope of securing the League with the Lodge reservations was through the election of the Republican candidate. "There is nothing," Taft concluded, "either of a real or a practical issue, which the election can settle in respect to the League."[36]

By October, Taft had become convinced that the League issue was even less important than he had thought it was in August. "As Mr. Wilson presents it," wrote Taft, "the League is a false issue, a mere academic ideal, and I hope you will not allow yourself to be misled into an effort, by the use of such an academic issue, from voting on the real issue of the campaign, which is whether you approve the Wilson administration and wish it to be continued, or whether you do not."[37] Just before the election, in response to a letter in which Taft was vigorously denounced for having forsaken his principles and betrayed his convictions, Taft justified his acts. Article 10, he said, was not one of the original planks of the League to Enforce Peace[38] and was not important, but was simply an idea of Wilson's. The Republicans would not support Article 10, but Wilson would not abandon it, and therefore Wilson was responsible for the defeat of the treaty. Taft therefore aban-

[35] Taft to Short, Aug. 7, 1920, *League Collection.*
[36] *Ibid.*
[37] Taft to James M. Howard, Oct. 17, 1920 (copy), *Taft MSS.*
[38] See above, pages 31, 129, 139.

doned Wilson and since Cox supported Wilson's position, Taft abandoned Cox also.[39] Nothing could be more revealing of the road that Taft had taken since May, 1919, than this explanation of his own course. After the President had secured changes in the Covenant to suit the suggestions of Taft and of others, Taft had supported the League vigorously. He had singled out Article 10 for special approval and had repeatedly declared that it was the heart of the whole League structure. Now he was willing to say that Article 10 was not important. Actually what Taft had abandoned was not Wilson or Cox, for he had never supported them; he had abandoned his own principles.

Taft's views were not approved by all the Republican members of the League to Enforce Peace. Thomas W. Lamont, for example, informed Lowell that efforts had been made to induce Harding to say definitely that he favored the League with the Lodge reservations. "But," said Lamont, "he is hopeless! Frightened by the headway which Cox has made in his speeches for the League, Harding has recently wobbled about a bit. But he is clearly against the League. One of his troubles is that he knows nothing whatsoever about the League Covenant or present organization and shows that he doesn't. Meanwhile Cox has done very well. Talcott Williams is mistaken in thinking that Cox is fighting for a Simon-pure Wilson formula. He is for proper reservations and says so frankly. He has told Mr. Wilson so. He seems to have a practical mind and to know when to compromise. Taft's attitude is that Harding has made a great blunder but that after the election he will see a light and come out for the Treaty and the League. George Wickersham writes me that he can blame no Republican for voting for Cox; but in general he thinks the Democrats are a sorry crew and so he will vote for Harding. But he is really distressed at the situation.... *The Evening Post* has come out for Cox and I must confess that I approve. It distresses me to turn my back on the Republican Party, but it is no longer our old party. It has turned its coat. It is now bowing down completely to Borah, Johnson, and Moses."[40]

[39] Taft to Rev. William H. Hargrave, Nov. 1, 1920 (copy), *Taft MSS.*
[40] Lamont to Lowell, Sept. 1, 1920, *Lowell MSS.*

George W. Wickersham, former Attorney-General, was distressed at the choice before him. He thought that Harding's record on the League was bad enough, but that his apparent willingness to accept Senator Knox's idea of making peace separately with Germany was something which he had supposed no one would seriously propose. But Wickersham disliked the idea of continuing the Democrats in office more than that of having Harding. "So," said Wickersham, "what a man who entertains the opinions I do upon international relations, and yet who so thoroughly despises the Democratic Party can do, is merely to retire to private life and cultivate roses."[41] Secretary Short distrusted Harding also. He noted that Harding was saying privately to people whom he supposed favored the League that the Republicans had to oppose it for political reasons but that they did not really oppose it and if the League's friends would just trust the matter to him he would secure the ratification of the treaty. Short felt that to support Harding on such grounds would be like "supporting the Devil in order to get to Heaven."[42]

Still other Republican members of the League to Enforce Peace felt that some positive and concerted action should be taken to support Cox. One of the most energetic of this group was Professor Irving Fisher of Yale University who was one of the first supporters of the League idea and who had devoted much of his time to the League to Enforce Peace. Professor Fisher visited both Harding and Cox. Harding told Fisher that he supported the League but that since the Republican Party was divided on the subject, strategy had to be used and that he was the Marshal Foch of the Republicans. Harding said that he wanted to have a conference of the nations who had joined the League and get them to agree to the Lodge reservations as amendments. This, he thought, would not be difficult. He impressed Fisher as being rather proud of the way his campaign was planned: (1) to use Johnson to denounce the League, (2) to sidetrack Johnson before he could be nominated for the presidency, (3) to get a clever straddle-plank in the

[41] Wickersham to Short, July 20, 1920, *League Collection*.
[42] Short to Sydney J. Bowie, Sept. 7, 1920, *League Collection*.

platform to keep Johnson in the party, (4) to stampede the convention for Harding, (5) to get Taft to support Harding, (6) to make an acceptance speech which introduced new puzzles, (7) and finally to enter the League after he had forced the world to change it to suit the Republican Party.[43] Professor Fisher was not convinced that Harding knew what he was talking about, and reached the conclusion that to aid Harding was to aid the bitter opponents of the League. He did not believe that Johnson, Brandegee, Borah, and Lodge would reverse themselves and that once Harding was elected he would say the League was dead.

Professor Fisher visited Taft but found him adamant in his belief in Harding.[44] As a result of the failure to influence Taft to force Harding to take a stand either for or against the League, Professor Fisher decided to launch a new movement called the "Pro-League Independents." Hamilton Holt and Theodore Marburg, who with Fisher had sponsored the dinner conferences that led to the organization of the League to Enforce Peace, joined Fisher's organization. Other prominent members were Charles Seymour, John F. Moors, Charles W. Eliot, President Henry C. King of Oberlin College, Herbert Parsons, Mrs. Emmons Blaine, President Mary E. Woolley of Mt. Holyoke College, Caroline Hazard, former president of Wellesley College, and Moorfield Story. The Pro-League Independents issued a statement calling upon the supporters of the League of Nations to vote for Cox. In support of the plea, they cited the history of the movement for the League, noted the change that had been made in the Covenant to please such Republicans as Root and Taft, and dwelt upon the fact that the League existed in fact. They declared that a refusal of the United States to assist in the League movement would permit the outbreak of another war and would be a betrayal of the American soldiers who had fought for a better world order. They dealt at length with Taft's argument for supporting Harding, which as they saw it was a theory that since the Senate majority opposed the

---

[43] Memorandum of the conversation with Harding, Aug. 2, 1920. Copy sent to the author by Professor Fisher.
[44] Fisher to Lowell, Sept. 21, 1920, *Lowell MSS.*

treaty, the way to support the treaty was to support the opposing majority. To a large extent, therefore, the Pro-League Independents represented the view of those members of the League to Enforce Peace who did not agree with the league policy in supporting the Lodge reservations and would not follow Taft in supporting Harding.

One of the most impressive statements made by a member of the executive committee of the League to Enforce Peace was the address of Herbert Hoover at Indianapolis on October 9. Mr. Hoover said that the Republican Party had promised "to undertake the fundamental mission to put into living being the principle of an organized association of nations for the preservation of peace.... The carrying out of that promise is the test of the entire sincerity, integrity, and statesmanship of the Republican Party." He continued as follows:

> If there be persons supporting the Republican Party today on the belief or hope that this party is the avenue to destruction of this great principle, that the party will not with sincerity and statesmanship carry out their pledges to bring it into effect, then they are counting on the insincerity and the infidelity of the Republican Party and its nominee for the Presidency. If by any chance it should fail, it will have made a deeper wound in the American people than the temporary delay in our adherence to the League of Nations. It will have destroyed the confidence of our people in party government, it will have projected us into the dangerous path of party realignment. Out of these grow radicalism, reaction, and the domination of extremists in government.[45]

By the time of Mr. Hoover's address most of the prominent leaders of the League to Enforce Peace had expressed their views regarding the political campaign. Dr. Lowell, however, had as yet not made a public pronouncement. In July, he had been alarmed over reports that Harding would conduct his campaign on the basis of opposition to the League with or without reservations, and he had appealed to Root to do something about it.[46] Lowell had not been blind to the clear mean-

[45] *The New York Times*, Oct. 1, 1920.
[46] Lowell to Root, July 17, 1920, *Root MSS*.

ing of the Republican Party platform. He noted that the anti-League forces in the convention had gained the ascendancy, that "Lodge either did not have the courage of his convictions or had no convictions to have courage for," and that the League plank in the platform, although intended to be non-committal, was "rather opposed to an assumption by this country of any binding obligations under a league."[47] Lowell was in Europe during the early part of the summer. On his return, early in September, he decided to support the election of Cox, for, as he saw the situation on the day he landed, Taft and Wickersham were supporting Harding on the assumption that he did not mean what he said.[48] Some of his friends urged him to support Cox,[49] but the majority of his Republican friends urged another course, trusting that Harding would favor the League if elected.[50] He decided to draft a statement calling upon Harding to make a positive commitment to a program of action, but he was unable to get anyone "at all prominent in Republican politics" to sign the statement.[51] Later in September, Herbert Hoover also initiated a movement to get prominent Republicans to sign a statement clarifying the language and purpose of the party plank on the League, but confined to one point, to pledge the Republican Party to the principle of the preservations of peace through international association, "my point being," said Hoover, "to make it perfectly clear to the country that any other action by the Republican Party will be a betrayal of its support."[52]

There seems to have been no doubt in the minds of the principal party managers such as George Harvey and Will Hays that Harding would be elected. But men like Hoover and Lowell, who were supporting Harding, became more and more dissatisfied with the company they were keeping when they observed one after another of those whom they called

[47] Lowell to W. Murray Crane, June 16, 1920 (copy), *Lowell MSS.*
[48] Lowell to Talcott Williams, Sept. 7, 1920 (copy), *Lowell MSS.*
[49] Henry B. Cabot to Lowell, Sept. 27, 1920, *Lowell MSS.*
[50] Lowell to Thomas W. Lamont, Sept. 9, 1920 (copy), *Lowell MSS.*
[51] Lowell to Samuel Colcord, Sept. 30, 1920 (copy), *Lowell MSS.*
[52] Herbert Hoover to Lowell (telegram), Sept. 30, 1920, *Lowell MSS.*

the best elements of the party go over to the Democratic side. They were distressed too at the trend of the Republican leadership away from the League of Nations, and the stronger this trend became the more untenable was their position. The upshot of this situation was that Hays asked Root to draft a statement that would be designed to induce the pro-League Republicans to remain in the party by satisfying them that Harding was really in favor of a league. Root's statement was discussed with Hays and probably with George Harvey before it was issued, and apparently Harding's approval of it was secured.[53]

Root's statement, later signed by thirty-one Republicans, was adroitly drawn and is one of the noteworthy documents of American political history. It declared that the main issue before the country was whether the United States should join an association of nations "under an agreement containing the *exact provisions* negotiated by President Wilson at Paris or under an agreement which omits or modifies some of those provisions that are very objectionable to great numbers of the American people." The declaration went on to affirm that the "round robin" senators did not oppose international organization, and that "good evidence" indicated that the Lodge reservations would have been accepted by the other nations but that Wilson had insisted upon the "agreement *absolutely unchanged*." The declaration affirmed that the principal change in the Covenant demanded by the Republicans was a change in Article 10, which would relieve the United States of obligations under it. This article, it was asserted, raised a vital issue, for "it certainly binds every nation entering into it to go to war wherever war may be necessary to preserve the territorial integrity or political independence of any member of the League against external aggression." The Republican Party, however, "was bound by every consideration of good faith" not to attempt the creation of a new society of nations but to enter the League of Nations after the offending Article 10 and "other objections less the subject of dispute" had been removed. The conclusion reached,

[53] *The New York Times*, May 23, 25, 1923.

therefore, was that the best way to "advance the cause of international coöperation" was to elect Senator Harding.[54]

The "Statement of the 31," which weighted its argument principally against Article 10, was in complete consonance with the later declaration of its author. Speaking at Carnegie Hall on October 19, Mr. Root declared that the world was "tired of alliances to prevent war by force," that the world could not "be made good by compulsion," and that the "only line of progress is through the growth of the moral qualities that make for peace." He declared that Article 10 would preserve in perpetuity the Treaty of Versailles, that it spoke the language of power but not of progress. He held that the conception that would make Article 10 the heart of a league to preserve peace was a "negation of the opinions held by the wisest, most experienced, and most devoted men who have labored in all civilized countries for generations to advance the cause of peace."[55]

Mr. Root had never been a member of the League to Enforce Peace, had coöperated with the anti-League forces, and had written the straddle-plank on the League for the Republican Party platform. His ideas, therefore, would not be particularly important in the history of the League to Enforce Peace if it were not for the fact that many of the prominent league members accepted his leadership when they signed his statement. What kind of banner did Root's followers march under when they rallied around his standard? The idea that force could not properly be used to preserve peace was in conflict with both the league's original program and its "Victory Program." The latter declared that peace should be ensured, among other ways, by "uniting the potential force of all members as a standing menace against any nation that seeks to upset the peace of the world." Mr. Root was apparently directing his shafts against President Wilson, but they were equally centered against the members of the League to Enforce Peace. It has been repeatedly noted that during the early history of the organization, Dr. Lowell had made it very clear that if the

[54] *The New York Times*, Oct. 15, 1920 (Italics mine).
[55] *Ibid.*, Oct. 20, 1920.

league removed the idea of the use of force, it simply removed from its program the one idea that made it significant. The league existed for the support of that idea or had no reason for existence at all. Mr. Root asserted that the conception that would make Article 10 the heart of the League was a negation of the ideas of the wisest and most experienced peace advocates. Thus he placed the members of the League to Enforce Peace, as well as all the statesmen of the forty nations that had joined the League, out of the category of wise and experienced men.

A notable feature of the "Statement of the 31" was the cleverness with which the attack was focussed on Article 10. It stated that the members of the League pledged themselves "to go to war whenever war may be necessary" to preserve the territorial integrity and independence of any member of the League. As a matter of fact Article 10 did not say anything about war, but stated that the members of the League "undertake to preserve against aggression the territorial integrity and existing political independence of all members of the League." While it was perfectly true that in fulfilling this pledge nations might resort to war, they were not pledged to do so, for the second sentence of Article 10 was no less important than the first. This sentence was as follows: "In case of any such aggression or in case of any danger or threat of such aggression, the *Council shall advise* upon the means by which this obligation shall be fulfilled." The rule of unanimity prevailed in most cases in the voting of the Council of which the United States would be a member. The actual situation, therefore, in which the United States might conceivably go to war in support of the independence of a league member was a far cry from what it was represented to be in Mr. Root's analysis.

There was no essential difference, except in the extravagance of language, between the "Statement of the 31" on Article 10 and the statement made by Harding in Akron, Ohio, a few days later. "Then," said Harding, "there was Article 10, which is a very simple thing, they say—proclaimed the 'Heart of the League.' I know it is the heart of the League,—the steel heart, hidden beneath a coat of mail. Article 10 creates a world government, puts America in alliance with four great powers to rule the world by force of arms and commits America to give her sons for all the battlefields of the Old World." He went on to say that a war would break out and the League would say, "Send us over 10,000 boys," and the United States would be obliged to send them.[56] This kind of imaginary example had been the stock in trade of Senator Lodge and of every out-and-out opponent of the League from the beginning of the contest. Speaking of the "Statement of the 31," *The New York Times* said editorially: "When Republicans of distinction allow themselves so to mistake and misrepresent the facts, what is to be expected of persons less scrupulous and more fanatically partisan?"[57]

Another signal characteristic of the "Statement of the 31" was the *ex parte* character of the quotations from the Republican platform and from Senator Harding's speeches. The quotations selected were those which tended to commit the party and the candidate to the idea of a league, but nothing was said about contradictory statements that had been made by the Republican candidate. If this is overlooked as being pardonable in a political document, a similar tolerance could scarcely be accorded to the approval given to a quotation from Senator Harding's speech of August 28. The quotation ran as follows:

> There are distinctly two types of international relationship. One is offensive and defensive alliance of great powers. . . . The other type is a society of free nations, or a league of free nations animated by consideration of right and justice instead of might and self interest, and not merely proclaimed an agency in pursuit of peace, but so organized and so participated in as to make the actual attainment of peace a reasonable possibility. Such an association I favor with all my heart. . . .

The fact that such a statement was made by Senator Harding was not significant beyond showing the quality of his thought. But the selection of this quotation by Mr. Root and the ap-

[56] *The New York Times,* Oct. 29, 1920.
[57] *Ibid.*

proval of it by "the 31" raised it in significance and invited an analysis of its meaning. Senator Harding was explaining why he opposed the League of Nations and favored the creation of a new association of nations. In doing this he defined the League and characterized the nations that were members of it. The League of Nations, as he defined it, that is, the type of organization he did not like, was a "defensive and offensive alliance" not of forty nations but of the "great powers," who were animated by considerations of "might and self interest" and united for purposes other than the pursuit of peace. Senator Harding would turn his back upon these nations and their alliance and would coöperate with the "free nations" of the world for the creation of an association based on right and justice. By Senator Harding's own definition, therefore, the "free nations" were those who, in 1920, were not members of the League of Nations. It could be argued, of course, that although this is what he said, it was not what he meant. But the only other possible meaning that could be read into his language would be even less complimentary to him. The only other meaning would be that he intended to ask the nations whose motives he questioned to abandon their League and join another league which, as soon as they had joined it, would transform them into free nations animated with motives of right and justice. The whole statement, therefore, revealed a confused mind, for under critical analysis the argument contained in it became absurd.

The most obvious criticism of the "Statement of the 31" was that it was inaccurate in asserting that the Democratic Party insisted upon the ratification of the treaty without any change. This assertion in the statement was not casual or general but was repeated and specific. The statement declared that the Democrats demanded the ratification of the treaty, "absolutely unchanged," and that they insisted upon the "exact provisions" of the agreements as negotiated by President Wilson at Paris. On this point the statement was as direct, and also as inaccurate, as Senator Harding's assertion that President Wilson demanded that the treaty be ratified without "dotting an 'i' or crossing a 't'."

The "Statement of the 31" was signed by five prominent members of the executive committee of the League to Enforce Peace. They were Herbert Hoover, A. Lawrence Lowell, Oscar S. Straus, Henry W. Taft, and George W. Wickersham. It was signed also by Elihu Root, Charles Evans Hughes, and Henry L. Stimson. Dr. Lowell's mail was filled with protests against his signing of the statement. One correspondent was "hurt and shocked" that Lowell had signed a statement that would not stand the light "of scholarly investigation."[58] Another inquired whether the statement could be explained by the fact that the signers of it had some private understanding with Senator Harding.[59] Still another supposed that the signers had been given misinformation and that in the light of Harding's recent speeches they would reconsider their support of him.[60] Some of Dr. Lowell's critics were bitter at his action; all of them were sorry that he had decided to ally with the Harding side. In answering his critics, Lowell stood his ground, both regarding the purpose of the statement and its phrasing. To one person he said that the word *exact*, when used in the statement that the Democrats demanded that the treaty be ratified exactly as President Wilson had signed it, did not refer to verbiage but to the refusal of Wilson to sanction "substantial changes."[61] To another he observed that the statement was "inaccurate" but not misleading.[62] And to still another he insisted that Harding, in his Des Moines speech, had said as much as he could for the League without displeasing Senator Johnson.[63]

Soon after the publication of the "Statement of the 31," Dr. Lowell received a letter from Senator Harding which could not have been very reassuring. Lowell had written to Harding expressing his confidence that Harding would support the entry of the United States into the League of Nations. He pointed out, however, that Harding would need the support

[58] John M. Gans to Lowell, Oct. 23, 1920, *Lowell MSS*.
[59] Oswald W. Knauth, Oct. 27, 1920, *Lowell MSS*.
[60] Dr. Lowell received many letters of this sort.
[61] Lowell to John S. Codman, Nov. 10, 1920 (copy), *Lowell MSS*.
[62] Lowell to George F. Peabody, Nov. 4, 1920 (copy), *Lowell MSS*.
[63] Lowell to Paul D. Cravath, Oct. 27, 1920 (copy), *Lowell MSS*.

CONFUSION AND FAILURE   197

of the men in the nation who did not act from "selfish motives," and that the impression had been growing that "men of high aspirations" were not following him.[64] Harding replied that he believed in popular government, and he was "deeply concerned that we shall not imperil it through needless adventures in search of a world millennium for which our present imperfect human nature finds us unfitted." "There is," said Harding, "an old proverb current among the Egyptians, I am told, which says that 'a camel going in search of horns lost both its ears.' "[65]

Shortly before the election, Dr. Lowell expressed, in a letter to Mr. Short, somewhat different reasons for signing the "Statement of the 31" than he had given earlier. "We are," said Lowell, "getting jolly well criticized and abused for signing the paper of the thirty-one; but from the point of view of the League of Nations, I think it has done a great deal of good. It has gone far to prevent a victory for Mr. Harding being taken as a decision against the League; and it has encouraged Republicans who were silent to speak in favor of it. Whether it has helped Mr. Harding or not I am rather doubtful. I am inclined to think it has stirred up more interest in the League, and this, with the popular current, has tended to make people vote for Cox."[66]

In the meantime Hamilton Holt and his group of executive committee members of the League to Enforce Peace had not been inactive. Theodore Marburg, Herbert S. Houston, Charles P. Howland, John Bates Clark, Edward A. Filene, Henry Van Dyke, and others were actively engaged in supporting the election of Governor Cox. Holt sent a questionnaire to the members of the executive committee and received replies from twenty-one of them, of whom fifteen were in favor of the Democratic candidate.[67] The available evidence suggests that none of the Democratic members of the League to Enforce Peace had any difficulty in deciding to support Governor Cox. The controversy within the organization was purely among

[64] Lowell to Harding, Oct. 12, 1920 (copy), *Lowell MSS.*
[65] Harding to Lowell, Oct. 20, 1920, *Lowell MSS.*
[66] Lowell to Short, Oct. 27, 1920, *League Collection.*
[67] *The New York Times,* Oct. 27, 1920.

Republicans. Holt and his group believed that Harding was absolutely unreliable, that the Republican Party was already in the grip of the Lodge-Johnson faction, and that in supporting Harding, men like Taft and Lowell were simply giving their prestige and their moral support to a group of unscrupulous people who would cynically disregard the ideal of the League to Enforce Peace as soon as Harding was elected. They believed that it was an utter illusion to think that the issue was Wilson vs. Lodge, that is, *the* League vs. *a* league, but that Lodge was really opposed to any league and that the issue was the League vs. no league.[68] They could point to the fact that Senator Johnson had cast scorn upon the "Statement of the 31" and had characterized those people who said that the Republican Party stood for *any* league, as people who indulged either in "rank misrepresentation" or "disingenuous interpretation."[69]

The Lowell-Taft group believed that Cox would lose the election, and if all the "pro-League Republicans" supported Cox, the anti-League Republicans could say that the election was a victory for their side and abandon the League. But if the pro-League Republicans supported Harding, then it would be clear that the election had not been a referendum on the League, and the anti-League Republicans would not be able to defeat the entrance of the United States into the League. The term "pro-League Republicans," was used to indicate those who supported the Lodge reservations. Lowell and Taft assumed that Lodge did not want to defeat the treaty but only to defeat the Democratic Party, that Harding was trustworthy, and that his denunciation of the treaty was only a "sop to Cerberus." They united, therefore, with the enemies of the treaty in order to elect Harding, who would be controlled, they believed, not by the enemies of the treaty but by its "true friends," the reservationists.

The conflict of views among the Republican members of the League to Enforce Peace explains how far the unity of the organization had disintegrated, and it explains also why it was

[68] A. Barr Comstock to Lowell, Oct. 15, 1920; Henry B. Cabot to Lowell, Sept. 27, 1920; Irving Fisher to Lowell, Sept. 21, 1920, *Lowell MSS.*
[69] *Springfield Republican,* Oct. 17, 1920.

unable to do anything for the cause of the League during the campaign. Early in the year, Secretary Short thought that the weight of the organization should be placed behind the candidate who most clearly supported the League.[70] Later he wanted to send questionnaires to the various candidates for national office with the intention of forcing them to take a direct stand on the League issue. This was in accordance with the policy that had been decided upon at the meeting, already referred to, which had taken place in Taft's office. Taft now objected to the questionnaire idea, demanded flatly that the league take no part in the campaign, and threatened to resign if any action were taken.[71] It was quite obvious that if questionnaires were sent, the Democratic candidates would make the more direct and unequivocal statements favoring a league. Mr. Taft was quite correct when he insisted that the League to Enforce Peace, under the terms of its Certificate of Incorporation, could not properly take a direct part in a political campaign. But nothing in the regulations prevented it from making statements of fact. After much deliberation, the league issued a statement in which it was affirmed that the League to Enforce Peace was a nonpartisan organization founded to secure "an association of nations" to minimize war, and that "both parties have confirmed the necessity and given assurance of the foundation of such an association."[72] The statement went on to explain what had already been accomplished by the League of Nations. Short believed that this statement gave "an undeserved bill of health to the Republican Party."[73] Other than the issuance of this statement and an occasional bulletin concerning League affairs in Geneva, the League to Enforce Peace took no official action during the election contest.

Taft was delighted with the results of the presidential election. He was pleased that the Wilson administration had been "rebuked," that the people had shown their opposition to "socialistic principles," and that the Republicans would control

[70] Short to Lowell, Apr. 14, 1920, *League Collection.*
[71] Taft to Short, Aug. 7, 1920, *League Collection.*
[72] *Minutes,* Executive Committee, Sept. 18, 1920, *League Collection.*
[73] Short to Sweetser, Sept. 20, 1920, *League Collection.*

the Senate.⁷⁴ He was glad, too, that Harry M. Daugherty would occupy a high position in the Harding administration, for he thought that Daugherty was capable and would tell Harding the truth about things he needed to know.⁷⁵ Most of all, Taft professed to be pleased at Harding's attitude toward the League of Nations. Harding's plan, he said, was to send a commission to Europe to induce the great powers to revise the treaty. "In other words," said Taft, "it becomes a mere matter of conference between the leading powers and the United States as to how near they can come to the League and yet satisfy the reservations that Mr. Harding desires."⁷⁶ Taft nonchalantly reported that Root would head the mission and that one member would be an irreconcilable opponent of the treaty. Taft suggested Knox, or Brandegee, but Harding, he said, had Senator Reed in mind.⁷⁷

Taft did not have to wait very long to discover how far astray he had gone. Senator Lodge and the opponents of the League soon revealed their true colors and proclaimed that the League, as far as the United States was concerned, was dead. Nevertheless some of the reservationist Republicans clung to their illusion that the Republican Party, under Harding's leadership, would bring the United States into a revised league. No doubt they based some of their hopes upon the fact that Charles E. Hughes, who had signed the "Statement of the 31," became Secretary of State, and Herbert Hoover, who had said that the pledge of the Republican Party to enter an association of nations was the test of its "entire sincerity, integrity, and statesmanship," also accepted a cabinet post. They persisted in their illusion, until President Harding, in his special message to Congress on April 12, 1921, pulled the props from under their feet. He denounced the Covenant, merely *hoped* for an association of nations, and proposed the ratification of the Treaty of Versailles with the Covenant deleted and with proper reservations and modifications that would commit the United States to nothing.

⁷⁴ Taft to Mrs. William Hooper, Nov. 8, 1920 (copy), *Taft MSS*.
⁷⁵ Taft to Charles D. Hilles, Dec. 18, 1920, *Taft MSS*.
⁷⁶ Taft to Lowell, Jan. 10, 1921, *Lowell MSS*.
⁷⁷ Taft to Lowell, Jan. 3, 1921, *Lowell MSS*.

CONFUSION AND FAILURE

Secretary Short had been restive even before April 12. He had written to Taft that if Harding capitulated to the "irreconcilables" and if the League to Enforce Peace stood by and said nothing, they would be "fearfully and lastingly discredited in the eyes of the moral and progressive forces in the country."[78] Taft, however, was as serene as ever and was ready with a reassuring and sanguine explanation. He did not think Harding's message was against the League, but that Harding was "merely postponing giving details," while he was "working out the situation as its necessities develop."[79] Taft opposed any attempt of the League to Enforce Peace to influence Harding, and, as of old, threatened to resign if it followed any other course.[80] Taft had already learned that President Harding intended to nominate him for the Chief-Justiceship of the Supreme Court.[81] When the nomination was made, Taft resigned his presidency of the League to Enforce Peace, and his place was taken by Dr. Lowell.[82]

Lowell, as President of the League to Enforce Peace, showed almost as much faith as Taft in the government and in Secretary Hughes. He felt confident that Hughes would lead the United States into a league and that their organization should do what it could to sustain his efforts.[83] But the State Department and the government moved in the opposite direction. A separate treaty of peace was negotiated with Germany, and Secretary Hughes scorned the League and all of its works.[84] In July, 1922, he wrote to Dr. Lowell, "The President does not think, and I entirely agree with him, that he should refer again, at this time, to his desire for an Association of Nations. . . ."[85] Secretary Hoover maintained an eloquent silence on the League question.

[78] Short to Taft, Apr. 9, 1921 (copy), *League Collection.*
[79] Taft to Short, Apr. 12, 1921, *League Collection.*
[80] *Ibid.*
[81] Pringle, *op. cit.*, II, 956.
[82] *Minutes,* Executive Committee, Oct. 19, 1921, *League Collection.*
[83] *Minutes,* meeting of the Executive Committee, Apr. 23, 1921, *League Collection.*
[84] See Denna Frank Fleming, *The United States and World Organization, 1920-1933* (New York, Columbia University Press, 1938), pp. 60-78.
[85] Hughes to Lowell, July 20, 1922, *Lowell MSS.*

In the meantime, the League to Enforce Peace had virtually ceased to exist. Moribund since the election of 1920, its income declined to the zero point, and it became inactive in April 1922, although it maintained a semblance of existence until October 21, 1923.

Slowly, to be sure, but inevitably, Dr. Lowell realized that he had been misled by those whom he had trusted, and that the "Statement of the 31" had been repudiated.[86] His position was indeed unenviable. He was the head of one of the world's great institutions of learning and he was a man of probity. Others might be content to remain silent or to decide not to "refer again" to their pledges, but he simply could not afford to follow their examples. And he did not intend to do so. Through his efforts, the signers of the statement were invited to a dinner meeting to be held in New York on May 16.[87] Lowell hoped that a declaration could be agreed upon demanding that the administration fulfill its solemn pledge concerning an association of nations. The meeting was held, some of "the 31" attended, but no action was taken. In demanding action, Lowell stood alone.[88]

On the day on which the dinner meeting was held, *The New York Times* published an extract of a letter from President Harding, written in answer to an inquiry about his promise to lead the United States into an association of nations. Mention was made in the inquiry regarding the promise of the famous "31." The President's answer was this:

> During the campaign of 1920, many men of many minds expressed widely varying views upon issues then before the public. The nominee for President expressed upon the subject which you present his own views and those which he expected to support in case he should be elected. The fact that some others should have placed a differing interpretation upon the issues of the campaign, was, of course, entirely their own affair. . . .[89]

---

[86] Lowell later wrote to Short that Hughes had accepted the aid of the pro-League Republicans and then abandoned them. Aug. 27, 1924 (copy), *Lowell MSS*.
[87] Lowell to Wickersham, Dec. 18, 1922 (copy), *Lowell MSS*.
[88] Lowell to John Grier Hibben, May 30, 1923 (copy), *Lowell MSS*.
[89] *The New York Times*, May 16, 1923. *The Times* did not print in full

CONFUSION AND FAILURE

Earlier in the year, in a message to Congress, President Harding had referred to the League thus:

> I have no unseemly comment to offer on the League. It is serving the Old World helpfully, more power to it. But it is not for us. The Senate has so declared, the executive has so declared, the people have so declared. Nothing could be more decisively stamped with finality.

In both of these statements, the President, in effect, denied that he had ever promised to lead the United States into an association of nations, or that he had ever approved of the "Statement of the 31." He gave the signers of that document the lie, and left them to choose whether they were frauds or dupes. This was too much for Dr. Lowell. If "the 31" would not act with him, he would act alone. His opportunity came when he was invited to deliver an address, under the auspices of the League of Nations Non-Partisan Association in Washington on May 23, 1923. His statement was very mild. The President, he said, in affirming that the American people had passed judgment against the League of Nations in the election of 1920, had "gone too far." Lowell then quoted passage after passage from the President's speeches in which Harding denied that the issue between himself and Governor Cox was the League or none, but affirmed that it was the League or a modified league.[90]

Dr. Lowell's address elicited considerable comment, particularly in the pro-League press, but only one signer of the "Statement of the 31" publicly came to Lowell's defense.[91] Other signers either could not be reached by inquiring newspaper men or had no comment to make. "Secretary Hoover," it was reported, "was busily engaged all day and no statement from him was obtained."[92] Dr. Lowell's address, which was a

---

the last sentence of Harding's letter. Continuing after the word "affair," the letter read: "but I think that would hardly be regarded as justifying the nominee, after his election by so decisive a majority, in changing his own attitude." The letter was dated Apr. 30, 1923 (copy), *Lowell MSS*.

[90] *The New York Times*, May 24, 1923.
[91] President John Grier Hibben of Princeton.
[92] *The New York Times*, May 26, 1923.

testimony to his own personal integrity, marked the end of the League to Enforce Peace, and the circumstances under which it was given demonstrated what had taken place in the moral structure of American political life.

Yet the story is not quite complete. An extract from a letter written by a member of the league on June 10, 1919, will suffice:

> As a returned soldier without, I hope, any too high opinion of the small part he played himself, I cannot escape the feeling that in this partisan dallying with the League of Nation's Covenant, this country is being trifled with, and all the mighty sacrifice of millions held a light thing.

CHAPTER SEVEN

Perspective

INSISTENT QUESTIONS have constantly hovered in the background of this study. Why were the American people apparently content with the default of their leaders? Why did the peace movement of a century and the enormous impetus given to it by the League to Enforce Peace and by President Wilson suddenly collapse, until, in Lowell's opinion at least, the people were grateful to those who had killed and buried the League of Nations? It is hoped that in the preceding pages many answers to these questions are implicit. Since, however, the League to Enforce Peace has been examined with close and minute scrutiny, it may be well, in leaving it, to take a backward glance and observe its stature against the sky.

President Wilson was anxious that the war should end as soon as his main objective, the complete military defeat of the Central Powers, had been achieved. Germany requested an armistice, that is a cessation of fighting, each belligerent remaining *in statu quo* until a treaty of peace could be negotiated. President Wilson refused this request. He negotiated with Germany, however, for the purpose of ending the war, and then negotiated with the Allies regarding their acceptance of his tentative arrangements with Germany. Further negotiations led to the Pre-Armistice Agreement, which was the precise legal basis for the treaty of peace. Under this agreement, Germany accepted military defeat. The terms of her *capitulation*, subsequently and improperly called the Armistice, were handed to her later. On their part, the Allied and Associated Powers agreed to make certain arrangements in Europe and in the world, and one of these was the establishment of a league of nations. The Pre-Armistice Agreement, therefore, was a *negotiated* peace in the sense that Germany surrendered on terms. When she had fulfilled her obligations, she had a right to expect that the Allies would fulfill theirs. Thus the "Peace Conference" at Paris was not exactly a *peace* conference, but rather a conference among the victorious powers for the purpose of carrying out what they had promised to do under the Pre-Armistice Agreement.

These are the facts, and they are inescapable, but confusion arose about them because circumstances inherent in the nature of the peace negotiations impeded the logical march of events. These circumstances should be noted with particular attention. If the Pre-Armistice Agreement had been called the treaty of peace and had been submitted to the Senate for ratification, one of two conditions would have prevailed. Hostilities would have continued while the Senate debated, or else an actual armistice would have been granted to Germany. To accept the former would have been to negate the purpose of the agreement which was to end the war without further bloodshed as soon as all American and Allied objectives had been achieved. To accept the latter would have given Germany a chance to reorganize and to prolong the war by refusing to accept the terms of capitulation. To put the matter in other words, Germany's acceptance of the Armistice terms, military surrender, was predicated upon the pledge of the United States and the Allies. In order to achieve his objectives, therefore, the President was obliged to make a political agreement and to pledge the good faith of his country for its fulfillment in the hope that when the pledge was actually fulfilled at the Paris Conference the Senate would approve what he had done.

In this complex situation, brought about partly by the peculiar constitutional situation in the United States and partly by the way in which the war ended, and involving the quasi-misuse of the terms "agreement," "armistice," and "peace conference," it is extremely doubtful that the American people realized what they were doing when they finally turned their backs upon the Treaty of Versailles. They placed the United States in the unfortunate position of having misleadingly induced Germany to surrender and of being the first, of all the nations involved in the war, to abandon its pledges. Germany, it must be noted, contributed to the confusion of American thought and profoundly assisted the anti-League forces in the United States. For, in utter blindness to her own interests, and in flat contradiction to her pre-armistice demands, she denounced the treaty instead of insisting upon America's acceptance of it. This was Germany's first and fatal blunder in the post-war world. The anti-League people, in their hatred of Wilson, joined their recent enemies, the Germans, and decried the treaty also. Thus the true perspective with which the treaty should have been observed was not easy to attain by the rank and file of the people, who naturally depended more upon the opinions of their leaders than upon their own analysis of such complex matters.

Another factor which contributed to the default of the United States in 1919-1920 was the tradition that had developed regarding the danger of alliances. There was no denying the fact that to join the League of Nations was to join an international alliance involving commitments to act in certain ways and limiting the nation's arbitrary freedom of action in other ways. When Senator Harding talked about having a league of nations effective for the preservation of peace, which at the same time would leave the United States free to do as it pleased in international affairs, he was talking utter nonsense. But the idea of entering upon an alliance frightened many people. The United States had never made but one alliance, that of 1778 with France. This was entered into at a time of great necessity for the American states during the Revolution, and served a useful purpose, but was abandoned with almost unseemly haste the moment it ceased to be essential. Certain "warnings" of Washington and Jefferson regarding alliances were familiar to the people, although the contexts in which these "warnings" appeared were not well known, and their irrelevance to the League was frequently not considered. Thus the mere word alliance had an ominous sound. Clear explanations were needed to point out the character of alliances such as Washington and Jefferson opposed and alliances for establishing balances of power, one group of nations against another, such as Wilson himself opposed, and the nature of a league system which by its very nature was also an alliance.

These two illustrations—and many more could be added—are probably sufficient to indicate the reasons why the mass of the voters simply could not be expected resolutely to steer a straight course through the welter of conflicting arguments regarding the Treaty of Versailles unless some leadership existed which could show them the way with such clarity of thought and language and with such compelling logic that they could not be misled. There were two possible sources for this leadership: President Wilson and the League to Enforce Peace. The President was supremely confident that the people were capable of understanding, and for the most part did understand, what the League of Nations really meant to the United States and to the world. Wilson believed that if he could talk to them, so to speak, he could dissipate their fears about alliances and other matters over which they were confused. For this reason he undertook his tour of the nation in behalf of the League. No one can say whether he would have been successful, for he became physically unable to complete his undertaking. In any event, the President's collapse, in addition to the failure of the League to Enforce Peace to remain a steadfast and clarifying agency of leadership, allowed the people to become the easy prey of those who promised them a league of nations which would have all of the advantages and none of the alleged liabilities of the existing League.

The crucial fact to keep in mind is that the majority of the American people, by May, 1919, were convinced that the United States should join with the other nations of the world in establishing *a* league of nations and were quite willing that it should be *the* League.

Some of the leaders of the Republican Party possibly thought that they could oppose the League without destroying the confidence of their political followers in the league idea. This was their tragic error, and it marked their failure as statesmen. For if the Covenant needed only minor changes, not only was the President willing to make them, but it was obvious also that the nation could safely adhere to the Covenant and rely upon the League itself to make such revisions. They were forced, therefore, in order to sustain their opposition to the Covenant, to declare that it was a dangerous alliance, that under it American freedom of action would be unwisely curtailed, that American sovereignty would be impaired, that the Monroe Doctrine would be endangered, and that the use of force in international affairs was evil. They succeeded in disseminating these fears, and once they had succeeded they could not undo what they had done without admitting that they had misinformed the people in the first instance. Thus the price of victory in defeating "Wilson's League" was the destruction of whatever hope they may have had of establishing "Harding's Association."

During the major part of its history, 1915-1919, the League to Enforce Peace spent its main effort in explaining the general principles of world organization and in advocating *a* league of nations. During this time it had various plans of its own: its original platform, its War Program, its Victory Program, and its design for an association of nations drafted by its Studies Committee. These various plans were given appropriate attention, but the league never insisted upon their adoption. They were practical examples of what could be done. Later the league urged the acceptance by the United States of *the* League of Nations. As long as the League to Enforce Peace advocated either *a* league or *the* League it maintained internal unity and met with great success. The very moment that some of its most prominent leaders ceased to support the government in its struggle for *the* League, and on their own initiative began to advocate, so to speak, their *own* league, by proposing amendments to the revised Covenant that had been adopted by the nations assembled at Paris, the League to Enforce Peace disintegrated. It not only dissipated its strength during the crucial contest for *the* League, which it had advocated, but actually transferred much of its prestige and influence to the anti-League forces. Thus by a curious and disastrous inversion of its policies it contributed substantially, and perhaps even decisively, to the defeat of its own objectives.

Until the League to Enforce Peace split into factions, its success was almost incredible. The President and the people of the United States were so fully in support of its cause that the establishment of a league of nations became their principal peace objective, one of the objectives of the Allies, and, it is probably safe to say, the hope of the civilized world. The League to Enforce Peace was not directly responsible for this world-wide situation or even solely responsible for the attitude of the United States. But it greatly influenced American thought, which in turn had a powerful impact upon the world.

There were, however, during this time of the league's success, ominous portents of its failure which were either not particularly noticed at the time, or, being noticed, were not considered insurmountable. Senator Lodge, taking particular care to emphasize his leadership in the Republican Party, abandoned the league's cause the very moment it was publicly espoused by President Wilson. He secured the elimination of a pro-league plank from his party's national platform in 1916, bitterly denounced the President's peace program during the political campaign of 1918, refused to suggest changes in the Covenant while changes were possible, and then demanded changes in the revised Covenant without having studied the document. Equally ominous were Taft's actions: his declaration in 1916 that the platform of the Republican Party endorsed the league idea, his attacks upon President Wilson, and particularly his collaboration with anti-league politicians in support of the election of anti-league congressmen and senators.

But these portents, as has been noted, were obscured by other events or circumstances. It has always been a characteristic of American political life that more consideration is given by the people to the words and acts of a political leader, especially a presidential candidate, than to the platform upon which he stands. Thus when Mr. Hughes announced his support of the league idea, the divergent action of his party's convention did not seem to be significant. Moreover, the mass of the people did not know, nor did the membership of the League to Enforce Peace know, that the pro-league plank had been withdrawn from the first draft of the Republican platform. This fact was known to Mr. Taft, but for some unexplained reason he chose to consider that the convention had endorsed the league. It could hardly be expected that as President of the League to Enforce Peace Taft would urge that organization to combat the action of the Republican National Convention when, as a private citizen, he had declared that no such action had taken place. And when Taft collaborated with anti-League politicians one day but advocated the League the next, his collaboration with the anti-League people, and even the fact that they were such, tended to be overlooked. And finally, when Taft was confronted with the anti-League tendencies within his party, he always asserted that the party would not *dare* oppose a league of nations at the end of the war and that if it did he would bolt the party. If it is remembered, too, that the most prominent leaders of the League to Enforce Peace were Republicans, that many lesser Republican politicians favored a league, and that a large number of the rank and file of the party were outstanding in their support of the league idea, it is not strange that these portents were not considered dangerous to the league's cause.

Between the end of the war and the end of the peace conference at Paris, the League to Enforce Peace steadfastly stood its ground. During that period it took the position, quite accurately, that, as Dr. Lowell said, the President had virtually staked his reputation before posterity upon his advocacy of a league of nations, and that the League to Enforce Peace could best serve its own and the President's cause by sustaining him both at home and abroad during the conference. This it did with great energy. Taft was in the forefront of the fight at home, while Holt and Straus led the fray in Paris. The league's agents in Paris denounced the rumor, instigated by Lodge and others, that the President was not supported at home and that the Republican Party, which controlled the Senate, would not support a league if one were adopted. Their most effective argument, and indeed the most positive fact they could cite in supporting it, was the character of the League to Enforce Peace: its size and influence, the cast of its leadership, and its pledge to support the President in his struggle for a league.

When the first draft of the Covenant was published, the leaders of the League to Enforce Peace publicly approved it. They were frightened, however, by the opposition that was being aroused against it and suggested several amendments which in their opinion would improve the Covenant, satisfy all reasonable objections to it, and insure its ratification by the Senate. These suggestions, *all of them*, together with others, were accepted by the President and were adopted by the Paris conference. As soon as this was accomplished, the League to Enforce Peace declared that, in the premises, further attempts to amend the Covenant would be the same as opposition to it, that reservations were not essentially different from amendments, and that the issue before the nation was *the* League or *none*. This declaration was consistent with the league's previous policies and acts. It could honorably do nothing else. For it had virtually prodded the President at every step on his pro-league course, had pledged him its support, and could not abandon him without stultifying itself.

Soon, however, the league faltered, and after a period of confusion, capitulated to the forces who by the league's own definition were the opponents of the League of Nations. Taft blithely led the way; Lowell followed; and they carried with them probably a majority of the league's leaders into the camp of their political associates, the League's opponents. In a sense, however, the damage had already been done when Taft was won over by the anti-League people. Thereafter the Lodge-Root-Borah coalition knew that they had nothing to fear from a divided League to Enforce Peace. In a sense, too, this capitulation was the beginning of the moral collapse of America in the postwar era. It was the prelude to the tragic default of the famous "31," and it was the first of many milestones along the road to Pearl Harbor.

The thesis may be presented that the failure of the League to Enforce Peace to remain steadfast in its original position regarding the Covenant was of less importance in the ultimate rejection of the Covenant by the Senate than is indicated in the preceding pages. No one can ever know what would have happened if it had remained steadfast, and therefore no one can disprove the assertion that the treaty would have been defeated no matter what the League to Enforce Peace did. This history is concerned with what happened and not with what might have happened, and with the League to Enforce Peace rather than with the whole American struggle over the League of Nations. It may well be, however, that the reasons for the collapse of internal unity within the League to Enforce Peace were also the reasons for the failure of the larger movement for the League. Indeed this is probably true.

It is doubtful that Taft ever really supported the kind of league that Wilson wanted. For the President thought of the League as an agency for extending internationally many of the ideas which had received national application during the earlier years of his administration. He saw in the League the end of imperialism, the reduction of armaments, the decline of militarism, the removal of trade barriers, the improvement of labor conditions, and the end of special privilege everywhere among nations as well as among individuals. People like Taft and Root were willing enough to have a league for the settlement of international disputes but they had no real vision of a world system which would not function properly without the abandonment of national policies which they had traditionally supported and still advocated. If this analysis is accurate, and it is only suggested here, then it provides a clue to the collapse of the League to Enforce Peace which is not indicated in its more formal and in its documentary history.

It seems reasonably clear that Lodge and Root intended not only to discredit the League in order to discredit Wilson, but also particularly intended to discredit Wilson's reform program. Taft was as anxious as Root or Lodge to discredit Wilson, and the former Progressives, such as Beveridge, Borah, and La Follette, all of them either isolationists or imperialists, were determined to defeat the League. Here then was the material for political combination that could be united for one purpose only, the defeat of "Wilsonism." If this line of thought is followed it is easy to see that Wilson, in opposing reservations, was not opposing alterations to the Covenant exactly, but was opposing the type of mind and the political forces that produced the reservations. To him there was little difference between no league of nations and a league dominated by men whose outlook was that of Lodge, Borah, or Beveridge.

Whenever the entire history of the struggle over the League in the United States is written it will be necessary to place that struggle into the larger American scene indicated above. But no matter how broadly the subject is conceived, it will be true that the League to Enforce Peace had the greatest opportunity of any organized group to direct the American people into a policy of enlightened world leadership. How that opportunity was gained and how it was lost must always be a significant if indeed a tragic chapter in world history.

In one sense, both the League to Enforce Peace and the League of Nations failed, for the United States did not join the League, which in turn was unable to prevent a second world war more far-flung and more barbarous than the first. But in another sense neither failed, for the League of Nations represented the greatest and farthest advance the world has ever known toward the goal of world peace, and the movement that created it came most clearly and directly from the United States. As these words are written the Second World War still darkens the earth. But when the war is won, the peace-loving nations will be able to take up their tasks of reconstruction with all the experience that the League's failures as well as its less appreciated successes have provided.

Appendix I

THE NATIONAL PROVISIONAL COMMITTEE FOR A LEAGUE OF PEACE

William Howard Taft, Ex-President of the United States
Jacob M. Dickinson, Ex-Secretary of War
Victor H. Metcalf, Ex-Secretary of the Navy
Oscar S. Straus, Member of the Hague Court
Judge George Gray, Member of the Hague Court
Theodore Marburg, Ex-Minister to Belgium
A. Lawrence Lowell, President of Harvard University
John Grier Hibben, President of Princeton University
James Cardinal Gibbons
John Sharp Williams, United States Senator from Mississippi
William Allen White, Editor of the *Emporia Gazette*
Andrew D. White, Educator and Diplomatist
Benjamin Ide Wheeler, President of the University of California
Edwin A. Alderman, President of the University of Virginia
John Mitchell, Labor Leader
James B. McCreary, Governor of Kentucky
Alton B. Parker, Jurist
John Bassett Moore, Professor in Columbia University
David Starr Jordon, Chancellor of Leland Stanford University
Homer H. Johnson, President of the Cleveland Chamber of Commerce
Darwin P. Kingsley, President of the New York Life Insurance Company
Harry A. Wheeler, Banker
Theodore S. Woolsey, Professor in Yale University
George Grafton Wilson, Professor in Harvard University
Charles R. Van Hise, President of the University of Wisconsin
Caspar F. Goodrich, Rear Admiral in the United States Navy
Rudolph Blankenburg, Mayor of Philadelphia
Alexander Graham Bell, Scientist and Inventor
James M. Beck, Ex-Assistant Attorney General
Henry A. Buchtel, Ex-Governor of Colorado

APPENDICES

Philander P. Claxton, United States Commissioner of Education
Hamilton Holt, Editor of *The Independent*
J. E. Ingraham, Railway Operator
William H. P. Faunce, President of Brown University
C. T. Tatman, Lawyer
Henry C. Morris, President of the Chicago Peace Society
John Hays Hammond, Mining Engineer
Irving Fisher, Professor in Yale University
Charles R. Brown, Dean of the Yale Divinity School
Lyman Abbott, Editor of *The Outlook*
William B. Howland, President of *The Independent*
Frederic R. Coudert, Lawyer
John A. Stewart, Chairman of the Peace Centenary Committee
Oliver Wilson, Master of the National Grange
Harold J. Howland, Associate Editor of *The Independent*
Frank Crane, Editorial Writer, Associated Newspapers
Rabbi J. Leonard Levy
Frederick N. Judson, Lawyer
Charles Cheney Hyde, Professor in Northwestern University
James B. Angell, Educator and Diplomatist
Rabbi Stephen Wise
William C. Dennis, Former Assistant Solicitor of the Department of State
Woodbridge N. Ferris, Governor of Michigan
Francis E. Clark, Founder of the United Society of Christian Endeavor
Rabbi Emil G. Hirsch
Luther B. Wilson, Bishop in Methodist Episcopal Church
George H. Prouty, Ex-Governor of Vermont
William H. Short, Secretary of The New York Peace Society
Victor Rosewater, Editor of the *Omaha Bee*
John H. Finley, New York Commissioner of Education
Winston Churchill, Author
George H. Blakeslee, Professor in Clark University
Warner Williams, President of the Colorado State Board of Peace Commissioners
John Bates Clark, Professor in Columbia University
George A. Plimpton, Publisher

APPENDICES 217

Albert Bushnell Hart, Professor in Harvard University
Nathan C. Schaeffer, Pennsylvania State Superintendent of Public Instruction
Franklin H. Giddings, Professor in Columbia University
Talcott Williams, Director of the School of Journalism in Columbia University
Joseph Swain, President of Swarthmore College
Leo S. Rowe, President of the American Academy of Political and Social Studies
Charles F. Thwing, President of Western Reserve University
R. Fulton Cutting, Financier
John M. Whitehead, Lawyer
Albert Shaw, Editor of *The American Review of Reviews*
John Barrett, General Director of the Pan-American Union
Henry St. George Tucker, Professor in George Washington University
Frank S. Streeter, Lawyer
Jeremiah W. Jenks, Professor in New York University
Edgar Odell Lovett, President of Rice Institute
Rowland G. Hazard, Manufacturer
Washington Gladden, Author, Clergyman
William Dudley Foulke, Former Member United States Civil Service Commission
Gutzon Borglum, Sculptor
William O. Hart, President of the Louisiana Historical Association
Isaac N. Seligman, Banker
Perry Belmont, Former Chairman of the Committee on Foreign Affairs
Jacob H. Schiff, Banker
Samuel P. Brooks, President of Baylor University
George Burnham, Jr., Civil Engineer
A. T. Clearwater, Lawyer
Samuel T. Dutton, Educator
Elmer E. Brown, Chancellor of New York University
George C. Holt, United States District Judge, Southern District of New York
Howard B. French, Manufacturer

Bayard Henry, Lawyer
Robert Sharp, President of Tulane University
Frederick Lynch, Secretary of the Church Peace Union
Samuel W. McCall, Governor of Massachusetts, 1916-1917
Samuel C. Mitchell, President of Delaware College
Cyrus Northrop, President Emeritus of the University of Minnesota
Odin Roberts, Lawyer
John C. Shaffer, President and Publisher of the *Chicago Evening Post*
William A. Shanklin, President of Wesleyan University
Edgar F. Smith, Provost of University of Pennsylvania
Everett P. Wheeler, Lawyer
John M. Thomas, President of Middlebury College
James L. Tryon, Director of the American Peace Society
W. H. Vary, Master of the New York State Grange
Anton C. Weiss, Editor of *The Duluth Herald*
Thomas Raeburn White, Lawyer
Henry Sturgis Drinker, President of Lehigh University
Andrew B. Humphrey, Secretary of the American Peace and Arbitration League

Appendix II

PLATFORM ADOPTED BY LEAGUE TO ENFORCE PEACE

AT THE "WIN THE WAR FOR PERMANENT PEACE" CONVENTION PHILADELPHIA, MAY 17, 1918

Assembled in a great Win-the-War Convention in this city of its birth, the League to Enforce Peace reaffirms its pledge to these two supreme duties, each essential to the other and both essential to the cause of human freedom:

I.—To make the world safe, by the defeat of Germany and German militarism.

II.—To keep the world safe by a League of Nations.

SUPPORT THE PRESIDENT

The League to Enforce Peace pledges unstinted support to the commander-in-chief of our army and navy, the President of the United States, and to all others in authority in all measures for victory over the military power of the Kaiser, realizing that such victory is the primary condition of lasting peace and the necessary basis for a League of Nations.

The League, standing for international law and justice, declares until Germany is overcome the paramount and pressing duty of the United States and the other free nations, with which this country is allied, is to fight with unconquerable determination for a victorious peace.

WARNING AGAINST A GERMAN PEACE

And, apprehensive of the lure of an inconclusive peace, which would enable the present masters of Germany to continue their dominion of Central Europe and sooner or later to menace again the peace and freedom of the world, the League feels that our people should be forewarned, in case Germany should propose to make peace on terms that might well deceive the unsuspecting. Suppose she should offer to retire from Belgium and France; to cede the Trentino to Italy; even to relinquish all claims to her captured colonies, and to promise some kind of autonomy to the various races of Central and Eastern Europe. Such an offer would be highly seductive, and if we are not prepared to understand what it means might well beguile the Allies into a peace which would be delusive; because unless the principle of militarism is destroyed, the promises would be kept no better than those broken in the past. Autonomy of other races would mean their organization for the strengthening of Germany; until she had control of the resources of a population of two hundred millions for her next war; and the abandonment of her former colonies would be made only with the hope of recoupment in South America on a more favorable occasion. Such a settlement would be a mere truce pending a strife more fierce hereafter. So long as the predatory militarism is not wholly destroyed no lasting peace can be made.

COÖPERATION OF LABOR

We welcome the declaration of the Representatives of Organized Labor in our convention and elsewhere that the workingmen of this country sympathize with these views, recognize the vital concern that they, in common with all who love liberty and equality of opportunity, have in the striking down of militarism and the formation of a League of Nations to maintain permanent peace. We rejoice in the pledge of the Leaders of Organized Labor that they and those for whom they speak will strain every nerve to secure top speed and one hundred per cent. efficiency in Labor's part of the needed production of war material. With them, we declare that all persons or groups of persons who in open or private collusion with persons in enemy countries attempt to initiate peace negotiations independently of the government are guilty of violating fundamental principles of Democratic government, based upon the consent of the people.

THE ULTIMATE AIM

Our fathers were wise because they looked the facts of their day in the face, discerning clearly the signs of their time; and we shall follow their example by doing the same in our day. The time has come for their heirs to take part in a League of Nations to maintain an enduring peace here and elsewhere. With faith in our purpose, with constancy in effort and sagacity in action, we must finish the work we have begun, until the principle for which we fight stands victorious and unquestioned; and then we must build a structure that, so far as human wisdom can reach, will banish the scourge of war from among men.

Appendix III

A LEAGUE OF FREE NATIONS

VICTORY PROGRAM

Adopted at a meeting of the Executive Committee, held in New York, November 23, 1918, as the official platform of the League to Enforce Peace, superseding the proposals adopted at the organization of the League in Philadelphia, June 17, 1915.

The war now happily brought to a close has been above all a war to end war, but in order to ensure the fruits of victory

APPENDICES 221

and to prevent the recurrence of such a catastrophe there should be formed a League of Free Nations, as universal as possible, based upon treaty and pledged that the security of each state shall rest upon the strength of the whole. *The initiating nucleus* of the membership of the League should be the nations associated as belligerents in winning the war.

The League should aim at promoting the *liberty, progress, and fair economic opportunity* of all nations, and the orderly development of the world.

It should ensure peace by eliminating causes of dissension, by deciding controversies by peaceable means, and by uniting the potential force of all the members as a standing menace against any nation that seeks to upset the peace of the world.

The advantages of membership in the League, both economically and from the point of view of security, should be so clear that all nations will desire to be members of it.

For this purpose it is necessary to create—

1. *For the decision of justiciable questions*, an impartial tribunal whose jurisdiction shall not depend upon the assent of the parties to the controversy; provision to be made for enforcing its decisions.

2. For questions that are not justiciable in their character, a *Council of Conciliation*, as mediator, which shall hear, consider, and make recommendations; and failing acquiescence by the parties concerned, the League shall determine what action, if any, shall be taken.

3. *An administrative organization* for the conduct of affairs of common interest, the protection and care of backward regions and internationalized places, and such matters as have been jointly administered before and during the war. We hold that this object must be attained by methods and through machinery that will ensure both stability and progress; preventing, on the one hand, any crystallization of the *status quo* that will defeat the forces of healthy growth and changes, and providing, on the other hand, a way by which progress can be secured and necessary change effected without recourse to war.

4. *A representative Congress* to formulate and codify rules

of international law, to inspect the work of the administrative bodies and to consider any matter affecting the tranquility of the world or the progress or betterment of human relations. Its deliberations should be public.

5. *An Executive Body*, able to speak with authority in the name of the nations represented, and to act in case the peace of the world is endangered.

The representation of the different nations in the organs of the League should be in proportion to the responsibilities and obligations they assume. The rules of international law should not be defeated for lack of unanimity.

A resort to force by any nation should be prevented by a solemn agreement that any aggression will be met immediately by such an overwhelming *economic and military force* that it will not be attempted.

No member of the League should make any other offensive or defensive treaty or alliance, and *all treaties* of whatever nature made by any member of the League *should at once be made public*.

Such a League must be formed at the time of the definitive peace, or the opportunity may be lost forever.

Appendix IV

TENTATIVE DRAFT OF A TREATY FOR A LEAGUE OF NATIONS

APPROVED BY THE EXECUTIVE COMMITTEE OF THE LEAGUE TO ENFORCE PEACE, NEW YORK, APRIL 11, 1918

1. The parties to this treaty hereby form a League of Nations for the promotion and preservation of future peace. The members of the League shall be the states that join the same at its formation, and any other independent states that may be at any time admitted by a majority (or two-thirds) vote of the Congress hereinafter described. Adhesion to the League, on the part both of the original and subsequent states, shall, in the case of each state, be ratified by the treaty making authority and approved by the legislative authority thereof; but such

ratification and approval shall not deprive any organ of government in any state of its constitutional rights.

2. There shall be three groups of members of the League: Those states which assume the full responsibilities of the League, with the duty, when its provisions are to be enforced, of using their whole economic and military power as provided in section 17.

States which in case of economic enforcement shall take the same commercial measures as the states of the first group; and in case of enforcement by arms shall declare war against the common foe and shall be under no obligation to furnish military forces except as they may find practicable. By reason of their lesser responsibilities they shall have a smaller representation in the organs of the League.

Neutralized states that are to take no part in the enforcement. These shall be perpetually neutral, and shall engage in no war, unless invaded, when they shall be defended by the whole force of the League. They agree to accept and carry out all decisions of both the Court and Council of Conciliation hereinafter described, and their neutrality is hereby guaranteed by the League and by every member thereof.

The group to which each member belongs shall be determined at the time it enters the League, and shall not be changed except by its own consent and by a majority vote of the Conference and of the executive body of the League.

3. All justiciable questions arising between the members of the League, not settled by negotiation, shall be submitted to a judicial tribunal, hereinafter called the Court of the League, for hearing and judgment; unless the parties to the controversy agree to submit the question to the Permanent Court at The Hague or some other special tribunal. The members of the League hereby agree to comply with the Decisions of the Court of the League.

4. All other questions arising between the members of the League and not settled by negotiation or arbitration shall be submitted to a Council of Conciliation for hearing, consideration and recommendation.

5. In case of a difference of opinion between the parties to

the controversy, or of doubt on the part of the Court or Council, whether the question is justiciable or not, that issue shall be submitted to a Court of Conflicts, constituted as hereinafter provided, whose decision thereof shall be final.

6. The members of the League shall jointly use diplomatic and economic pressure against any state, whether a member of the League or not, that threatens war against a member of the League without having first submitted its dispute for international inquiry, conciliation, arbitration or judicial hearing, and awaited a conclusion, or without having in good faith offered so to submit it. They shall follow this forthwith by the joint and several use of their military forces against that state if it actually goes to war with, or commits acts of hostility against, any member of the League before the matter in controversy shall have been submitted to the Court or Council as provided in the foregoing paragraphs, or within twelve calendar months after such submission; or, if the decision or recommendation has been made within that time, within six months after it has been made.

7. There shall be established a Court of Claims, to which any persons or corporate bodies may, with consent of their own government and any other governments involved, present their claims for adjudication and report.

8. From time to time as hereinafter provided there shall be held a Congress of the League, one of the objects being to formulate and codify rules of international law, which, unless one-third of the members of the League shall signify their dissent within twelve months, shall be established as international law and thereafter govern in the decisions of the Court of the League.

9. The Organs of the League shall be as follows: The Court of the League, the Council of Conciliation, the Court of Conflicts, the Court of Claims, the Congress and the executive body of the League.

The Court of the League shall be a permanent tribunal continuously open. It shall consist of not more than sixteen judges, whereof the members of the League of the first group shall each appoint one judge for six years, and the members of the second and third groups shall each appoint a judge to sit for one, two or three years, so arranged that the total number of judges from these groups shall not exceed eight in all. A judge appointed by a member of the League that is a party to a controversy before the Court shall not sit in the case; nor shall any judge sit who has a direct or indirect personal or pecuniary interest in a question to be decided, or has acted as counsel or judge therein. In case of a vacancy, or of a personal disqualification of a judge, the member of the League by which he was appointed may appoint a substitute for the duration of the vacancy or disqualification.

Except as provided herein, or in the convention establishing the court, or by subsequent regulation by the Congress of the League, the Court shall make its own rules of procedure. Decisions shall be made by an absolute majority of judges sitting in the case, and if the Court is equally divided the presiding judge shall have a casting vote in addition to his vote as a judge. The presence of a majority of the judges shall be necessary and sufficient for a quorum.

The Court shall elect one of its members President, and shall determine which of its members shall preside in his absence.

Each judge shall receive from the League a salary of oooo a year and shall receive, while a judge of the Court, no other compensation, title, honor or decoration from any government.

A judge may be removed for misconduct, disability or incompetence by a two-thirds vote of the members of the Congress present and voting.

10. The Council of Conciliation shall also be a permanent body. It shall sit at least twice a year, and at any other time when a session is demanded by any member of the League. It shall consist of not more than sixteen persons appointed for the same periods and by the same method of representation as the judges of the Court of the League; provided that no one shall be at the same time a member of both bodies. So far as possible the states entitled only to intermittent positions on the two bodies shall not be represented on both at the same time. Any member of the League may at any time recall its representative and substitute another. The representative of a state that

is a party to any question pending before the Council shall not be disqualified from sitting; and any state that is a party to such a question and is not at the time represented on the Council may, whether a member of the League or not, appoint an additional member to sit for that case.

Each member of the Council shall receive from the League a salary of   a year; and at the same rate for any fraction of a year, including therein the time usually required for travel to and from the country which he represents. A special member appointed as aforesaid shall receive compensation from the League at the same rate. No member of the Council shall during his period of service receive any other compensation, title, honor or decoration from any government.

The Council shall choose its own President and Vice-President, and except as provided herein or in the Convention establishing the Council, or by subsequent regulation by the Congress of the League, the Council shall make its own rules of procedure. Any action it may take of a general nature, or in a special case, shall be by a majority of the members voting thereon, and in case of a tie the presiding officer shall have a casting vote, in addition to his vote as a member of the Council. The presence of a majority of the members shall be necessary and sufficient for a quorum.

11. The Court of Conflicts shall consist of three judges of the Court of the League elected by the judges thereof, three members of the Council of Conciliation elected by the members thereof, and of a seventh member chosen by these six. In case they fail to make a choice on the first day, the seventh member shall be the President of the Congress, or, in case of his inability to be present in two days thereafter, that Vice-President of the Congress, in the order of his rank, who is present at that time. The seventh member shall preside, but shall have no vote except in case of a tie when he shall have a casting vote.

12. In any case pending before the Court, the Council or the Court of Conflicts, such body shall have authority to make an order restraining any party, whether a member of the League or a state having a controversy with a member of the

APPENDICES

League, from doing any act which in the opinion of the body issuing the order will cause an irreparable injury or render the final attainment of a just result extremely difficult. The order shall be effective until one month after the body issuing it has made its decision or recommendation, and it shall be enforced as hereinafter provided.

13. The Court of Claims shall be composed of five judges of the Court of the League, each of the parties to the controversy selecting two, and the fifth being selected by the Court of the League.

14. The Congress shall be composed of representatives of the members of the League. Each member shall have at least one representative. At the outset the members of the first group shall have six representatives each, and the others a smaller number according to a ratio based upon population and upon commercial and other considerations. The number of representatives shall be changed from time to time on the admission of new members to the League, but so that the number to which the members of the first group shall be entitled shall never be less than one-half of the total authorized membership of the Congress. The members of the League shall have the right to withdraw and replace their representatives as they see fit.

The Congress shall elect by plurality vote its President, and First, Second and Third Vice-Presidents. The Court, Council and Congress shall each organize its own secretariat, and shall prescribe the salaries of the officers thereof, which shall be paid by the League.

The Congress shall make its own rules of procedure. In addition to dealing with international law it may consider the reduction of armaments and any matter affecting the tranquillity of the world or the progress or betterment of human relations, and it may make recommendations on the subject. Any action shall be taken by a majority of the votes cast thereon; the presiding officer having only his vote as a member of the Congress, except on questions of procedure when he shall in case of a tie have a casting vote in addition.

15. The Congress may appoint a commission or commissions

to inspect and report upon the work of international administrative bodies. It may also appoint commissions to control and administer such of these international matters as may be intrusted to it by treaty.

16. Unless otherwise provided the Court, the Council, the Court of Conflicts and the Congress shall hold all their meetings at The Hague, but nothing herein shall abrogate the acts of the Conferences hitherto held at The Hague, or prevent the holding of similar ones hereafter.

17. The executive body of the League shall be composed of representatives of the states of the first group. The representative of each state shall be the chief executive thereof, or a substitute appointed and removable by him at pleasure and acting under his instructions. The representatives shall meet every year on the first Monday in May, and at any other time at the request of any one of the states of the first group. In case of emergency, the executive body of the League may act upon the instance of any member, without convening in person, after communication with all its members.

In case any state, whether a member of the League or not, goes to war with, or commits acts of hostility against, any member of the League before the matter in controversy has been submitted to the Court or Council as herein provided, it shall be the duty of the executive body to call upon all members of the first group to use forthwith jointly and severally against such state their economic and military forces, or such military forces as may be agreed upon; and upon the members of the second group to declare their belligerency against such state with its economic consequences. If a doubt arises whether such state has gone to war, or committed acts of hostility, that question shall be decided by the executive body, and such decision shall be conclusive of the fact.

In case any state, whether a member of the League or not, threatens war, disobeys a restraining order issued as hereinbefore provided, or fails to comply with a judgment rendered by the Court of the League, the executive body shall consider and decide what action shall be taken to prevent war or enforce compliance with the order or decision.

APPENDICES

18. The expenses of the Court, Council and Congress shall be defrayed by the members of the League in the proportion of their contributions to the Universal Postal Union. If a payment due from any member is at any time one year in arrears, that member shall forfeit all right of representation in every organ of the League until its dues are fully paid.

19. No member shall withdraw from the League except upon twelve months' notice, nor while any controversy, brought by it or against it, is pending before the Court, Council or Court of Conflicts, nor until it has complied with all restraining orders, issued as aforesaid, and all judgments rendered by the Court of the League.

20. The signatories agree to conclude, as soon as possible, conventions organizing in conformity herewith the Court, the Council and the Congress.

Index

Akron, Ohio, Harding's speech at, 193
Alabama arbitration, influence on peace movement, 6
Alber, Louis J., assists league in war effort, 89
Algeciras Conference, U. S. participation in, 16
Alliances, U. S. entangling opposed, 37; fear of stressed, 43, 207; Jefferson's reference to explained, 49
Allison, William B., favors arbitration, 7
American Academy of Political and Social Science, meets to discuss world peace, 65; meets to discuss American foreign policy, 85
American Federation of Labor, favors ratification of treaty, 172
American Peace Conference, Fifth, meeting of in San Francisco, 46
American Peace Society, founded, 4; sponsors conference on arbitration, 7; divided on league, 45; Wilson a member of, 52; extends pacifist opposition to league, 70
American Society for the Judicial Settlement of International Disputes, established, 17
Anglo-American, friendship opposed by Irish and Germans in U. S., 19; alliance advocated, 65; alliance opposed, 81
Anglo-French Treaty, negotiated, 18
Anglophobes, oppose league, 48
Arbitration, *Alabama* claims settled by, 6; proposals for, 6, 7; national conference on, 7; Olney-Pauncefote Treaty of, 8; permanent court of, 13; Hague Convention on, 14; Judicial Court of, established, 17; American Conference of International, 18; treaties for negotiated by Hay, 18; Taft treaties on, 19; compulsory advocated, 36; uses of explained, 45; limits of explained by H. C. Lodge, 50; limitations of noted by Charles E. Hughes, 58; treaties of denounced by Lodge, 78; discussed in *Covenanter* articles, 129
Armistice, effect of on league

activity, 96; purpose of explained, 205
Army and Navy League, cooperates with league, 89
Article 10, basis for in League Covenant supported by Taft, 50; principle of supported by Wilson in 1914, 52; principles of supported by Theodore Roosevelt, 56; defended by Henry W. Taft, 129; denounced by Root, 138; regarded as essential to League, 140; Taft's amendment to, 143; nullified by Lodge reservations, 161; Hitchcock's reservation on acceptable to Wilson, 172; discussed in "Statement of the 31," 191
Articles of Confederation, pattern for world organization, 28
Astor Hotel, peace society meetings held in, 32
Association of Nations, favored by Harding, 183
Austria, relations with Germany strained, 12
Axson, Stockton, Wilson's conversation with concerning peace, 52

Baker, Newton D., attends first meeting League to Enforce Peace, 39; supports U.S. entrance into war in order to make proper peace, 82; says soldiers favor League, 137
Baltimore, Md., league meetings in, 64
Baruch, Bernard M., contributes funds to league's Washington bureau, 149
Beard, Charles A., leader in League of Free Nations Association, 111
Beck, James M., attends fourth Century Club conference, 35; doubts American adherence to league idea, 86; opposes League, 87
Bernstein, Herman, Sir Edward Grey's letter to, 67
Bethmann-Hollweg, Theobald von, announces Germany's willingness to join a league, 67
Beveridge, Albert J., opposes league, 73; denounces internationalism, 99
Bickett, Thomas W., opposes Taft's political actions, 109
Bieberstein, Marshal von, opposes disarmament, 17
Blaine, Mrs. Emmons, joins "Pro-League Independents," 188
Blakeslee, George H., supports league, 62
de Bloch, Jean, treatise of on war, 12
Borah, William E., opposes Bryan's conciliation treaties, 23; opposes Wilson's peace plans, 75; attacks League to Enforce Peace, 76; denounces league idea, 109; anti-league influence of counteracted at Paris, 119; bargains with Lodge to oppose peace treaty, 132; satisfied with Harding's opposition to League, 183
Boston, Mass., league meeting in

INDEX

Symphony Hall, March 8, 1916, 63
Bourgeois, Léon V. A., attends first Hague Conference, 13; activity of at Paris conference, 119
Boxer Uprising, suppressed, 16
Bristow, Joseph L., opposes Bryan's conciliation treaties, 23
British League of Nations Union, league coöperates with in Paris, 116
Brooks, Phillips, little interest in world peace, 5
Bryan, William Jennings, negotiates conciliation treaties, 16, 22; opposes league, 69; debates league issue with Taft, 70; opposes preparedness, 72; support of for league sought, 77; suggestions of for changes in Covenant, 122
Bryce, Lord James, peace proposals of considered by third Century Club conference, 35; leads peace study group in England, 66
Burton, Theodore E., favors second Hague Conference, 17
Bush Terminal Sales Company, gives floor space to league, 98
Butler, Nicholas Murray, refuses to join League to Enforce Peace, 43; given pro-league statement for use by Republican Party, 57

Capper, Arthur, suggestions of for change in Covenant, 122
Carnegie, Andrew, urges Theodore Roosevelt to work for peace, 27
Carnegie Endowment for the Advancement of Peace, 17
Central Organization for a Durable Peace, meeting at The Hague, 38; "minimum program" of, 65
Century Club, New York, peace conference dinners in, 33; conference of Jan. 25, 1915 held in, 34; conference of March 30, 1915 held in, 35; resolutions of third conference, 35; fourth conference, 35; resolutions of fourth conference, 37
Chamber of Commerce, U. S., supports program of league, 46
Chamber of Deputies, French, supports arbitration with the United States, 7
Chautauqua, Coit-Alber System, used by league in war work, 89
Chicago, Ill., league meetings in, 64
China, intervention in, 16; progress of, 24
Choate, Joseph Hodges, favors third Hague Conference, 25
Church Peace Union, meeting of, 46; coöperates with league in war work, 89, 97
Cincinnati, Ohio, Wilson's speech at, Oct. 26, 1916, 60
Civil War, influence of on peace movement, 5
Clark, John Bates, discusses plans for world peace, 30; ac-

tive in New York Peace Society, 32; attends first Century Club conference, 34; attends fourth Century Club conference, 35; speaks for League to Enforce Peace, 38; supports Cox for presidency, 197

Clark, J. Reuben, attends fourth Century Club conference, 35; favors U.S. isolation, 37

Clemenceau, Georges, at Paris conference, 119

Clergymen, U.S. Protestant, work of for league, 97, 128

Cleveland, Grover, supports arbitration, 8

Colby, Everett, writes articles supporting League, 129

Collective security, advocated by Lowell, 45

Colt, Le Baron B., dislikes attitude of Republicans on League, 157

Committee on Foreign Relations, U.S., amends arbitration treaty, 9

Commonwealth of nations, advocated by Wilson, 51

Conciliation, Bryan treaties of, 16, 22

Confederation of European States, proposal for, 6

Congress, U.S., supports arbitration, 6; appeal for election of Republicans to, 100

Constant, Baron d'Estournelles de, attends first Hague Conference, 13; at Paris peace conference, 119

Constantinople, post-war position of considered, 85

Convention for the Pacific Settlement of International Disputes, signed at The Hague, 15

Covenant of League of Nations, opposed in Senate, 120; Wilson accepts amendments to, 122; Lodge-Lowell debate on, 123-124; resolutions favoring, 128; explained by league officials, 129; Root's suggestions on, 135; amended to suit critics, 136; published in U.S., 136; misinterpreted by Harding and in "Statement of the 31," 192-196. *See also* Treaty.

Covenanter, The, written to support League, 128

Cox, Jacob D., supports League, 182

Crane, Frank, attends first Century Club conference, 34; makes speaking tour for league, 127

Cremer, William Randall, works for arbitration, 6

Crimean War, influence on peace movement, 5

Croly, Herbert, leader in League of Free Nations Association, 111

Cuba, controversies over, 10

Cullom, Shelby Moore, 18

Cummings, Homer S., delivers key-note address at Democratic convention, 178

Cummins, Albert B., opposes Wilson's league program, 78

Dana, Richard H., conversation of with Lodge on League, 161

Daniels, Josephus, urged to se-

INDEX 235

cure Bryan's support for league, 77
Daugherty, Harry M., praised by Taft, 200
Davison, Charles S., urges Republican Party to support league, 57
"Declaration of Interdependence," designation of Wilson's first pro-league speech as, 55
Democratic Party, leaders of support league, 56; support of for league sought, 56; endorses league in 1916 platform, 59; position of on league upheld, 79; committed to support of a league of nations, 85; national chairman of supports league, 98; leaders of in Senate support Wilson's peace program, 104-105; Wilson requests support for, 107; defeat of sought, 146; position of on treaty, 158; views of leaders on reservations, 160; supports Wilson on League issue in 1920 campaign, 178; 1920 platform of favors League, 179-180; position of misrepresented, 195
Democracy and world peace in 19th Century, 23
Dennis, William C., attends fourth Century Club conference, 36
Des Moines, Iowa, speech of Harding at, Oct. 7, 1920, 181
Detroit, Mich., league meetings in, 64
Dewey, John, leader in League of Free Nations Association, 111

Dickinson, Jacob M., attends first meeting League to Enforce Peace, 39
"Dollar Diplomacy," use of, 16
Duggan, Stephen, leader in League of Free Nations Association, 111
Dutton, Samuel T., opposes league idea, 80

Economic pressure, urged as sanction for peace, 47
Education, U. S. public, not effective for peace, 5; liberal, influence of, 23
Elections, U. S. political, of 1916, influence on League to Enforce Peace, 60; of 1918, analysis of results of, 111
Eliot, Charles W., advocates extension of league's aims, 69; joins "Pro-League Independents," 188
Eliot, Samuel Atkins, speaks for League to Enforce Peace, 38
Emergency Campaign Committee of League to Enforce Peace, established, 114
England, interest in arbitration treaties, 19; peace groups in, 66
Europe, committed to league idea, 77
European Federation, proposals for, 25

Fabian Society, reports league idea, 66
Fall, Albert B., opposes Bryan's conciliation treaties, 23
Far East, Russo-British relations in, 12; U. S. agreements in, 16

Farm journals, support League, 130

Federalist Papers, used as model for *The Covenanter*, 128

Fess, Simeon D., attacks Wilson's peace program, 106

Fieldman, Soloman, organizes Taft-Bryan debate on league, 70

Filene, Edward A., influences U. S. Chamber of Commerce to support league, 46; speech of at first national assembly of league, 50; gives $25,000 to league, 61; speech at league's Philadelphia meeting, 94; makes speaking tour for league, 115; seeks information on league's attitude toward reservations, 148; supports Cox for presidency, 197

Fisher, Irving, supports world organization, 29; attends first Century Club conference, 34; analyzes Harding's views on League, 187-188; organizes "Pro-League Independents," 188

Force, international use of favored, 28; advocated by Lowell, 36; use of debated by Bryan and Taft, 71

Ford, Henry, pro-league candidate for Senate, 106

Foreign Press Association, Sir Edward Grey speaks before, 67

"Four Minute Men," provided with league literature, 89

"Fourteen Points," speech by Wilson, 91; basis for discussion of peace terms, 106

Fourth Liberty Loan, opening of, 103

Frank, Glenn, thinks interest in league declining, 90

Frankfurter, Felix, leader in League of Free Nations Association, 111

Free trade, declared to be cause of war, 96

French, interest in arbitration treaties, 19; leaders support strong league, 117; struggle of Wilson with, 117-119; U. S. alliance with abandoned, 207

French Society for a League of Nations, league coöperates with in Paris, 116

Frost, Edward W., supports league's decision concerning reservations, 153

Gadsden, Philip H., attends first national assembly of league, 49

Gallinger, Jacob H., opposes Wilson's peace plans, 75

Gardner, Augustus P., opposes league, 81

Garrison, Lindley M., opposes league idea, 80

Geneva League of Peace and Liberty, proposals of, 6

Gerard, James W., makes speaking tour for league, 115

German-American, relations strained by *Lusitania* sinking, 38

Germanophiles, oppose league, 48

INDEX 237

Germans, in U. S. oppose Anglo-American friendship, 19; in U. S. oppose Wilson in 1916, 81

Germany, relations with Austria strained, 12; U. S. efforts for arbitration treaties with, 19; refuses to state peace aims, 68; renews submarine warfare against U. S., 83; admission of to a league opposed, 96; accepts Pre-Armistice Agreement, 113; U. S. default in pledges to, 206-207

Gibbons, James Cardinal, declines invitation to speak at Philadelphia convention, 93

Giddings, Franklin H., attends first Century Club conference, 34

Governors, U. S. state, favor league, 96

Great Britain, *Alabama* arbitration, 6

Great Lakes, naval armament on, 129

Grey, Sir Edward, supports league idea, 66; conversation with James M. Beck, 86

Hague Conference, first, called, 11; accomplishments of, 12, 15

Hague Conference, second, promoted by U. S., 16; meeting of, 17

Hague Conference, third, proposed, 25

Hallowell, James Mott, organizes Massachusetts branch of league, 62

Hammond, John Hays, host at Century Club dinners, 33; attends second Century Club conference, 34

Harding, Warren G., confused on League issue, 162; comments of in Senate on League, 169; promises establishment of an "association of nations," 181-182; schemes of analyzed by Fisher, 187-188; speech of at Akron, Ohio, 193; explains position on League to Lowell, 197; plans of for entering League, 200; abandons league idea, 200; denies having promised association of nations, 203; confused ideas of, 207

Hartford, Conn., league meetings in, 64

Harvey, George, confers with Root on amendments to Covenant, 135; convinced of Harding's election, 190

Hawaiian Islands, annexation of, 10

Hay, John, instructions to U.S. delegates to first Hague Conference, 14; favors arbitration, 14; negotiates arbitration treaties, 18

Hays, Will H., side-steps league issue as chairman of Republican National Committee, 98; denounces Wilson's administration, 100; calls for election of Republican Congress, 101; asks Root for statement on League, 135; views of on Root's reservation on peace treaty, 139; coördinates Republican opposition to treaty,

144; convinced Harding will be elected, 190; seeks Root's support for Harding, 191

Hazard, Caroline, joins "Pro-League Independents," 188

Hearst, William Randolph, newspapers of oppose league, 110, 131

Henry IV, peace proposal of, 26

Hitchcock, Gilbert M., supports Wilson's peace note, 74; suggests changes in Covenant, 122; makes speaking tour for league, 127; misled by Lodge, 159; lists reservations acceptable to Democratic senators, 168

Holt, George C., attends second Century Club conference, 34

Holt, Hamilton, influence on Roosevelt's Christiania address, 27; leader of peace movement, 27, 30-31; Baltimore address of, 28; plan for world peace, 28-29; host at Century Club dinners, 33; member of resolutions committee at first meeting League to Enforce Peace, 39; speech of at Philadelphia meeting, 42; elected vice-chairman executive committee League to Enforce Peace, 43; comments on influence of league, 66; confers with Colonel House on league issue, 77; interview of with Colonel House, 82; speaks for league's war program, 89; elected chairman Committee on Churches and Moral Aims of the War, 97; leader in League of Free Nations Association, 111; agent of League to Enforce Peace at Paris conference, 116, 118, 211; makes speaking tour for league, 127; opposes league's decision to support reservations, 151; joins "Pro-League Independents," 188; believes Republican Party controlled by Lodge faction, 198

Holy Alliance, compared with League to Enforce Peace, 79

Hoover, Herbert C., opposes reservations, 150; address of at Indianapolis, Ind., Oct. 9, 1920, favoring League, 189; signs "Statement of the 31," 196; abandons support of League, 200-201

House, Col. Edward M., favors league, 53; affirms Wilson's strong support of league idea, 77; observes growth of partisanship on league issue, 82; explains Wilson's position on league, 91; aided by league's agents at Paris, 118

House of Commons, supports arbitration, 6

House of Representatives, U. S., resolution supporting arbitration, 7

Houston, Herbert S., elected treasurer League to Enforce Peace, 43; prepares pamphlet for league, 45; speaks at first national assembly of league, 49; makes speaking tour for league, 115, 127

Howland, Charles P., host at

INDEX 239

Century Club dinner, 33; supports Cox for presidency, 197
Howland, Harold J., attends first Century Club conference, 34
Hughes, Charles Evans, as Republican presidential nominee in 1916 supports league, 58, 210; ceases to support league, 82; declines invitation to Philadelphia convention, 93; suggestions of for changes in Covenant, 122; supports Root on reservations to peace treaty, 139; signs "Statement of the 31," 196; as Secretary of State abandons League, 200
Hull, William I., attends first Century Club conference, 34
Hutchinson, Charles L., favors league, 64

Immigration, fear of European control of expressed in Senate, 78
Imperialism, support for in U. S., 10; advocated in U. S., 15; supporters of against league, 73
Independence Hall, meeting at to launch League to Enforce Peace, 37; meeting of league in, 93
Indianapolis, Ind., Wilson's speech at, Oct. 12, 1916, 59; League to Enforce Peace dinner in, 81; Beveridge's speech at opposing league, 99; Hoover's speech at, Oct. 9, 1920, 189

Institute for International Law, founded, 6
International arbitration, American Conference on, 18
Internationalism, advocated, 10; acceptance of in the U. S., 60; influence of doubted, 73
International Law, development of, 13
International Peace Bureau, opened at Bern, 6
International police force, establishment of advocated, 36
Interparliamentary Conference, meeting at St. Louis, 17
Interparliamentary Union, work for arbitration, 6
Intervention, U. S., in Santo Domingo, 16
Irish, in U. S. Oppose Anglo-American friendship, 19; oppose League, 131
Isolation, U. S., shown at first Hague Conference, 15; denounced at Century Club conference, 36; opposed by Wilson, 54, 60; opposed by Charles E. Hughes in 1916, 59; feared by Sir Edward Grey, 67; supported by Borah in Senate, 76; opposed, 79; as issue in election of 1918, 110; supported by Root, 138, 192, 193

Japan, 22
Jefferson, Thomas, phrases of used by isolationists, 48; principles of debated by Bryan and Taft, 71-72; ideas of misunderstood, 207

INDEX

Jenks, Jeremiah W., attends second Century Club conference, 34

Johnson, Hiram, works against League, 133; satisfied with Harding opposition to League, 183; influence of, 196; scorns "Statement of the 31," 198

Johnson, Robert Underwood, discusses plans for world peace, 30

Jones, Andrieus A., opposes Bryan's conciliation treaties, 23

Kansas City, Mo., speech of Harding at, Oct. 8, 1920, 182

Kant, Immanuel, essay on *Perpetual Peace* referred to, 42

Kellogg, Frank B., position of on treaty, 150

King, Henry C., joins "Pro-League Independents," 188

Kingsley, Darwin P., elected chairman committee on finance League to Enforce Peace, 43

Kirchwey, George W., active in New York Peace Society, 31; favors calling peace conference, 32

Knox, Philander Chase, negotiates arbitration treaties, 19; opposes establishment of a league in peace treaty, 110, 133

Labor, U. S. organized, supports League, 128

La Follette, Robert M., isolationist, 213

Lake Mohonk Conference, organized, 7; conference of 1915, 38

Lamb, Frank, member of Washington bureau of league, 148

Lamont, Thomas W., supports treaty, 149; opposes Taft's view on Harding, 186

Lansing, Robert, opposes Wilson's speaking at league meeting, 53

Latin America, protection of supported by Bryan, 72; not expected to approve Monroe Doctrine reservation, 165

League of Free Nations Association, organized, 111

League of Nations, idea of supported by Century Club conferences, 37; idea of supported by Wilson, 52; idea of endorsed by Democratic Party in 1916; establishment of as U. S. war aim, 84; struggle for at Paris conference, 117; Covenant of opposed in Senate, 120; defeat of in Senate, 173; denounced by Harding, 181-182; abandoned by Harding's administration, 201; significance of, 214

League of Nations Covenant. See Covenant of the League of Nations.

League of Nations Non-Partisan Association, Lowell's speech at, 203

League of Nations Society, organized in England, 66

League of Peace, proposed by Theodore Roosevelt, 26

INDEX

League to Enforce Peace, origin of, 30; meeting at Philadelphia to launch, 37; first platform of, 40; beginning of Elihu Root's influence on, 44; favored by U. S. Chamber of Commerce, 47; first national assembly of in Washington, 48; principles of supported by Wilson, 52; fails to secure Republican Party support in 1916, 58; membership in, 60; income and expenditure for 1916, 61; state branches of, 62; local organization of, 63; influence on world opinion, 69; character of opposition to analyzed, 73-74; attacked by Roosevelt, 77; not a pacifist organization, 87; "war program" of, 88; principles of included in "Fourteen Points," 91; convention at Philadelphia, 92-96; "Win the War" conventions organized, 96; adopts "Victory Program," 111; ideas of accepted in Pre-Armistice Agreement, 114; organizes new campaign to influence public opinion, 114; activity at Paris peace conference, 116; agents of assist Wilson at Paris, 116; influence of at Paris, 120; holds "congresses" supporting League, 121; supports League Covenant as amended, 126, 212; analyzes strategy of League opponents, 132; opposes reservations to peace treaty, 145; compromises with Taft, 147; executive committee of decides to support reservations, 151; action in support of reservations analyzed, 155-156; effect of disunity in, 159; principles of in relation to Lodge reservations, 171-172; begins to disintegrate, 173, 212; policy of in election of 1920, 175; Root's influence on, 192; inactive during 1920 campaign, 198; principles of abandoned by Harding's administration, 201; end of, 202; lost opportunity of, 207-214; early success of explained, 209; partisan conflict in, 210-212

League to Enforce Peace Days, proclaimed in Massachusetts, 63

League to Enforce Peace Sundays, establishment of urged by league, 63

Legislatures, U. S. state, resolutions in favoring league, 96; resolutions of favoring League, 130-131

Lewis, David J., offers to introduce league resolution in Congress, 56

"Liberty Day," league provides speakers for, 88-89

Liberty Loan, Fourth, opening of, 103; Wilson's speech concerning commented on, 103-104

Lippmann, Walter, states belief concerning post-war organization, 86

Lodge, Henry Cabot, against

Olney-Pauncefote Treaty, 10; opposes Wilson, 11; opposes Taft's arbitration treaties, 20; opposes Bryan's conciliation treaties, 22; supports league at its first national assembly, 50; removes pro-league plank from Republican platform, 57; opposes Wilson's peace plans, 75; denounces Wilson's peace program of Jan. 22, 1917, 78; reasons of for opposing league indicated, 81; explains his opposition to league, 82; denounces Wilson's peace program, 101, 104; ideas of for peace analyzed, 105; scheme of for defeating league, 108, 146; anti-league influence of counteracted at Paris, 119; refuses to suggest changes in Covenant, 122; debates with Lowell on Covenant, 123; admits public opinion favors League, 132; explains difficulty in defeating treaty, 161; prevents acceptance of compromise reservations, 173; praises Senate for defeat of treaty, 175; denounces League in Marion, Ohio, speech, 180; leader of anti-League forces, 210-212; intentions of in opposing Wilson, 213

Lodge reservations, listed, 163; approved by League to Enforce Peace, 164; analysis of, 164-165, 170-171.

Lowell, A. Lawrence, attends fourth Century Club conference, 35; explains use of force, 36, 70; elected chairman executive committee League to Enforce Peace, 39; speech of at Philadelphia meeting, 42; urges Root to join league, 44; prepares pamphlet for league, 45; confers with Wilson on league, 56; speaks for league in Boston, 63; speaking tour of, 1917, 64; speaks for league's war program, 89; confers with Wilson on Philadelphia convention, 93; works with Committee on Churches and Moral Aims of the War, 97; urges Wilson to work for league, 102; makes speaking tour for league, 115, 127; urges Wilson to secure strong league at Paris, 118; suggestions of for changes in Covenant, 122; debates with Lodge on Covenant, 123; writes articles for *The Covenanter*, 128-129; appeals to Root to support League, 133-134; approves Root's suggestions on Covenant, 135; opposes acceptance of Taft's resignation from league's presidency, 147; supports reservations, 148, 150; seeks Republican support for League, 190; decides to support Harding, 191; signs "Statement of the 31," 196; succeeds Taft as president of league, 201; calls meeting of the "31," 202: criticizes Harding for abandoning League, 203

INDEX

Lusitania, sinking of, 38
Lyceum, provides outlet for league speakers, 89
Lynch, Frederick, discusses plans for world peace, 30; attends first Century Club conference, 34

McAdoo, William G., opposes league's decision to support reservations, 152
McCormick, Vance C., as chairman of Democratic National Committee supports league idea, 98; opposes league's decision to support reservations, 152
McCracken, Henry N., discusses plans for world peace, 30
McCumber, Porter J., viewed as favoring League, 150; opposes reservations, 150-157; analyzes Lodge reservations, 150; joins Democrats in opposing reservations, 164
McKinley, William, supports arbitration, 8
McNary, Charles L., declares Covenant satisfactory, 137
Mahan, Captain Alfred Thayer, opposes arms limitations at first Hague Conference, 14; opposes Taft's arbitration treaties, 20; social ideals of, 21; influence of on imperialists, 73
Mandates, under League, discussed in *Covenanter* articles, 129
Marburg, Theodore, leader of peace movement, 28; attends first Century Club conference, 34; speaks at Lake Mohonk Conference, 38; speech of at Philadelphia meeting, 41; elected vice-chairman executive committee League to Enforce Peace, 43; speaks at first national assembly of league, 49; confers with Wilson on league, 56; works for league in England, 66; reports to Taft on conference with Grey, 66; opposes league's decision to support reservations, 152; joins "Pro-League Independents," 188
Massachusetts, organization of league in, 62-64; situation in regarding league, 81; legislature of favors league, 97
Massachusetts Peace Society, founded, 3; supports league, 62
Max of Baden, Prince, initiates peace negotiations, 106
Mediation, use of, 14
Militarism, supported by Lodge, 78
Milwaukee, Wis., league meetings in, 64
Minneapolis, Minn., league meetings in, 64
Monroe Doctrine, expansion of favored, 34; mentioned, 51; Wilson's peace plans declared to be violation of, 75; abandonment of feared by Borah, 76; expansion of urged by Wilson, 78; departure from feared, 79; Covenant amend-

ment concerning, 124-125; relationship of to League, 129; reservation on advocated by Root, 138

Moody, Dwight L., little interest in peace, 5

Moors, John F., joins "Pro-League Independents," 188

Morgenthau, Henry, makes speaking tour for league, 115

Morrow, Dwight W., makes speaking tour for league, 127

Mount Vernon, Wilson's speech at stating peace aims, 102-103

Munitions, private manufacture of opposed by Wilson, 52

Myers, Denys P., member of Washington bureau of league, 148

Napoleonic War, influence on peace movement, 3

National Peace Conference, meeting in Chicago, 38

National Security League, cooperates with league, 89; opposes Wilson's administration, 100

Navy, U. S., world cruise of, 16

Neutrality, U. S., violated by Germany, 83

New, Harry S., ceases to support league, 82

Newberry, Truman H., anti-league candidate for Senate, 106

Newspapers, little concerned over peace movement, 5; support of league idea in 1916, 64; German-American oppose league, 81; show favorable trend toward league idea in America, 89; support league's Victory Program, 95; attitude of toward Wilson's peace program, 103; attitude of toward League, 130

New York, league meetings in, 64; Wilson's speech at discussing peace aims, 103; Wilson's speech at discussing League Covenant, 121

New York Peace Society, founded, 3; leads movement for a league of nations, 30; Plan of action Committee's report, 31; assists League to Enforce Peace, 61

Nobel Peace Prize, Theodore Roosevelt's acceptance address, 26

Olney-Pauncefote Treaty, defeat in Senate, 9

Olney, Richard, negotiates arbitration treaty with Britain, 8; describes defeat of Olney-Pauncefote Treaty, 9

"Open Door," negotiations, 16

Owen, Robert L., reservation of on Article 10, 172

Pacifism, advocated, 10

Pacifists, definition of, 4; oppose league, 45; principles of stated by Bryan, 70; arguments of used by imperialists, 73

Pan-American, extension of influence favored by Wilson, 34

Pan-American Pact, supported by Wilson, 52

Parker, Alton Brooks, elected

INDEX

chairman committee on home organization League to Enforce Peace, 43; opposes league's decision to support reservations, 153

Parsons, Herbert, joins "Pro-League Independents," 188

Partisanship, U. S. political, need for avoidance of, 80; growth of in U. S. on league issue, 82; avoidance of in political campaign of 1918, 98; rapid development of, 106-108; shown in Senate's vote on treaty, 160

Pauncefote, Rt. Hon. Sir Julian, negotiates arbitration treaty with United States, 8

Peace aims, requested by Wilson, 67

Peace conference, Paris, activity of league at, 116; accepts U. S. amendments to Covenant, 125; character of explained, 206

Peace Congress, U. S. National, 27

Peace Movement, in the nineteenth century, 3; growth of in U. S., 4-16. *See also* Peace.

Peace, progress of in 19th Century, 23, 25; premature peace with Germany denounced, 94; Wilson's program for debated in Senate, 104-105. *See also* Peace Societies.

Peace Societies, founding of, 3; number in the U. S., 4; disagreements among, 4; activities of, 16; support Taft's arbitration treaties, 27; New York supports movement for a league of nations, 30; conferences of held in 1915, 38; divided on League to Enforce Peace, 45

Pearl Harbor, prelude to, 212

Perry, Bliss, supports league, 62

Philadelphia, league meeting of 1918 in, 93

Philippine Islands, annexation of, 10

Pittman, Key, supports Wilson's peace program, 104-105; states view of Democratic senators on reservations, 168

Plimpton, George A., attends first Century Club conference, 34

Poindexter, Miles, opposes Bryan's conciliation treaties, 23; works against Wilson's peace program, 108; anti-league influence of counteracted at Paris, 119

Police force, international, establishment of advocated, 36; French support for at Paris conference, 118

Political parties, support of for league sought, 56; position of on league issue, 80-81

Portland, Oregon, Taft's speech at supporting League, 121

Portsmouth Peace Conference, U. S. interest in, 16

Pre-Armistice Agreement, includes promise for a league of nations, 113; character of, 205

Preparedness, advocated by Wilson, 72

Pritchett, Henry L., favors U. S. isolation, 37

Progressive Party, support of for league sought, 56; platform of favors league, 57

"Pro-League Independents," organized to support Cox, 188

Pro-League Republicans, views of Lowell on, 198

Public opinion, in U. S., believed by Wilson to favor a league, 34; expressions of for league, 115, 128; shown as supporting League, 130, 131; favorable to League in 1919, 208. *See also* Newspapers.

Puerto Rico, annexation of, 10

"Ratifying Conventions," organized by League to Enforce Peace, 127

Republican Party, leaders of favor league, 55; support of for league sought, 57; fails to endorse league, 58; appears to support league, 59; position of on league analyzed, 79; National Chairman of side-steps league issue, 98; leaders of in Senate oppose Wilson peace program, 104-105; leaders of denounced by Taft, 110; represented as supporting league at Paris conference, 119; leaders of urged to oppose treaty, 136; organizes to oppose treaty, 144; 1920 platform of on League, 176-177; policies of analyzed by Hoover, 189; platform of understood by Lowell, 190; prominent members of support Cox, 190-191; divided on League issue, 198; policies of explained, 208-209

Rickey, Harry N., directs Washington bureau of league, 148

Rights, fundamental of nations, 54

Rogers, John J., opposes league, 81

Roman Catholic, clergymen invited to assist league, 93; support sought for league, 114

Roosevelt, Theodore, mediation of Russo-Japanese War at Portsmouth Conference, 16; policies concerning Panama, 16; favors second Hague Conference, 17; removes Hay arbitration treaties from Senate, 18; opposes Taft's arbitration treaties, 20; address at Christiania, Norway, 26; refuses to organize peace movement, 27; advocates principles of league, 55-56; reconciliation of with Taft, 59; writes article against league, 74; attacks Wilson's peace plan, 77; opposes internationalism, 99; denounces Wilson's administration, 100; calls for election of Republican Congress, 101; supports election of Newberry to Senate, 106

Root, Elihu, negotiates arbitration treaties, 18; opposes Taft's arbitration treaties, 20; refuses to join League to Enforce Peace, 43; remains aloof over league issue, 82; denounces Wilson's administration, 100; calls for election of

Republican Congress, 101; suggestions of for changes in Covenant, 122; reasons of for favoring reservations, 131; formulates amendments for Covenant, 134-136; coöperates with Lodge to oppose ratification of peace treaty, 136-137; proposes further revision of Covenant, 138; efforts for reservations successful, 158; helps write Republican Party platform, 176; writes statement in support of Harding, 191; speech of in New York, Oct. 19, 1920, 192; signs "Statement of the 31," 196; intentions of in opposing Wilson, 213
Root-Takahira agreement, 16
Rotary Clubs, invited to assist league, 93
"Round Robin," signed by Republican senators, 120; views of signers explained, 191
Rowe, Leo S., attends fourth Century Club conference, 36; writes articles supporting League, 129; opposes league's decision to support reservations, 153
Russia, calls first Hague Conference, 11

Salt Lake City, Taft's speech at supporting League, 121
San Francisco, Cal., Taft's speech at supporting League, 121
Santo Domingo, U. S. intervention in, 16
Saratoga, N. Y., reconciliation of Taft and Roosevelt at, 99-100
Scott, James Brown, opposes league, 48
Sea, freedom of advocated by Wilson, 55
Second Liberty Loan Campaign, supported by league, 88
"Secret treaties," opposed, 65
Senate, U. S., debates Olney-Pauncefote Treaty, 8; control of by imperialists, 11; amends Hay arbitration treaties, 18; rejects Taft arbitration treaties, 19; debates league issue, 74, 78; debate in on Wilson's peace program, 104-105; election of Republican majority to, 111; ideas on peace influential at Paris conference, 117, 125; majority of favors peace treaty, 137; Committee on Foreign Relations drafts amendments to peace treaty, 142; votes on peace treaty, 167
Seymour, Charles, joins "Pro-League Independents," 188
Shadow Lawn, Wilson's speech at, Nov. 4, 1916, 60
Shaw, Albert, attends fourth Century Club conference, 35
Shaw, Anna Howard, makes speaking tour for league, 127
Sherman, John, favors arbitration, 7
Short, William Harrison, secretary of New York Peace Society, 32; elected secretary League to Enforce Peace, 43; services to league, 61; confers

with House on league issue, 77; explains reasons for league's Philadelphia conventions, 92; works with Committee on Churches and Moral Aims of the War, 97; explains league's views on League, 145; explains break-up of league, 173-174; views of on support of Harding, 187; views of concerning duties of league, 201
Simmons, Furnifold M., reservation of on Article 10, 172
Smiley, Albert K., organizes Lake Mohonk Conference, 7
Smith, Alfred E., supports treaty, 149
Socialism, opposed by Taft and Mahan, 21
Society for the Promotion of Permanent and Universal Peace, founded, 3
Spanish-American War, 10
St. Louis, Mo., Taft's speech at supporting League, 121
St. Paul, Minn., league meetings in, 64
"Statement of the 31," analyzed, 191-196; repudiated by its signers, 202-203; default of signers of, 212
Stewart, James A., attends first Century Club conference, 34
Stimson, Henry L., advises Republican Party on League issue, 135; signs "Statement of the 31," 196
Story, Moorfield, joins "Pro-League Independents," 188
Straus, Oscar, seeks support of Progressive Party for league, 57; agent of League to Enforce Peace at Paris conference, 116, 118, 211; surveys press opinion on Covenant, 122; criticizes Root's attitude on peace treaty, 140; supports reservations, 148; signs "Statement of the 31," 196
Submarine warfare, unrestricted use of renewed by Germany, 83
Sweetser, Arthur, views of concerning reservations, 165-166

Taft, Henry W., writes articles for *The Covenanter*, 129; statement of on Root, 138-139; criticizes Root's attitude on peace treaty, 141; opposes league's decision to support reservations, 153; signs "Statement of the 31," 196
Taft, Horace D., criticizes Lodge and "mild reservationists," 160
Taft-Katsura agreement, 16
Taft, William Howard, favors arbitration, 19; attends fourth Century Club conference, 35; edits Century Club resolutions, 37; elected president League to Enforce Peace, 39; speech of at Philadelphia meeting, 41; prepares pamphlet for league, 45; speech of at first national assembly of league, 49; confers with Wilson on league, 56; claims Republican Party has endorsed league, 58, 211; reconciliation

of with Theodore Roosevelt, 59; speaks for league in Boston, 63; speaking tour of, 1917, 64; debates league issue with Bryan, 70; speaks for league's war program, 89; confers with Wilson on Philadelphia convention, 93; speech at league's Philadelphia meeting, 94; works with Committee on Churches and Moral Aims of the War, 97; denounces Wilson's administration, 100; calls for election of Republican Congress, 101; urges Wilson to work for league, 102; supports election of Newberry to Senate, 106; coöperates with anti-league politicians, 108; misrepresents Wilson on league issue, 109; denounces anti-league Republicans, 110; makes speaking tour for league, 115, 127; urges Wilson to secure strong league at Paris, 118; supports Wilson on League Covenant, 121; suggestions of for changes in Covenant, 122; defends Article 10 in *Covenanter* article, 129; opposes amendments to peace treaty, 132; defends Article 10, 141; denounces treaty's opponents, 142; changes attitude on treaty, 143; works with treaty's opponents, 144; offers resignation to league, 145; joins anti-League forces, 146; misrepresents Wilson's position on reservations, 167;

supports election of Harding, 184; thinks Lodge should be secretary of state, 184; opposes Article 10, 185; threatens to resign from league, 199; outlines Harding's plan for entering League, 200; resigns presidency of league, 201; activities in league summarized, 210-212

Tarkington, Booth, answers arguments of Beveridge against league, 99

Tariff, cause of war, 24; opposed by Filene, 50; lowering of denounced by Republicans, 106; Covenant amendment concerning, 124

Territorial integrity, guarantee of supported by Wilson, 52; Wilson's ideas concerning opposed in Senate, 76

Thompson, R. E., states opposition to league, 96

Thompson, William O., makes speaking tour for league, 127

Topeka, league meetings in, 64

Treaty, Olney-Pauncefote, 8; Anglo-French of 1903, 18; of arbitration negotiated by Elihu Root, 18; on arbitration negotiated by Hay, 18; Taft's arbitration, 19; Rush-Bagot referred to, 129; Versailles, Root's proposed amendments to, 139-140, defeat of in U. S. Senate, 173, abandoned by U. S., 200, significance of American action concerning, 206-207. *See also* Conciliation; Peace conference.

Tryon, James L., attends first Century Club conference, 34

Underwood, Oscar W., states Democratic Party's position on treaty, 158
Union against Militarism, American, Wilson's speech before, 53
Union College, H. C. Lodge speaks at, 50
United States, dispute with Great Britain settled, 6; position on armaments, 14; Far Eastern agreements, 16
Universal Peace Congress, work of for arbitration, 6
Universal Peace Union, founded, 5

Van Dyke, Henry, makes speaking tour for league, 115; opposes league's decision to support reservations, 153; supports Cox for presidency, 197
Venezuela, boundary controversy, 7
Versailles Treaty, League of Nations to be part of, 103, 110. *See also* Treaty.
"Victory Program" of League to Enforce Peace, adopted, 111

Wadhams, William H., urges Republican Party to support league, 57
Walsh, Frank P., makes speaking tour for league, 115
War, Napoleonic, influence on peace movement, 3, 5
War, arguments against, 4; U. S. Civil, 5; Crimean, 5; Spanish-American, 10; First World, influence on Bryan treaties, 22; support of by U. S. political leaders, 100; Napoleonic, 3, 5; of 1812, influence on peace movement, 3
Warner, Charles D., member of Washington bureau of league, 148
Washington bureau, League to Enforce Peace, activity of, 148; opposes reservations, 150
Washington, D. C., league meeting in, Jan. 13, 1920, 172
Washington, George, false tradition of denounced, 36; phrases of used by isolationists, 48; warnings against alliances explained by Lodge, 51; principles of debated by Bryan and Taft, 71-72; advice of misunderstood, 207
Wheeler, Everett P., attends second Century Club conference, 34
Wheeling, W. Va., league meetings in, 64
White, Andrew D., attends first Hague Conference, 13; favors third Hague Conference, 25
White, Henry, asks Root to suggest improvements in Covenant, 134
White, Thomas Raeburn, chairman of first league meeting at Independence Hall, 39
Wickersham, George W.,

INDEX 251

writes articles for *The Covenanter*, 129; appeals to Republicans to support League, 133; opposes league's decision to support reservations, 153; disappointed at Republican opposition to League, 186-187; signs "Statement of the 31," 196

Willard, Daniel, supports treaty, 149

Williams, Talcott, works with Committee on Churches and Moral Aims of the War, 97; member of Washington bureau of league, 148; explains position of league after Senate vote on reservations, 174; mistaken regarding Cox, 186

Willoughby, Westel W., attends first Century Club conference, 34

Wilson, George Grafton, attends first meeting League to Enforce Peace, 39; makes speaking tour for league, 115; writes articles supporting League, 129

Wilson, Henry Lane, urges Republican Party to support league, 57; resignation of as league worker, 81

Wilson, James F., favors arbitration, 7

Wilson, Woodrow, opposed by H. C. Lodge, 11; favors conciliation treaties, 22; favors creation of a league of nations, 34; favors expansion of Pan-American influence on Monroe Doctrine, 34; speech of at league's first national assembly, 51; member of American Peace Society, 52; conversation with Axson concerning peace, 52; early support of principles of Article 10, 52; speech of favoring league, 54; lists fundamental rights of nations, 54; fears partisan opposition to league, 56; speeches of in behalf of league idea, 59-60; advocates preparedness, 72; league endorsement of attacked in Senate, 76; address to Senate of Jan. 22, 1917, 77; discouraged over reception of peace proposals, 83; second inaugural address, 83; war message, 84; confidence of in people of U. S., 87, 208; opposes formation of specific program for peace, 90; "Fourteen Points" speech, 91; consulted by league on Philadelphia convention, 93; phrases of concerning peace misrepresented, 100; denounced by Republican press for advocating election of Democratic congressmen, 101; difficulties of in securing unified allied command, 102; outlines ideas for a league, 103; appeals for election of Democratic congressmen, 107; peace program of stated in Pre-Armistice Agreement, 113; secures acceptance of league idea at

Paris peace conference, 116; defends League as part of peace treaty, 121; secures amendments to Covenant, 125; offers to accept reservations on treaty, 172; views of on reservations misrepresented in "Statement of the 31," 191; reasons for negotiating armistice, 205; objectives of in supporting League, 213

Wise, Stephen S., makes speaking tour for league, 127

Woolley, Mary E., joins "Pro-League Independents," 188

Woolsey, Theodore S., attends first Century Club conference, 34

Worcester, Mass., league meeting at, Nov. 28, 1916, 63

World Alliance for Promoting Friendship through the Churches, coöperates with league in war work, 89, 97

World Court, advocated by U. S. Chamber of Commerce, 47; idea of supported by Wilson, 55

World Court Congress, Cleveland meeting of, 38

World Peace Foundation, established, 17; distributes Lowell's article on league, 45; supports league, 45; assists League to Enforce Peace, 61; distributes *Covenanter* articles, 129

World War I, influence on the League to Enforce Peace, 3; influence on peace movement in America, 38; Wilson's aims in, 84

Wrong, George M., gives Canada's view on reservation, 165n.

www.ingramcontent.com/pod-product-compliance
Lightning Source LLC
Chambersburg PA
CBHW021122300426
44113CB00006B/248